# San Juan Islands
# WILDLIFE

A Handbook for Exploring Nature

# San Juan

# Islands Wildlife

## A Handbook for Exploring Nature

*Evelyn Adams*

EVELYN ADAMS

*Illustrations by*
Jim Hays

THE MOUNTAINEERS/THE SAN JUAN PRESERVATION TRUST

Published by The Mountaineers
1011 SW Klickitat Way
Seattle, Washington 98134

In cooperation with The San Juan Preservation Trust
Box 327, Lopez Island, Washington 98261

© 1995 by Evelyn Adams

9 8 7 6 5
5 4 3 2 1

Published simultaneously in Canada by Douglas & McIntyre, Ltd., 1615 Venables Street, Vancouver, B.C. V5L 2H1

Published simultaneously in Great Britain by Cordee, 3a DeMontfort Street, Leicester, England, LE1 7HD

Manufactured in the United States of America

Edited by Ellen O. Setteducati
All photographs by Becky VavRosky
Cover design, book design, and typography by The Mountaineers Books

Cover photographs: *main image:* great blue heron, © Vince Streano/Allstock; *Insets: (left to right):* orca © Fred Felleman/Allstock; starfish, Orcas Island © Karl Weatherly/Allstock; fawn lily © Fred Sharpe

Library of Congress Cataloging-in-Publication Data
Adams, Evelyn.
    San Juan Islands wildlife : a handbook for exploring nature /
Evelyn Adams : illustrations by Jim Hays.
        p.  cm.
    Includes bibliographical references (p.   ).
    ISBN 0-89886-420-8  (paper)
    1. Natural history--Washington (State)--San Juan Islands.  2. San Juan Islands (Wash. )  I. Title.
QH105.W2A33   1995
508.797'74  dc20                                                94-43483
                                                                  CIP

Printed on recycled paper

*For Ilsa and Gary*
*and the big cedar*

◆ ◆ ◆

*"The people created after the flood prophesied that a new language will be introduced into our country. It will be the only language spoken, when the next change comes. When we can understand animals, we will know that the change is halfway. When we can talk to the forest, we will know that the change has come."*

*Andrew Joe, Swinomish Tribe,*
*relating a Skagit creation myth in*
**Indian Legends of the Pacific Northwest**
*by Ella Clark*

PATO

WALDRON

STUART

SPIEDEN

*Haro Strait*

SHAW

SAN JUAN

48°30'

*Strait of Juan*

123°

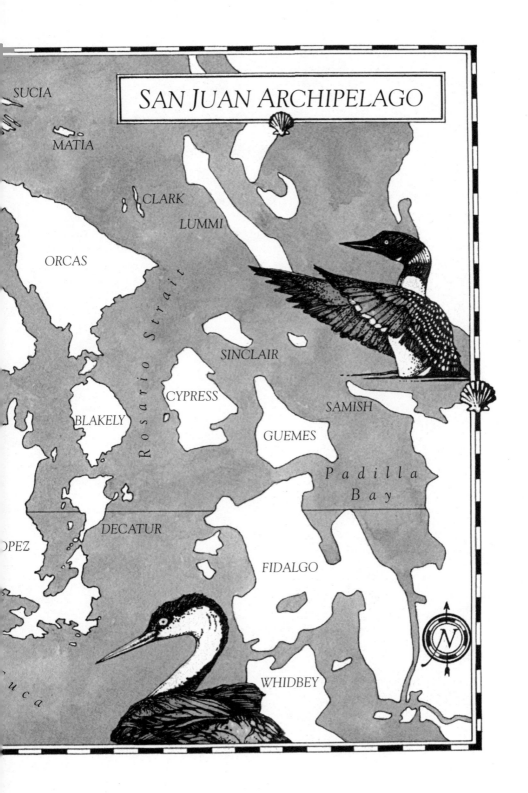

# SAN JUAN ARCHIPELAGO

SUCIA

MATIA

CLARK

LUMMI

ORCAS

*Rosario Strait*

SINCLAIR

CYPRESS

BLAKELY

SAMISH

GUEMES

*Padilla Bay*

DECATUR

OPEZ

FIDALGO

uca

WHIDBEY

N

## A NOTE ABOUT SAFETY

Safety is an important concern in all outdoor activities. No guidebook can alert you to every hazard or anticipate the limitations of every reader. Therefore, the descriptions of roads, trails, routes, and natural features in this book are not representations that a particular place or excursion will be safe for your party. When you follow any of the routes described in this book, you assume responsibility for your own safety. Under normal conditions, such excursions require the usual attention to traffic, road and trail conditions, weather, terrain, the capabilities of your party, and other factors. Keeping informed on current conditions and exercising common sense are the keys to a safe, enjoyable outing.

*The Mountaineers*

# CONTENTS

# PART 3
## Furthering the Relationship
### *Resources for Wildlife Study 139*

# PART 4
## Wildlife Reference Section

# ACKNOWLEDGMENTS

A book such as this one is heavily dependent on the field and laboratory work of others, and I acknowledge my debt to all those I've never met but who have been my teachers and, many times, my inspiration. I'd also like to thank those with whom I did meet and talk for the generous sharing of their time and knowledge, as well as for a passionate commitment to wildlife, which I hope will move readers as much as it has me. There are a few others who shared their expertise with me but are not mentioned in the followings pages; I am grateful to Dr. Eugene Kozloff, Lou Falb, Art Kermoade, and Mike Davison for their help and to Martha Jordan, from whose lectures came much of the information on trumpeter swans.

I'd also like to thank Becky VavRosky (who good-naturedly crawled through muskrat trails and suffered bee stings to take the book's photos) for her perserverance and staunch support; Dean, chiropractor, and Allen, computer whiz, for keeping me and my machine going; Ellen Conlee for her encouragement; and husband, daughter, and dog for putting up with me.

# PREFACE

Let me begin with a disclaimer: I am not an expert on any aspect of wildlife. I have, however, spent so many hours in the islands' wildlife haunts that the police called to check on a concerned local's suspicion that I was trapping beavers. Nonetheless, the more I delve into the world of nature, the more I discover the extent of my ignorance and so cannot justly claim for myself any title other than "beginner."

That's all right by me. One of the reasons I wrote this book was to learn more. Another reason is that during two and a half years of writing about the San Juan wildlife scene, I grew frustrated with the immense and scattered variety of local information. This book is an attempt to collect much of that information for easier access and offer a wide-angle view too seldom seen. It is also my way of paying homage to the naturalists and wildlife groups working to safeguard the fragility of this hugely popular area.

Many of those people speak on the following pages, sharing not only their knowledge but their love for wildlife as well. This passion for plants or whales or waterfowl is at least as important as migration schedules or dietary needs, if not more so, for the purpose of this book is less to instruct than to excite. I'm hoping you'll be enough inspired by the wonderful tapestry nature has woven for us here in the San Juans to set the book down and go out and follow the threads that interest you.

The opportunities here are endless. Many islanders trek off to more exotic areas each year, but there isn't a boater in the Caribbean or a sojourner in Kathmandu who has anything on the San Juan naturalist. In truth, we live in a foreign land from the moment we step outside our doors. The woods, the water beyond the madrones, the very soil in our garden plots—what do we really know of life beneath the waves or in an inch of soil? The frog's song is familiar and yet always strange, a language we can only guess at night after night—no Berlitz book simplifies the challenge here. No Rand McNally guide can map the mystery of a breaching orca or the bloom of a calypso.

I also trust that with your new knowledge and discoveries will come respect for our wild neighbors. Working on the premise that we destroy what we don't understand, I hope that in understanding lies the way to wonder and the preservation of life.

There is an image I like to hold in my mind, not a dream, but a picture of the Washington state ferry stopping to pick up a waterlogged eagle. Here was an hour or so when human agendas took a backseat and the civilized world lumbered to a halt to reach out and restore the balance a bit. It's a picture that sustains as I search for others and work to add my own.

A word or two more about this book. The intention was not to write a field guide but rather to give an overview of island wildlife from forest to swamp to salt water. Field guides complement the book by providing more in-depth study in subjects that may pique the reader's interest, ideally encouraging a handshake acquaintance to become more intimate and profound.

The territory covered includes the islands of San Juan County (the San Juans proper), as well as those areas as far east as Padilla and Samish bays. The boundary separating the western islands from the eastern (Fidalgo, Guemes, Cypress) has always seemed to me rather arbitrary; in this book, the territory is not separated into counties but is defined by a similarity of flora and fauna. It is true that species exist on Fidalgo and Guemes, for instance, that don't exist in the "official" San Juans; those cases are so noted.

Obviously, the book is not all-inclusive or you wouldn't be able to lift it off the shelf. It necessarily reflects my own interests, knowledge, and explorations, and so you will find much more on slugs and frogs than on mushrooms. Again, I have many times felt overwhelmed by my inadequacy to attempt such an overview and perhaps should close, as Hal Borland once did, with these lines from Gustav Linnaeus, the father of modern biological classification:

"If you have remarked errors in me, your superior wisdom must pardon them. Who errs not in perambulating the realm of nature? Who can observe everything with accuracy? Correct me as a friend, and I as a friend will requite with kindness."

Come, then, and let's walk together as friends eager to share the incredible wild riches of our island world.

*Evelyn Adams*

# WILDLIFE VIEWING ETHICS

Maintain a respectful distance while watching or photographing wildlife. Constant flushing of feeding birds, especially migratory species such as swans, can lead to stress-induced disease. Use binoculars or spotting scopes for viewing.

Leave nesting birds alone. Disturbances may result in nesting failures, and approaches to occupied nests may alert predators.

Use your car as a blind when possible. Staying inside avoids stressing and scaring wildlife away, as well as ruining the experience for other wildlife watchers.

Avoid creating dangerous traffic situations: pull completely off the road to view wildlife.

Move slowly and quietly around wildlife when hiking. Avoid brightly colored clothes; wear drab greens and browns instead. Mammals are generally color-blind, but birds are not.

Camouflage shirts can often be found in thrift shops, and insulated coveralls work well for cool-weather sits. (You're likely to see more if you stay quietly for a time in one place. The optimum times for viewing are dawn and dusk, and the best places are where two or more habitats meet.)

Respect property; don't trespass through fields, yards, or private beaches, and don't litter in either private or public areas.

Do not pick wildflowers or trample over their habitats. When picking berries or rose hips, be careful not to break canes. Stay on the trails.

Shoreside, refill all holes and return large rocks to their original positions. Observe limits on the collection of edible species, and forgo the collection of others for souvenirs. Handle tidepool creatures gently and briefly, and return them to their original places.

Report marine mammal harassment to the National Marine Fisheries Service, (206) 526-6133, or the Whale Hotline, 1-800-562-8832, with the vessel's name and identification number. Federal guidelines prohibit vessels from approaching marine mammals more closely than a hundred yards or doing anything that substantially disrupts the normal behavior of these animals.

Educate others about ethical wildlife observation—"spread the word."
(These guidelines were developed with the help of the Washington State Department of Fish and Wildlife.)

# PART I

# Getting Acquainted

## A Seasonal Introduction to Wildlife

*"While I enjoy the friendship
of the seasons, I trust that nothing
can make life a burden to me."*

**—Henry David Thoreau**

*Italicized flora and fauna may be referred to in the "Wildlife Reference Section" for additional information.

# Chapter 1

# SPRING

SPRING IN THE SAN JUANS IGNORES THE CALENDAR as it washes over the islands like an incoming tide. In early February the first waves bring the siren beginnings: the courtship flight of mating bald eagles, the deep blush of red-flowering currant, the ruby throat of a returning hummingbird.

The next waves leave in their wake a scattering of wildflowers, catkins furring the willows, and insects rousing from sleep only to be rushed upon by returning swallows. High tide mark is the full flush of the season: warblers splashing the woods with song and color, otter kits tumbling along the shore, and flocks of evening grosbeaks mobbing the feeders. Pressing insistently up to the very walls of island homes, the waves of spring swell and crash with life as frogsong floods open windows, cliff swallows plaster nests under eaves, and balls of baby spiders wriggle in corner-hung webs.

A heady mix of noise, color, and motion, the return of spring stirs emotion in us as does no other seasonal event. Bound up in the first full-throated frog chorus and glimpse of jeweled hummer are the hopes of our own rejuvenation and endlessness. In spring, the heart leaps, moved by each small sign of rebirth.

Many of us look for that one sure sign or moment that heralds the season's return. For the swallows and flycatchers that wing in now, spring comes as insects fill the air. For mourning cloak butterflies, spring arrives as the sun warms them out of hibernation and into flight. For many islanders, spring comes softly, with the first peach-fuzz catkins of the willows. Or it may come brassily, with the blaring notes of the red-winged blackbird, or delicately, with the first fawn lily on the mossy rocks.

For me, spring comes with the frogs. In the first week of March, when mating calls fill the wet fields nearby, my windows go up no matter how chilly the night air, for to me early spring sings no sweeter lullaby. When the bird chorus fades at dusk and frogsong continues the spring rhythm, folks up the road who have their priorities in place and whose home borders a wetland invite friends over to sit on their porch and enjoy a natural concert. Still other neighbors confess to being driven "crazy" by the noise. Would they feel that way, I wonder, if they knew a bit more about the creatures behind the exuberant croaks?

The singers are male *Pacific chorus frogs* calling to attract mates. Bright green with a black eye stripe, these frogs are tiny fellows, not more than an inch or two long, with suction disks on their toes for climbing slippery surfaces such as skunk cabbage leaves. This species was once placed in the tree frog genus, and many still refer to it as the Pacific tree frog, but I like the switch to chorus frog because the frog's song is so much more familiar to me than its face. And I have yet to find one in a tree.

When it sings its hopeful serenade, the frog pumps air over the vocal chords in its throat pouch, which balloons out and greatly magnifies the sounds. Singing usually starts at dusk and continues through the night, although I have heard near-deafening choruses on warm afternoons.

After the singers have succeeded in attracting mates and the eggs have been laid, the females return to the woods, followed by the males a few weeks later. By May or June, frogsong no longer fills the ponds and puddles, although the lifelessness is deceptive. In early June, when you look into a shallow pond, you'll often find frogsong made visible, the water thick with tadpoles swimming in what resembles a murky apostrophe soup.

*Pacific chorus frog*

Frogs aren't the only amphibians that lay their eggs in the wetlands. If you pull a branch from a pond in early spring, you may find that with it comes a jellylike egg sac the size of a woman's fist, clear, quivering, and filled with the black dot embryos of the western long-toed salamander, our earliest egg-laying amphibian. Although the egg masses are a common find in the spring, you're not as likely to see the adult salamander on your wetland walks as you are to come across its close relative, the *rough-skinned newt*. This long-lived creature, dark brown above and bright orange below, returns each spring to its birthplace to spawn. It's sometimes difficult to spot newts as they crawl along a trail, because they blend in so well with the forest floor; watch for them especially on cooler, cloudy days.

Spring in the islands can sometimes be rather gray and waterlogged, just right for newts but perhaps not so for those of us who crave the sun. Head out into the wetlands, then, to find your rays gleaming in the mud and murky waters. Molded from light, Indian pond lilies are the spring suns of the wetland, while *skunk cabbage* rises above both its bleak name and the mud to provide one of the earliest spring shows. I know of one large patch impossible to pass without smiling; out of the muck shoot dozens of startlingly yellow tongues to lick the spring air and lift the spirits.

These brilliant yellows are some of the first flags of spring. Even when the air temperature falls below freezing (not too likely here in the spring but still interesting to note), these plants can sustain an inner temperature of 68 degrees Fahrenheit, creating a perfect nursery for newly hatching insects. Look down into those spires and you're almost certain to find a few tiny flies.

Does the smell put you off? The plant's heat also serves to spread its infamous odor, the purpose of which is not to offend but to attract—perhaps not *you* but insect pollinators, which in this case are far more important than yourself.

Local tribes once harvested the large leaves of the skunk cabbage and rolled them into cups for drinking and holding berries. They also boiled the roots for medicinal purposes. One Northwest tribe farther south, the Kathlamets, tells a tale about skunk cabbage in the ancient days, a bleak time when there wasn't yet any salmon to feed the people. Tribal members instead subsisted on roots and leaves, especially those of the skunk cabbage. When the salmon finally appeared, he rewarded the skunk cabbage for feeding his people by placing the plant in the soft soil of riverbanks. The salmon then wrapped the skunk cabbage in an elkskin blanket (the yellow spathe) and gave it a war club (the stalk, or spadix) to proudly hold aloft.

With the lengthening days of spring, island ponds and wetlands come into their fullness. Water striders skim the surface of the water, fiddleheads uncurl, dragonfly and damselfly nymphs hatch. The cuplike *Indian pond lily*, well represented on island ponds, provides protection for insect and amphibian eggs, as well as food for other species. Waterfowl and muskrats feed on the plants, as did Native Americans, who ground the seeds to flour or roasted them.

A common early spring sight is pairs of *hooded mergansers* gliding among the lilies, even when the ponds are still partially iced over. You may be lucky enough at this time to see them engage in territorial disputes, which can be rather dramatic as the drakes rear back and throw long, rippling croaks at each other.

These territorial and courtship displays spice up the spring days. Bald eagles and male hummingbirds charge those who intrude on their space, male common snipes whirl and dive above the wetlands, fanned tails noisily fluttering, and the forest echoes with the drumming of woodpeckers declaring themselves.

One of the earliest signs of spring is the piercing *conkaree* call of the *red-winged blackbird*, possibly the most numerous land bird in North America and surely one of the most loudly territorial. This bold bird with the flashing red shoulder epaulets stridently defends his nesting territory starting in early February. The red-wing's calls and aggressive behavior aren't limited to warding off interlopers of his own species but extend to hawks, cats, and even humans.

Spring speaks in many voices: frog croak, insect hum, and, perhaps most eloquently, birdsong. From the ringing call of the red-wing to the cries of soaring red-tails and the delicate, dry notes of warblers in the woods, a San Juan spring is a natural, noisy symphony.

Songs during the breeding season are from males courting females and declaring territories. The notion that these songs are the happy expressions of birds greeting the return of spring is charming but largely mistaken. The singers are engaged instead in the serious business of warding off competition that would hinder their nesting success. Still, who can say for sure that a bird never extends its tune on a spring dawn out of sheer *joie de vivre?*

As I took a walk through woods bordering a wetland, the March air was filled with the trilling of winter wrens, the nasal calls of nuthatches, the blasting of red-wings, and the drawn-out note of a varied thrush sounding like a police whistle in the midst of a noon rush hour. Nervous little songbirds called warblers passed through, filling the spring woods with bright colors and beguiling music. More than other birds, warblers move about in the trees and so are harder to spot. They've come back, as have the swallows and flycatchers, to feed on the spring insects. About eight species migrate through the islands in the spring and fall, with a few remaining to breed through the summer.

A friend who visited the Midwest for some time one spring returned here with the comment that she'd felt a bit disoriented on her visit. Unnerved by all the unfa-miliar bird sounds, she likened the experience to listening to a foreign language.

So that you do not feel a stranger in your own land, now is a good season to learn the language of our island birds. Start listening early in spring, when the migrants have not yet arrived to confuse your ears and the trees have not fully leafed out to hide the singers. Early morning and late afternoon are best; birds sing loudest in the dawning hours, with another, less intense chorus toward evening.

As you listen, try to put phrases to the sounds, or make comparisons to other familiar sounds to aid your memory. For instance, the hooting call of the *California quail* is a three-note "Where ARE you?" You'll rarely see the olive-sided flycatcher in the canopy of the spring woods, but you'll know it's there from the whistled "SEE you!" or "I SEE you!" If you hear an upward-sliding creak, somewhat like the open-ing of a door that needs oiling, you'll know you're listening to a *rufous-sided towhee.* A nasal "Yeah, yeah, yeah" in the trees will be the red-breasted nuthatch, and a fast, frantically loud "Wait, wait, wait, wait, wait! . . ." identifies a *northern flicker.*

Bird tapes can help your efforts, but remember that the songs given are usually only the most common ones; birds make different sounds at different times, and most songbirds have repertoires that include two or more different songs. We even have our imitators here, such as the Steller's jay, which gives a good rendition of a red-tailed hawk. You may be throwing up your hands at this point and wondering, Why bother? Indeed, why not just enjoy the bird sounds—is the experience any the less for not knowing the singers?

When a bird is hidden away in the treetops, our knowing its song can bring up a mental image of the singer and, one hopes, some knowledge of its habits, which magnify the experience. There are those who cringe at classifying nature, believing that the result is a diminished experience and, indeed, the wonder may be lost if one's focus is solely on checklists and memorization. But the labels themselves should be the least of it. If behind them lies an understanding of the intricacies of nature, then wonder escalates to an eye-popping pitch. So take some time to really hear those birds; they're as much a part of our island home as are summer tourists and sunset and mountain views. Birdsong is a great gift that not only charms us but also anchors us more firmly to our special spot on earth. Who can truly call a place home who doesn't know the songs of its birds?

Another bird sound you'll often hear during the springtime is a surprisingly feeble one, considering the bird from which it comes. I remember the letdown the first time I attached the *bald eagle's* cry to its source; I was amazed at its wavering and, to my mind, wimpish quality. Surely such a bird should blast forth with the strength of a great blue heron's squawk or at least the steady *scree* of the red-tail.

In no other area, however, does the bald eagle disappoint (except perhaps in its thieving manner of bullying an osprey out of its catch). More often it inspires, and never so much as when one is lucky enough to observe the eagle's nuptial flight. Eagles mate for life, spectacularly reaffirming their relationship in early February by climbing higher and higher in ever-narrowing circles and then folding their wings and rocketing downward. Or they may lock talons together and plunge to the earth, breaking their fall just a few breathless yards from land or water.

Nest sites are commonly in old-growth Douglas-firs, especially those with good visibility close to water, since fish and waterfowl are the eagle's primary food. The islands have about ninety-four pairs of nesting eagles, one of the largest populations of breeding balds in the continental United States, thanks primarily to good habitat: lots of shoreline, upland nesting grounds, and wide foraging areas. Scan the treetops along the shore and watch for the gleam of white that says eagle.

Despite the healthy number of eagles here, only about one out of every four fledglings will survive to adulthood. The primary cause of death is starvation, although these birds are opportunistic feeders: a Whidbey Island landfill hosts eagles waiting each day for spoils from a Safeway truck, and the former landfill on Orcas was a good, if less than poetic, spot to see eagles in the spring.

This utilitarian adaptation of eagles may surprise some, such as the person I once heard ask a biologist why eagles need such careful protection when habits such as dump foraging "prove" they can adjust to man. The biologist replied, rather wistfully, I thought, "What kind of eagles do we want, urban nesters and dump feeders?" Most of us, I think, prefer the eagle the way we see it in the islands in early spring— bold, unchained, and remote. Long may it remain so.

Walk the meadows in spring and savor the stirring life: fresh mole tunnels through the grasses, scattered sprays of wildflowers, foraging hornets and bees. *Western yellow jacket* queens are laying thousands of eggs and workers are out finding food for the larvae. Fat bumble queens wing their way low over the grasses looking for a place to build a nest for their eggs. Watch also for the yellow sparks that are goldfinches hunting for seeds, although these birds will wait for the high seed productivity of late summer before building their nests.

Meadow wildflowers are just coming into bloom now: buttercups, spring gold, prairie stars, blue-eyed Marys, and a host of others. The large, starry purple blooms of great camas are a common spring sight in island meadows; Lummi Indians used to hunt for the best bulbs in May on Matia, Spieden, Clark, and Barnes islands. The plant was highly prized by Northwest natives, who used the bulbs for sweetening.

As we slip from winter to spring in our evergreen islands, the change lacks the drama felt in other parts of the country where the world suddenly turns from ash gray to lacy green. But walk through the woods now and you may feel a new brightness before you realize its source.

In spring, the greens glow. Tufts of bright new growth hang from the tips of hemlock and fir branches. The stems of red huckleberry gleam green, the tips of cedar boughs are a much lighter shade, and even salal shrubs sport bright lime-colored leaves among the dark older growth. On one spring hike, I stopped to admire a young hemlock about 4 feet high that looked like a small Christmas tree, so full was it of bright green tips that hung like glowing balls—only here it was spring that had done the decorating.

Trees are growing new layers of wood, red alder and big-leaf maple are filling out with leaves (the maples drip with cascades of yellowish flowers), and many shrubs of the understory are heavily dusted with pollen. One of our earliest spring bloomers is the *red-flowering currant*, which provides a good source of nectar for returning hummingbirds. The osoberry, or *Indian plum*, is another early bloomer, easily recognized by drooping white blossoms that have a rather rank odor (thus earning it another name, skunkbush).

Although there is no poison ivy or poison oak in the islands, *stinging nettle* pushes up fast along the trails, growing to 8 feet high in some conditions. This perennial scourge spreads quickly by rhizomes: shallow, rootlike stems that run horizontally underground and send up shoots.

Whereas nettle once served coastal tribes who wove its fibers into gill nets and brewed tonics for various ailments, today it's far more famous for causing discomfort. Hikers in the area quickly learn to wear long sleeves and pants even in the warmest weather when tramping through moist, disturbed woodlands.

The stems of the nettle and the undersides of its leaves are covered with fine hairs that act as tiny syringes filled with a pressurized acid mix. When the hairs penetrate the skin and break, they inject a toxin that may burn for a couple of hours to a couple of days. For certain tribal seal hunters who rubbed nettle over their bodies to insure wakefulness during a hunt, this toxin was a boon. Nature-lovers who stumble into nettle and want to sleep in peace can rub thimbleberry leaves on the sting to relieve it or try the remedies in "Mac Smith: All the World's a Garden."

Forest trails are edged more enjoyably with spring wildflowers: dainty starflower, peppermint-striped candyflower, and white fawn lilies standing apart and alone, heads drooping heavily on hair's-breadth stems. Many small woodland plants must do their blooming in the early spring, while the sun's rays can still reach them through the budding canopy. Spires of white foamflower splash the spring woods, grounded cousins to the newly emerging *ocean spray* blooms overhead. What wonderfully descriptive names to remind us of our salt-washed islands even in the deepest woods.

Queen of the forest and still another reminder of our saltwater surroundings is the exquisite calypso, named for a sea nymph who lured the legendary Ulysses to her island with promises of immortality. If any flower could be said to promise wonders, it's this bewitching orchid, as exotic and surprising on the forest floor as a jewel dropped in the mud.

Morels are pushing up now, and creeping along the trails in the moist spring woods are the millipedes, snails, and *banana slugs*. One of the surest signs of spring is having to walk the trails with head bowed to avoid squashing the slugs, snails, newts, and snakes slithering underfoot. Snails and slugs are mating now; look for their pearly egg clusters under rocks and debris. If you try to handle a snail, it will hurriedly shun your company and slam its door: a hornlike appendage called an operculum that exactly fits the shell opening.

The most often seen millipede is black and edged with yellow along its segments; watch the lovely motion of its pairs of legs as they undulate through the mud. Gently pick one up and it will immediately curl into a defensive ball and likely emit a strong-smelling, brownish fluid to discourage your attentions.

Raccoon kits are born now, as are fawns, squirrels, and foxes. There are small populations of *red fox* on San Juan Island (where they were released years ago to control the number of rabbits) and on Fidalgo. Foxes use maternity dens in the spring but rarely den up during the rest of the year. *Raccoons* may be found nesting in vacated fox dens, hollow trees, or other natural cavities. The *Douglas squirrel* mates in early spring and bears its young in May and June in tree holes or balled nests of mosses, twigs, and shredded bark high in the branches.

*Rufous hummingbird at red-flowering currant*

Mating and birthing are in full swing shoreside now, too. *Harbor seals* begin breeding in mid-April, as do *river otters*. Although you might not expect river otters to be saltwater creatures, these are the otters you'll find frolicking in the rocky coves of the islands, as well as in lakes and marshes. (Sea otters are found only along the outer coast; pictures often show them resting on their backs in the water, something river otters rarely do.) River otters mate in April or May, but the kits aren't born until the following spring.

Deep within the waters, *bull kelp,* which has overwintered as an almost microscopic plant, attaches itself to rocks and begins to grow again. *Northern sea lions*, having spent the winter in the islands, leave to breed on rocky islets along the coast, while elephant seals pass through on their way to northern feeding grounds. Far offshore, gray whales migrate past our islands from Baja California to the Bering Sea. The migration tapers off after mid-April, with some grays veering off to forage in the islands during the spring and summer.

*Common loons* will be around until May, when they leave for nesting grounds. You'll often see them from the shore, molted into a dazzling black-and-white breeding plumage, and perhaps you'll be lucky enough to hear their haunting tremolo. For ages, people have believed that something more than a mating invitation was communicated in that eerie call. An old Native American legend says that when the world was new, two fishermen quarreled at sea. One knocked the other unconscious, cut out his tongue, and robbed him of his catch. The thief was turned into a crow by the Great Spirit for his crime, and the other became a loon whose sad warbling cries still tell the story of betrayal to all who will hear.

Migration is one of the strongest pulse beats of spring, drumming its song in whales, *salmon*, salamanders, and, of course, birds. Winged comings and goings are especially numerous, making spring probably the most exciting season for birdwatchers. With the arousal of insects from eggs and cocoons come the birds who love to dine on them: first the swallows (tree swallows, then the violet-greens, cliff swallows, and barn swallows, the only ones with forked tails). Next come the warblers and then the flycatchers. (It's interesting to note that in earlier times people didn't believe such small birds were capable of long migrational flights. Instead, a popular theory was that they hibernated in caves or hollow trees through the winter.)

Marshes and lakes come alive with the return of red-winged blackbirds, hooded mergansers, and blue-winged and cinnamon teals, while other ducks such as wigeons, canvasbacks, and shovelers head north. Loons and grebes and many raptors wing their way north, although springtime is when you'll see the return of the turkey vulture and the osprey. But let's look now at a visitor hardly bigger than a swallowtail butterfly yet just as fascinating as its larger traveling companions: the *rufous hummingbird*.

One spring I recorded the first of these birds with the glinting red-sequined throats as early as March 4 at my feeder; another was reported out at Cattle Point on San Juan a day later. The males arrive from Mexico before the females and can be easily identified by their flashing throat patches, or gorgets (named for medieval armor worn on the throat and made up of tiny mirrorlike pieces), and reddish brown backs. Females are duller, with green backs, light bellies, and rufous sides.

The males are aggressive at this time, seeking out and defending territory from not only other hummers but also much larger birds and even humans. If you hear what sounds like a giant bee dive-bombing your head, you've encountered one of these males, which may simply want to check out a red button on your shirt. The humming comes from the bird's incredible wing beats, up to 200 per second if necessary, although more usually between 70 and 80 whipped furiously in a figure-eight pattern. The bird's shoulder joints are uniquely made to rotate 180 degrees, and its breast muscles are proportionately large to provide power. Although this tiny dynamo weighs no more than a nickel, it expends more energy for weight than any other animal in the world. Hummers depend on nectar for high sugar content and eat aphids and spiders to build muscles. Island flowers especially favored include honeysuckle, columbine, and hedge nettle, all of which have nectaries (tubes that secrete nectar) too long for bees to penetrate but perfect for a hummingbird's needle bill. In our fairly cool area, the birds store food in their crops before dark and slowly digest it overnight to stay warm.

This is perhaps as good a place as any to leave our spring rambles. Watch the tiny jeweled bird, one of the first to announce the season, as it draws a long sip of nectar from the blossom of the red columbine. Feel the faint breath of its wings as the bird flutters before you, and drink up with it a honeyed foretaste of the full, ripe days of summer.

---

## SPRING WILDLIFE HAPPENINGS

- Pacific chorus frogs fill the night with mating songs.
- Willow catkins emerge, turning from gray to yellow with pollen.
- Rufous hummingbirds arrive in February (males about three weeks before females).
- Bald eagles mate in mid-February and lay eggs in March. Chicks hatch in April. Numbers decline somewhat as transient eagles move north to breeding areas.
- Brant population returns to Padilla Bay to feed on its way to nesting grounds in Alaska.
- Spring-run salmon return to freshwater streams to spawn.
- Wildflowers are blooming now, as well as skunk cabbage and pond lilies, honeysuckle, wild roses, and berry plants such as red-flowering currant and salmonberry.
- Morels push up in woods.
- Swans, snow geese, Canada geese, and the majority of loons, grebes, pintails, shovelers, wigeons, canvasbacks, scaups, scoters, buffleheads, oldsquaws, ring-necked ducks, and green-winged teals head north.
- Seabirds such as murres, rhinoceros auklets, puffins, and pigeon guillemots gather in nesting colonies.
- Turkey vultures return, as do ospreys, swifts, swallows, flycatchers, warblers, vireos, and cedar waxwings.
- Transient hawks such as rough-leggeds, northern harriers, kestrels, and merlins head north, while local hawks begin courting.
- Bees and hornets lay eggs.
- River otters mate but don't give birth till following spring.
- Foxes build dens; fawns and raccoons are born; muskrats bear first litter.
- Snails and slugs mate and lay egg clusters.
- Newts and salamanders return to birthplace in wetlands to spawn.
- Black-tailed deer begin to grow new antlers.

- Harbor seals breed offshore on rocks and secluded beaches.
- Bull kelp spores attach to rocks and begin to grow.
- Madrones bear masses of fragrant white blossoms April to May.
- Northern sea lions and elephant seals migrate south.

## BACKYARD WILDLIFE ACTIVITIES

Plant a butterfly garden now. Especially good choices include buddleia; herb combinations such as sage, thyme, peppermint, and catnip; and flowers like sweet alyssum, lilac, zinnia, statice, and marigolds.

Set out nesting materials such as bits of yarn, thread, dryer lint, fur, and hair, or hang them from a tree limb in a loose mesh bag.

Don't keep suet out as the season advances. When it gets greasy it can mat feathers and thereby reduce birds' waterproofing. It can even cause the loss of facial feathers—downy woodpeckers who feed on sun-warmed suet may become barefaced.

Clean and set out hummingbird feeders now. Red food coloring is unnecessary and unsafe, and use no more than one part sugar to four parts water; this ratio may be reduced to 1:6 once the birds find the feeder. Boil the water before adding sugar to slow mold growth, and let the solution cool before filling the feeder. Do not use honey (which helps fungus grow) or artificial sweeteners (which have no calories). Change the solution every four or five days, more often in warmer weather—fermentation may result in enlargement of livers in hummingbirds.

In addition to providing feeders, plant flowers—especially red or orange tubular blossoms—to attract hummers. Fuchsias are popular, as are hollyhocks, larkspurs, gladioli, honeysuckle, and flowering red currant.

# MAC SMITH

## *All the World's a Garden*

As it does for so many of us, a San Juan spring holds a special place in Mac Smith's heart. "Spring for me starts in February, because that's when I see plants coming back, like the flowering red currant and willows and Indian plum," he says. "It's just like, heeere it comes!"

Mac is an expert in the ethnobotany (the uses of plants) of the Pacific Northwest. He discovered the San Juans when he moved to Bellingham in 1976 and spent most of his free time hiking and kayaking through the islands. The area is especially good for botanizing, he feels, because of the variety of habitats (woodlands, grassy knolls, shoreline) and mild temperatures: "You get a lot of late bloomers out here, a lot of layover plants. It's real mild for them, they don't freak out much in the fall." A good example is yerba buena, his favorite herb, gone by summer's end in most places but still blooming at his Orcas home in October.

Another reason the islands are so botanically blessed is that plants such as soapberry, lodgepole pine, juniper, and madrone can exist here but normally aren't found in the more rainy areas on the mainland. These singularly placed plants are "like me," Mac says with a grin. "They like open, sunny, south-facing, low-rainfall slopes. When I'm out with groups, it's nice to 'ooh and ah' people with rare things. We have this added treat of plants that are special and only grow in this area."

Although Mac has been studying plants for over twenty years now, there are a few rare ferns and wildflowers on his Orcas property that he has never encountered before. This is all the more amazing when one learns that his botany professor at Western Washington University "could never bring in a plant to our class that I didn't know—my claim to fame! He had to go east of the mountains to gather plants for our test, and I still knew them."

Mac's proficiency comes from having thumbed through thousands of plant books over the years. His interest in botany began when he worked at a tree nursery in California, learning shrubs and trees from all over the world. At the same time, he became interested in wild edible plants for survival ("in case I ever had to leave home in a hurry") and bought a set of descriptive plant cards, which he memorized and tried to match to the plants he found in the field. "Every time I was out on a hike or walk, I'd see what was out there, then go back home and look it up in the cards or books. I'd see if I could find a use for it and then write all that down." He smiles and shrugs. "My personality is very compulsive. I just got so far into it, I couldn't get out."

Once in Bellingham, he began taking pictures of plants, "thousands and thousands of pictures. Bellingham is still a rural area where you can ride your bike or walk down an alley and see all these wild plants, so it was a good place for me to do my surveys. I'd ride my bike and pull over in fields and walk around." In 1981, he started teaching and sharing his excitement about plants with others.

Today, when he leads plant walks, Mac is lucky if he can move a hundred yards in three hours. Plant after plant is pointed out with the constant query, What's it good for? He encourages the snail's pace: "Stop and take bird steps and poke your nose down in areas. That's part of my philosophy of teaching plants—stop and look and smell it, look around it, and get all the clues you can about a plant, because it may help you later."

As we walked the rocky outcrop of Orcas's Madrona Point, Mac pointed to a withered patch of plants. "Twenty years ago, I'd look down here and see nothing but grass. Now I look and I see great camas all over." Although in the spring the blooms of the benign great camas and its poisonous cousin, the death camas, are easily identified by color, now there was only a dry brown uniformity at our feet. So what omniscient knowledge does Mac draw upon to determine that we're standing over the fair instead of the foul?

From experience, he knows how to tell great from death camas in their dried states by shaking the seeds out of their pods: the former has round black seeds; the latter's are flat and golden brown. "I know I can come here in March or April and see a wonderful display of camas, whereas if you didn't notice these, you might just see a nice grassy knoll."

He urges folks not to limit themselves to springtime displays but to look at plants in all of their stages. "Once you know that this is a different cycle of a plant you see in the spring, it adds more dimension to just looking at a plant in bloom. I always tell people, go to a favorite, easily accessible place if you want to learn about plants, and go there every three months. Try to look at those same plants and watch the way they change." He notes that even though plants don't fly away while you're studying them (a decided advantage over bird-watching), they are not completely static. "They do change, they do have variations, they're not just one picture in one book. The more you get out there and watch, the more clues you look for, the more you'll see how they're dynamic things. They move, they migrate, they change. They even become disturbed or extinct in certain areas."

To really get to know the plants, go out in the early spring and try to identify sprouts, and then in late fall look at the fruits, seeds, and dried plants. For an added challenge, try to pick out plants from a distance simply by their colors. "I identify plants from sometimes hundreds of feet away, just by knowing there's that certain shade of yellow fall foliage, that's a serviceberry. Or there's a little bit of orange in those autumn leaves, that's the crabapple. You can be driving down the freeway and see a certain shade of rust and know that was a patch of sheep sorrel in bloom, just by the shade of color."

Mac hauls along a hefty supply of books on his plant walks, and the ones he favors are full of color plates. "I gave up the technical stuff while teaching," he says. "Especially in the last few years. When I've concentrated on things I think people would like, I've had a lot of comments like 'You're the first botanist who hasn't confused me with technical jargon or talked down to me.' Because I'm just sharing stuff I want other people to be excited about." To those who really want to get serious about identifying plants, he stresses the importance of learning scientific names and systematic botany, but otherwise he doesn't use the technical terms while teaching unless asked. "A lot of the good reception I get from my courses is, wow, you can just look at a plant, learn a little bit about its natural history and its use in a general, fun way, without getting wrapped up in botanical lingo and scientific names."

Most people are visual learners, he feels, including himself. The tomes he touts are the picture books he has learned from, such as the one he now pulls from his pack, the *Golden Guide to Weeds*. "I use the Golden Guides extensively," he says. "This one on weeds, I learned *tons* of stuff about plants, just by a picture. You can take this out in the field with you, and you can look at weeds and learn them just by osmosis." He admits you won't be able to do this with all the plants, however. Some remain a mystery until you finally break down and pull out the Hitchcock or, better still, find someone who's familiar with the plant.

His all-time favorite book is Lewis Clark's *Wildflowers of the Pacific Northwest*, a huge volume of wonderful close-ups, excerpts of which are also published in smaller field guides of different habitats: sea coast, marsh and waterways, forest and woodland, field and slope. Any spare time in college found him leafing through this volume and imprinting many of its photos on his mind. "To this day I can be hiking around and find a plant that I've never seen before in my life, but I'll remember seeing it in that book. If you're going to get into this for a long period of time, that's a good investment, just to let a lot of this stuff go in at your leisure."

Many of the problems in identifying plants come from not taking enough time to discover all the clues about a plant; instead of concentrating on just one leaf, for instance, Mac suggests looking at both the mature and young leaves, at a couple of different bushes of the plant, or at a different part of the plant. Plants do not always follow a book's description exactly, and one must allow for that. "It might have smaller leaves, or the leaves might be a little greener, or the plant might be a little taller or stubbier or lankier. The flowers might be bigger."

Mac also teaches classes on foraging. On one five-day backpacking trip on the Olympic Peninsula, he chose to forage his way up the coast. His students brought their own meals, and although one might think Mac's pack would have been far lighter than theirs, he brought as much weight in condiments as they did in food. He acknowledges that everything could be eaten plain, but he's a bit of a gourmet on the trail and finds that garnishing wild plants helps many people get past their hesitancy about digging in. He also likes to experiment with different ways of fixing wild foods, serving up salads, soups, and stir-fries to the "guinea pigs" in his classes.

"When I say *edible*, I don't necessarily mean *palatable*," he's careful to point out. "You have to use your imagination with wild foods. You don't go to a grocery store and buy a bag of vegetables and take them home and eat them all raw. You cook some of them, put some of them in salads, add dressing to some, put cheese on some, put them in soups. You've got a hundred different things you do with vegetables. Same thing with wild plants. Find out how to bring out their best attributes."

Seaweeds are a favorite of his: "There's hundreds of different kinds of seaweed and they lend themselves to all different kinds of cookery: steaming, baking, drying, stuffing, soups and stews, fresh in salads." Mac loves to snorkel and bring up a batch of tasty weed for the table. Some types he slowly dries over a campfire for a smoked-salmon flavor. Others have a nutty taste and still others are like spinach greens or beef jerky. Some are so gelatinous they can be turned into puddings.

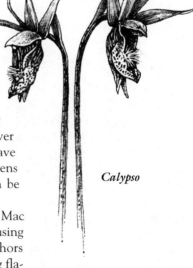

*Calypso*

When he was first learning marine cuisine, Mac took a class where the entire meal was prepared using different seaweeds: main dishes, salads, and hors d'oeuvres. "Someone made a nice white pudding fla-

31

vored with vanilla," he says, almost smacking his lips. Someone else made an energy bar with nuts and honey layered with dried nori. "It tasted just like baklava. After that class, I thought, Well, *there's* a whole new part of the plant kingdom I'm surely including in my foraging list!" Should you still harbor reservations about dining on seaweed or salal, remember that wild plants are high in nutritive value. Dandelion leaves contain six times the amount of vitamin A in lettuce, and just three rose hips can have the same amount of vitamin C as one orange, according to Mac. "Seaweed gives you almost every mineral you need, many different vitamins, and protein, but it's low-calorie. A good nutritional source."

Mac stops at a large orangish shrub at the head of the trail and picks through the branches for one of his favorite wild foods. He explains how the Pacific crab-apple is at its ripest when yellow on one side and orange on the other. Our only wild apple, it's a rather tart, grape-sized fruit that makes good sauce if you can collect enough of them. To make a tasty, purplish applesauce, Mac mixes in an equal portion of another favorite berry, salal.

"A lot of times I'll introduce people to [salal berries] and they'll go, 'Ugh, I've eaten that before and I've hated it.' Or 'My mother always told me that was poisonous.'" Salal berries are edible, but to taste flavorful, they need to be picked at the right time. "I think a lot of people don't eat berries when they're ripe," says Mac. "They'll try a wild berry and maybe it wasn't ripe or was growing in a bad place, and from then on, it's like, oh, that's a terrible berry." Salal berries ripen in August, and for the sweetest, Mac recommends collecting from plants growing on a sunny south slope. Combine them with crabapples, eat them raw, or dry them like raisins. His favorite solar dehydrator in the summertime, by the way, is simply the dashboard of his car.

He's often asked about madrone berries, which mature in the fall, and says that, again, you have to get them when ripe and you have to cook them. "On one tree, there might be ripe berries and unripe berries that are similar in color," he says. "You have to find the ideal color and texture; you kind of feel it. It's like fruit in the grocery store. You look for color, smell, texture." About the madrone berries, he says, "I steam them with oatmeal, which seems to work okay."

Mac has also munched on cambium, the growing green layer just under a tree's outer bark. Cambium was a major source of starch for the Native Americans, who would remove the outer bark and then scrape out the inner layer. "It actually peeled off like rolls of cooked lasagna noodles." He has experimented with the cambium of western hemlock and describes it as a very sweet and chewy substance that looks and smells like pasta. A film-canisterful provided hours of chewing. "It was good. It was filling." When collecting cambium, he stresses, be sure to take it only from wind-fallen trees. Pulling a piece of bark off a living tree can harm it, and taking a ring of bark from the trunk will kill it.

There are a few other caveats to remember when foraging for wild food, number one among them to know what plant you're working with—"absolutely no experimentation on anything you don't know." Even after twenty years of stalking the wild salal, Mac says he still comes across situations that can be dangerous. A case in point was the Oregon crabapple shrub on which we had just indulged ourselves. Entwined among its branches was a honeysuckle vine, the fruit of which is poisonous. The berries are reddish like the apples, smaller but not impossible to confuse with them, especially for the novice or someone not fully alert. "Make sure you're eating what you think you're eating," he warns.

Two of the most poisonous plants in North America make their home here: poison hemlock, which looks like wild parsley or wild carrot, and water hemlock, which looks like parsnips. Avoid any parsley-parsnip plant, Mac says, unless you're absolutely certain of what it is, and he takes his own advice. "I can make mistakes. I've looked at wild carrot and poison hemlock together. I can see the difference, but what if I had a bad day or was kind of sleepy?" Once he picked bunches of greens with some poison hemlock mixed in; the deadly plants had been growing with the edible ones, but they escaped his notice until he went through the clusters and found two little sprigs of the poison "parsley" hidden among them.

Collect only the young, fresh sprouts of wild edible plants (the bigger they are, the more bitter and tough), and when trying new plants, eat sparingly at first to avoid concentrating elements that may be harmful in large quantities or cause allergic reactions. He urges people to find plants that are "user-friendly." Skunk cabbage, for instance, is a dangerous plant to try because it contains calcium oxalate crystals. One part is edible if steamed, "but if you eat the wrong part or you don't steam it long enough, it could swell your throat shut. So do you want to experiment with this plant?" he asks. "Or do you want to find something like yerba buena that you can make a wonderful tea with?"

Wild teas are a favorite with Mac. A confessed coffee lover, he'll sometimes mix up thirty herbs to make a strong, flavorful brew so full of vitamins and minerals it's "like drinking brewer's yeast but with a different flavor." (Thank goodness!) And not only herbs go in but also rose hips, dried wild strawberries and Oregon grapes, blackberries, western hemlock and grand fir needles, and three or four wild mints. "It's wonderful, when you're done drinking, to try and figure out what you just drank by all the dried parts in it. It's like reading tea leaves, only this is reading tea *parts*, flowers and berries and bits of stems and leaves." Mac sees gathering his wild teas as a way to enjoy the rich plant life of spring and summer and the fruits and berries of fall throughout the dark winter. "Go out in the spring, summer, and fall. Collect herbs and dry them, and then have this wonderful tea all winter while waiting for spring to come," he urges.

Bear in mind that collecting should never be done on private property or in parks or biological preserves and should be limited to abundant plant populations. Use your common sense when collecting and take only the parts needed; never collect rare or delicate plants or those which number only a few in the area.

Many local wild plants have uses other than as food. Their purpose may be medicinal, as in the case of the cascara, or the "Ex-Lax tree," as Mac calls it. "I teach elderhostels too, and you bring that up and they'll go, 'Oh, my mother used to give me cascara juice.'" Snowberries, scorned by most birds and mammals, are nature's Go-Jo, or waterless hand cleaner. When he's working around a campfire, Mac uses the berries daily to scrub the grime off.

Stinging nettle may have been useful to early Northwest natives, but woods walkers today find it far more bane than boon. Sometimes there seem to be nearly as many remedies for nettle stings as there are plants, but the "all-time best cure that I've ever found," says Mac, who has seen it work time and time again, even in severe cases, "is broad-leaf plantain, the weed that grows in driveways and along trails." He does a lot of string making with nettle on his field trips, and his hands often get badly stung. But he has noticed that when he cracks the nettle stem open to take off the fiber, if he rubs the inner pith of the stem over his numbing fingers, that cures the sting. So next time the plant attacks and there's no plantain to be had, remember it carries its own cure, if you've the mettle to split the nettle.

Mac's 5 acres on Orcas, Yerba Buena Gardens, are covered with his favorite herb. "The reason I've always liked it is because I'm really into the smells of plants," he says, inhaling deeply as he rubs the square stem of the mint. "It's got a powerful odor and a beautiful little flower." He notes that simply the herb alone makes a wonderful tea, and that San Francisco was once almost named Yerba Buena, which means "good herb," because the plant grows all over down there. It grows all over his property, too, much to his delight. In places it has literally taken over and carpeted the land, "with wild strawberries growing in it, and twinflower, and five varieties of wild orchids. You can crawl along and eat strawberries and smell yerba buena and look at wild orchids," he says. "It's like . . . *nirvana*."

One can almost see him sitting on a favorite grassy knoll (south-facing), surrounded by wildflowers, sipping his yerba buena tea and munching on cambium and seaweed bars, transported. "I'm one of those people who get so excited with any flower, even the wild geranium, which is a weed."

He smiles. "I love that little thing."

---

The now shabby deck of cards Mac began with years ago is called "Edible and Poisonous Plants of the Western U.S." (Calvin P. Burt and Frank G. Heyl, Lake Oswego, OR 97034, 1973). In addition to the Golden Guides, he also recommends the western edition of the *Audubon Field Guide to North American Wildflowers, Western Region,* by Richard Spellenberg (New York: Alfred A. Knopf, 1979): *Mountain Wildflowers,* by Ron Taylor (Portland: Binford & Mort, 1975), and *Wildflowers 1: The Cascades,* by Elizabeth Horn (Beaverton, Ore.: Touchstone Press, 1972). Nancy Turner's book *Food Plants of British Columbia Indians,* parts 1 and 2 (Victoria, B.C.: British Columbia Provincial Museum, 1978) was a real inspiration for him. For discovering whether or not a plant is edible, Mac recommends *Wild Edible Plants* by Don Kirk (Healdsburg, Calif.: Naturegraph, 1970) as the most compact exhaustive guide.

# Chapter 2

# SUMMER

NOW THE FLUTTERY HEARTBEAT OF SPRING HAS SLOWED to the peaceful rhythm of rolled-up-pants days along summer shores. Animals drowse in the afternoon heat, and seeds drift lazily on the breeze. Years ago, Samish and Lummi Indians made summer food migrations through the islands, carrying cattail mat shelters and filling their nets with fish and their baskets with roots and berries. Now islanders try to hold onto golden dawdle days amid the relentless press of tourism.

Boats fill the harbors as fully as the leaves fill the trees. Hikers and bikers cover trails and roadsides, crowding every corner along with animals whose broods, clutches, and litters creep and fly forth. But summer's essence is no fragile flower easily trodden under by too many feet. Most of us still find the time and opportunity to soak up rich sun-washed moments that will rise again in us like sap during the wet gray chill of winter.

At this latitude, summer's daylight lasts forever. Walk into a meadow as the sun is sinking and watch for *little brown bats* streaking after insects. In the meadow, you're not so far away as you might think from the waters in which you may have sailed that afternoon. As you watch the bats, ask yourself what, if anything, they have in common with whales. How is a winged, mouselike creature (the Germans call it a "flitter-mouse") in any way like the mighty orca that in summer closes in on the islands in pursuit of migrating salmon?

The bat, our only true flying mammal, hunts the dimming summer sky; the orca, a fellow mammal, tracks its prey through the dusky saltwater depths. Neither is favored with the owl's night vision, so how do they make so many unerring strikes?

Echolocation is the four-star word binding these two species. Bats and whales locate their prey by bouncing high-frequency sound waves off different objects and receiving back a "sound picture" by echo; this lets a bat, for instance, know if it's headed toward a telephone wire or an insect. Try to fool one by tossing a pebble into the air. It may initially charge toward it, but won't long be deceived into catching a mouthful of rock for supper.

It was once thought that bats avoided obstacles and zeroed in on their prey through acutely sensitive nerves in the wing, and it's not hard to see how this idea originated. The bat's wing is an amazing structure, a huge webbed membrane stretched between long bony fingers. Were our fingers as long in proportion to our bodies as a bat's, they would measure an incredible 4 to 5 feet.

Bats have long suffered an unjust reputation as harbingers of evil and carriers of rabies. The Wolf Hollow Wildlife Rehabilitation Center once received a rather dramatic report of a "rabid bat, foaming at the mouth," on a Friday Harbor sidewalk. The tiny creature was sick but far from "foaming" and posed no threat even to flies at that point. According to Wolf Hollow, the chance of a bat carrying rabies is minute—less than 1 percent—and if a bat *is* a carrier, it will sicken and die of the disease. The precaution, then, is simple: should you find a bat on the ground unable to fly, leave it alone. Perhaps, though, if you remember that the little brown bat can eat up to three thousand mosquitoes in a night, you'll call in help for this sadly maligned friend.

Return to the meadow on a summer's afternoon and take a moment to relax among the tall grasses; summer is the time to enjoy again a child's close-up view of the world. Bend the stiff grass stems in your fingers; then let your hand float through their frothy tops and watch their shadow patterns play over your bare legs. Listen to the music of the meadow, a ripe, humming chorus of bee buzz and grasshopper crackle. As frogsong was spring's natural symphony, so insectsong becomes the serenade of summer.

Sun-worshipping sylphs are floating over the grasses and flowers; look for showy swallowtails, meadow fritillaries, skippers, and painted ladies, among others. It's a lovely happenstance that as birdsong fades with the summer, butterflies fill our sunny days, silent but fluttering just as gaily as bird notes through the air.

Many grasses and plants of the summer meadow have died back, leaving behind a legacy in seed, and wonderful are the ways in which those seeds seek out new homes. The lazily drifing parachutes of the dandelion are a familiar sight, but other seeds are more secretive in their journeys. They may ride unharmed in the digestive tracts of birds or stick tenaciously to the coats of furry hosts. One abundant mustard, shepherd's purse, has a particularly fascinating dispersal method. Its sticky seeds attract ants; unable to pull loose, they soon die and become food for the growing plant.

Atop the fluffy-headed thistle can be found our state bird, the sunny goldfinch. The male's golden plumage sparkles in summer as in no other season in this late nester's bid to attract a mate. His canary yellow is set off by black wings and a black cap set rakishly on his head, a sporty outfit that will disappear in the fall. Goldfinches are fond of the seeds of many wild grasses, but especially covet the thistle's downy fluff to line their nests with in August. Once the clutches hatch, goldfinch flocks may be seen foraging among the grasses in late summer to feed the hungry nestlings.

Birdsong will wane with the summer as parents concentrate on feeding and otherwise tending to their young, but in late May and early June, rise early and listen to the dawn chorus. In the earliest hours, not long after midnight, the swallows call and are soon followed by robins, vireos, and warblers that greet the sun as it rises over Mount Baker.

You may miss the excitement of the spring sky, when migration and mating rituals stirred the air, but summer brings two winged visitors to our islands who will not disappoint.

*Turkey vultures* return in the spring and are seen frequently in the islands until their departure in September. Over a thousand birds leave Victoria in the fall, cross over Lopez and San Juan islands, and continue on down Whidbey Island to Puget Sound and the mainland.

The flight pattern of the vulture easily distinguishes this bird from the eagle. Look for two-tone wings held in a vertical V (just remember "V for vulture") and a rocking motion in flight. The bird's naked red head and gruesome diet make it about as appealing as a slug's underside to many, but turkey vultures are a beautiful sight as they soar, and they also perform a vital janitorial chore in the islands.

An interesting aside: it may happen that one day we'll no longer call these hulking, small-headed birds turkey vultures—a Harvard ornithologist has discovered by examining the bird's DNA that it is more closely related to storks than to vultures.

Another large raptor that makes the islands its summer home is the *osprey*, sometimes known as the fish hawk. Flying in from Central and South America about the same time as or a little later than the vulture, in April, it too takes its leave in September, spending the interim nesting near water. The osprey is one of the most widely distributed birds on earth, but its presence in the islands is rather less than overwhelming, perhaps because of a preponderance of bald eagles that would rather steal an osprey's dinner than catch their own.

Perhaps the eagle knows that the osprey is far better suited to fishing. The jointed wings of an osprey fold in as it torpedoes toward the water; the bird hits feet first to grasp its slick prey with talons wonderfully designed for fish catching. Most hawks have three toes forward

*Osprey*

and one backward; the osprey is the only diurnal raptor that can move one of those front toes to the back, leaving it with two forward and two behind, like an owl's foot but covered with spicules, or tiny spikes, to further secure the slippery fish. Sometimes this hawk will completely submerge itself in the water, its nostrils closing down as it goes under. When it finally emerges, the osprey maneuvers along the surface until it breaks free of the water and takes to the air.

Look for large, bulky nests on the tops of tall snags near a shore. (Like eagles, osprey pairs return to the same nest each year.) The bird is easy to distinguish by its brown back, white front, and white head with a dark streak from the eye down to the neck. In flight, watch for a long, strongly crooked wing like a stretched-out M, and listen for a high-pitched *kyew, kyew, kyew*.

I watched an osprey one early June morning as it flew over Cranberry Lake to a tall, thin snag along the shore. A moment later, a bald eagle cried and landed in the trees near the osprey's perch. Perhaps both had eaten, for they remained peaceably on their perches while I reveled in the sights and smells of a wetland where beavers make their home. The cotton grass was in bloom on the bog islands, and the warm, humid air hummed with insects. It was so quiet I could hear the whir of dragonfly wings and the industrious gnawing of a beaver against the sound of a foghorn in the distance. A river otter poked its head out of the water to stare, and a hummingbird buzzed the bushes.

The summer wetland is a lush, languid place, redolent with the musty smell of beaver and muskrat and the scent of dense vegetation. Duckweed is thick on the ponds, and purple fluffs of hardhack mix with dark green salal along the edges. Swallows dart across the water after insects, and brilliant blue slashes of damselfly pairs zigzag through the air clasped together in mating embraces. Female *dragonflies* skim the water's surface, dipping their bodies regularly into the water to deposit eggs.

Dragonflies and damselflies are familiar residents of the summer wetlands, sometimes disconcertingly so to those of us who grew up knowing them as "darning needles" that might sew up the mouth of a misbehaving child. If such was the case for you, don't let the recalled drivel of exasperated adults keep you from fully enjoying these fascinating insects. They can be easily told from each other, much as moths are told from butterflies: damselflies hold their wings upright over their bodies while at rest, whereas dragonflies hold their wings horizontally. Dragonflies are also larger, and they have two sets of wings to the damselflies' one.

*Dragonfly and damselfly*

Look for them on sunny days by ponds and lakes; when the sun disappears, usually so do these winged sprites. But with our typical abundance of bright days, dragonflies are easier to observe than the summer birds, and they often display much of the same types of behavior, such as curiosity and a strong territoriality. Supposedly, they often return to the same perch for several days, and you may be able to gradually condition them to your presence enough for some truly close-up viewing.

Watch dragonflies as they mate in the air, still flying while holding tight to each other. An egg hatches into an aquatic nymph with a huge lower lip that folds under the head and can dart out like a frog's tongue to catch prey. The nymph sheds its skin as it grows. When ready for the final molt, the tiny creature climbs out of the water on the stalk of a plant one spring or summer night; then it swallows air to expand its body until the skin splits, releasing a new adult ready to fly at dawn.

Dragonflies possess perhaps the finest aerodynamically tuned bodies in the world; they can hover, fly backward, or rocket along at speeds up to 35 miles per hour. As you watch one, know that its antics are not only the source of many a lazy day's trivial contemplation but also the object of serious study by engineers who hope to apply the dragonfly's secrets to planes and even NASA spacecraft. Studies have shown that a dragonfly creates the equivalent of tiny whirlwinds by twisting its wings on the downstroke, and scientists may use that discovery to redesign aircraft now dependent on steady, rather than turbulent, airflows.

Oddly enough, dragonflies, with one of the most ancient of histories, live only a short time, five to ten weeks. Long before dinosaurs walked, the dragonfly winged its way through a three-hundred-million-year-old sky, above horsetails the size of trees, flapping wings that reached 2 to 3 feet across. Watching them, it's easy to feel a sense of disconnectedness and imagine their prehistoric ancestors gliding over a steaming primordial soup.

Other creatures besides the dragonfly are enjoying the summer ponds and swamps. Look for *garter snakes* sunning themselves along wetland paths. A garter may be lethargic enough to stroke with your finger, but remember that although it's not poisonous, it may try to bite when handled and will also give off an unpleasant discharge. Kids often squeal that a snake has "peed" on them, which is not far from the truth, since the secretion comes from the anal glands.

A bulge along the snake's body indicates a recent meal of slugs, fish, frogs, or small mammals. One summer day, a friend and her son were chilled by what sounded like a kitten yowling in distress down by their creek. Instead, the two found what was probably a red-legged frog, screaming as it was being swallowed back end first by a snake. Unable to walk away, especially with a four-year-old urging heroics, the mother prodded the snake with a stick to loosen its grip—no easy task. Freed at last, the frog swam off downstream with the snake in hot pursuit. Finally, the frog froze in the water, and the snake, tricked, glided swiftly by.

Snakes are the only animals able to swallow creatures larger than themselves, thanks to a hinged mouth and elasticized body walls. Snakes themselves are taken by skunks and raptors. I've seen more than one red-tailed hawk rise from a field or even just off the side of a road with a wriggling specimen clutched in its talons.

Sometimes you may find the old skin of a snake, a ghostly reminder of its owner, which sheds the skin as much as two or three times a year. Molting begins at the head; the skin peels backwards until a reversed remnant is left, like a glove finger pulled inside out. One summer after the tarp was taken off the woodpile, it seemed that wherever I didn't find one of the heat-loving creatures, I at least found the shadow of its former self.

Cut stems of marsh plants floating on the water or left on shore are clues to another wetland inhabitant, the *muskrat*. Remember, though, you won't always find a muskrat or any other animal where it's "supposed" to be; Nature delights in the double take. For instance, a friend who lives on Cypress was walking along a beach one day when she saw a furry animal swim out of the salt water and collapse exhausted onto the shore. Her description made me suspect a muskrat, although one would not generally expect a marsh animal to come in with the tide. Perhaps an eagle had snagged the hapless critter and, finding its prey too much of a burden, had dropped it over the water.

The muskrat's natural habitat is the marsh or shallow lake, where it builds a conical house of mud-plastered cattails and sedges (rather than the sticks beavers use in their lodges), or it may burrow into a steep bank if available. Look for it especially in cattail-dominated wetlands, where the plants provide not only prime building material but a favored food source as well. The lodges are built in late summer and have a nest chamber above water with one or more underwater entrances.

In the summer, despite their many wildlife attractions, marshes and swamps must give way to salt water as the major drawing card. Summertime for many islanders and visitors means shore time. Now is the season when the *orca* pods close in on the islands for the salmon runs, and some don't count it truly summer until they see those first whales come through in June.

Fewer sights inspire more excitement than tall black dorsal fins slicing through the waves, but more commonly you may be walking along a shore or out on a ferry and see a group of much smaller dark fins. Could it be a group of baby whales, a wandering "nursery pod"? Juvenile orcas are always in the company of adults, so what you're actually looking at, then, are not whales at all but *Dall porpoises*.

These porpoises have black-and-white bodies similar to, though a good deal smaller than, those of orcas, and a much smaller dorsal fin, which is often white-tipped. You can also identify them by the "rooster-tail" spray they throw up when surfacing to breathe. Dall porpoises love to play in the bow waves of boats and are our fastest cetacean, having been clocked at speeds of up to thirty knots. When sailing, I most often spot the Dall porpoise in the Strait of Juan de Fuca; the waters around San Juan Island will also likely produce sightings of this playful companion.

You might see another large shape in the water with a disproportionately small dorsal fin set farther back on the body than either the orca's or porpoise's center-set fin. This is the minke whale, the most commonly seen baleen whale in our waters. Unlike orcas, which have teeth, minkes have plates of baleen (a flexible, horny substance hanging from the upper jaw) that act as huge food strainers, releasing water and capturing the multitudes of herring and plankton these whales need to survive. At least a couple of dozen minkes visit our island waters in the summer.

One of the most happily common offshore sights here is the sudden surfacing of a *harbor seal's* round shining pate. Dark eyes that seem strangely large for its head appear to study you carefully before disappearing as soundlessly as they arrived. The eyes of the depths are firmly upon you, although the seal doesn't have as good vision above as below the water, where it can see better than we do on land.

You may also see a seal smack the water's surface with its tail. I watched one for at least an hour one summer's afternoon, slapping and splashing and making the small harbor ring with its revels.

The doe-eyed harbor seal is gray with black spots and lacks external ears. These characteristics will help you distinguish it from the *sea lion*, which has external ears but no spots, and which you may also hear barking on some offshore reef. Harbor seals don't bark; their most vocal period is during their days as young pups, when plaintive cries and sheeplike *ma-a-as* help mother seals reunite with their offspring. You'll also know you're watching a seal and not a sea lion if you're able to observe the animal's movements on a haulout. Seals are extremely awkward on land, unable to do more than hitch themselves along with their flippers. Sea lions, on the other hand, can more or less walk by rotating their hind flippers forward.

Another possible source of confusion is the elephant seal, which you may spot either in the water or hauled out now for its annual molt. Adult males have distinctive elephantlike snouts, and neither sex of this species is spotted like the harbor seal.

Our most common marine mammal and a year-round resident here, the harbor seal hauls out on intertidal rocks for several hours of rest each day. Having less blubber and fur than other pinnipeds, these seals need haulout time to conserve energy. As you watch through your binoculars, you may see them stretch and yawn, nurse their pups, or simply rest in their rather distinctive, awkward-looking pose, belly-down or tilted to the side with tail curved upward.

The peak number of pups on haulouts occurs here during the last week of July and the first week of August, unfortunately coinciding with the height of the tourist season. Approaches by boats from cruise ships to dinghies will spook the seals into the water, possibly separating pups from mothers and at the very least stressing the animals. The youngsters need to nurse now to build up the body fat that will see them through the winter ahead.

A pup may sometimes be left alone on shore while its mother forages in the water, and it should not be disturbed by well-meaning but misguided rescuers. If the pup remains alone after a 24-hour waiting period, contact Wolf Hollow on San Juan Island or call the Whale Museum, either of whom will in turn contact the Marine Mammal Stranding Network.

If you're walking along a rocky shore, plunge into the tidepool world and make the acquaintance of creatures more bizarre and wonderful than any of your imagining. Look for *sea urchins*, those koosh balls of the tidepool, sculpins—tiny, aggressive fish that can climb partially out of the water—and feeding *sea anemones* with tentacles like tiny pale fingers waving hello. Try to catch the *barnacles* opening up to feed as water comes in to cover them; there are tiny creatures in those shell fortresses that, in a curious twist somewhere along the evolutionary line, "chose" to live more as plants than animals.

Peer over the rocks that face the water and pick out the *sea stars* left behind by a receding tide. The ones you'll see most often are large, stubby stars that are brown, orange, or purple, all of which are the same species, the common purple (or ochre) star. Should you try to pull that star off the rocks, you'll find it tough going because the suction cups on its arms exert a tremendous force. This creature relies on such strength because a crashing surf could otherwise easily dislodge it.

Those powerful arms and suction cups can also pry open shellfish equally stubborn but usually not as strong. Eventually, a clam or mussel meets its undoing as it relaxes a bit under the star's relentless pull. When the shell finally opens, a truly amazing thing happens. Does the sea star push an arm through the crack and slap a sucker on the meat to pull it back out? Does it flick some sort of tonguelike appendage into the opening, perhaps barbed like a woodpecker's, to spear its prey?

Nothing so mundane as all that for this fellow. As the sea star hunches over the clam and finally cracks it open, the star's stomach pushes through its mouth on the underside of its body and into the open shell. Inside the shell, the meat is dissolved and its juices are absorbed until the stomach's satisfied owner pulls it back once more through the mouth. If you pause for just a moment and really consider this behavior, you must agree that the things we've devised to divert ourselves in life utterly pale in comparison to a close-up look at nature.

Minks are fairly common along island shores, although hard to spot. A more familiar companion of our shoreside walks is the gull, but don't let its abundance lull you into a shrugging acceptance. Gulls are one of the easiest birds to observe, whether from behind a ferry window while they whirl and dive for food scraps tossed from an upper deck or as they noisily congregate at a fishing site or scout around your shoreside picnic spot.

A ferry ride is a particularly fine way to watch gulls; where else can you travel shoulder-level to a bird, with the possible added bene-fit of peering into its nest?

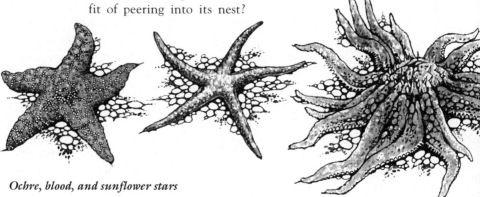

*Ochre, blood, and sunflower stars*

My daughter observed several chicks in a nest atop a piling at the Orcas ferry landing through the course of one summer, so don't forget to check the pilings for some close-up views of parent-chick behavior.

The most common gull in the islands and our only breeding species is the *glaucous-winged gull,* which lays its eggs by the end of May. Note the bright red spot on the adult's lower mandible; it serves as a pecking target for chicks anxious to prompt parents to release meals. Chicks and juvenile gulls have black bills and ashy gray plumage; adults have yellow bills and the familiar white breasts with gray wings. There are several species of gulls in the islands, and a good field guide can help you sort them out if that's your desire.

Sometimes the confusion isn't only between gull species. Both the Bonaparte's gull and the common tern migrate southward beginning in mid-July and may easily be mistaken for each other since both are black-headed, though the gull has more of a hood than the tern's cap. Look at the tail and then you'll be sure of what you're seeing. If it's deeply forked, somewhat like a barn swallow's, the bird is a tern. Gulls' tails are fan-shaped.

Although often called sea gulls and even believed by some to be the spirits of dead seamen, this family is not strictly a seafaring one. Gulls flock to flooded fields as well as salt water, taking advantage of both land and water environments. Special sets of nasal glands at the base of the bill extract excess salt from the gull's body, allowing it to drink both fresh and salt water.

Highly gregarious, gulls communicate with a variety of calls. Listen to them sometime, not simply as the ever-present background noise of the shore but as creatures with something to say, if only "Back off from that shellfish, buddy." (Not every gull's a Jonathan Livingston, of course.)

Summer's wildest song is the cry of the gull, a freeing call that coaxes us to warm-weather wanderings. Watch the gull and let your spirit join its exulting whirls and dips. Breathe deep the blossom-scented air, soak up the season's nectar, revel in the honeyed days of a San Juan summer, and then turn the corner, fortified, to welcome the frosts of autumn.

---

## SUMMER WILDLIFE HAPPENINGS

- Orca pods close in on the islands in June.
- Turkey vultures and ospreys summer here.
- Birds raise young now; young fledge through summer.
- Bald eagles leave the islands as summer wanes to fly inland for river salmon runs.
- Goldfinches nest in August.
- Snakes bear young about the size of 6-inch earthworms in late summer.
- Fall-run salmon return to spawn, beginning in July.
- Bats are out in the summer dusk.
- Bonaparte's gulls and common terns pass through on southward migration beginning in mid-July.

- Peak numbers of harbor seal pups on haulouts in mid-July.
- Migrant elephant seals haul out to molt.
- "Baby season" in islands: young of beaver, otter, deer, raccoon, fox tumbling about in woods and wetlands.
- Ripening up: salmonberries, thimbleberries, currants, Oregon grape, salal, soopolallie, serviceberries, and elderberries.
- Some plants blooming now: ocean spray, wild roses, yarrow, twinflower, thistle, monkeyflower, self-heal, columbine, Columbia lily, fringecup, Indian pipe, spotted coralroot, hardhack, pearly everlasting, mullein, fireweed.

## BACKYARD WILDLIFE ACTIVITIES

Create pools and other water sources now for dragonflies, frogs, newts, and others. A water source can be as simple as an overturned trash-can lid filled with water, an old tub sunk in the ground, or a shallowly dug, lined pool with potted water lilies and edge plants such as cattails.

Build rock piles or walls on a 1:6 incline (one measure in for every six up) for frogs, snakes, salamanders, and lizards.

Set out bat houses to encourage these insect eaters to roost near your home. A low-wattage light set at least a dozen feet off the ground will attract insects and may encourage foraging bats.

Don't cut down dead or dying trees, but leave them as snags for cavity nesters such as woodpeckers, nuthatches, chickadees, owls, squirrels, and bats. If safety is a consideration, remove the treetop and leave a 10-foot or higher stump.

# TIM RANSOM

## *In the Company of Otters*

At anchor one warm July day in Stewart Island's Prevost Harbor, I watched an otter dive for food and then surface with a fish, which it soon swallowed, whiskered snout pointed skyward. Later that day, when dusk was beginning to blend into the water, resounding splashes broke the stillness, and I could only guess the noisy revels meant the otter had returned.

A summer stroll along San Juan beaches or a day in a quiet anchorage may be enlivened by an otter or two sporting in a cove or running over shore logs. Although often seen in salt water, these members of the weasel family are not sea otters (which are larger, with light gray faces) but river otters, equally at home in freshwater lakes and wetlands and sometimes even beneath islanders' living rooms.

"People were always asking me how to get rid of otters," says Tim Ransom, a former curator of the Whale Museum in Friday Harbor. River otters don't build dens but instead use natural cavities or other animals' abandoned holes to curl up in. The birthing area, where the kits stay for approximately three months, may be sited well away from the water. The prospective mother heads inland—up to 60 yards from shore—to give birth in a cozy protected spot, such as a crawlspace. It's common for islanders to find nests under their homes made snug and warm with the latest in ripped-off insulation.

"As long as you don't recognize the long-term implication of breathing insulation," says Tim, "short-term is that it's a perfect place to have a den." In response to those homeowners unsympathetic to a mother otter's needs, he advises prevention. "Reducing access to the space is really the best thing. Close it up as much as you can, and put something like ammonia in there when she's looking for a den in the spring." Otters have extremely sensitive noses, and once they catch the first whiff of a bowl of ammonia, they won't stick around for a second.

One homeowner with a nesting family in his crawlspace successfully routed the mother, which exited carrying her kits. When a nest is already active, Tim urges folks to let it alone for the season and later beef up prevention. "We just have to remember that we're sharing their space and not vice versa," he remonstrates gently.

In the trauma of the mother otter's exodus, one youngster was left behind. The forgotten kit eventually ended up at the Wolf Hollow Wildlife Rehabilitation Center, where she was christened Pogo. Eventually the otter was released off San Juan Island with Albert, another orphan, and Tim was present at the release, paddling a kayak out into the bay to monitor the otters' behavior. Albert "charged off doing his own thing and later decimated a crab population where we had released him, even though he'd never seen or eaten crab before. It was amazing."

Pogo, on the other hand, kept trying to climb into the kayak. Eventually she went off with Albert but returned and "was approaching people all the time. It was a potentially bad situation." Wolf Hollow recaptured the friendly otter, and for a while she became a surrogate mom for otter foundlings until she was successfully released a season later off Patos Island with Peter, one of the orphans she had mothered.

Before Pogo's release, however, "we had the opportunity to do a little unnatural observation with her." It was a unique chance for a man who calls his usual methods of observation "radically natural."

Most of the information we have about river otters comes from trapping studies, but these provide very little data besides basic physical traits and diet. Capturing otters and transferring them to an unnatural environment such as a zoo is not much more helpful, for little is revealed about their behavior in the wild (river otters in zoos, for instance, do not usually reproduce). Only slightly more positive about releasing otters with implanted radio-tracking devices, Tim, who has a doctorate in animal behavior, describes his preferred methodology as one he used when living with baboons for two years in Africa: "basically just putting in the time to go and be there so that you're part of the environment when they come by."

The idea is to build up over a period of time an animal's awareness of you as a benign part of its environment. Such an approach is far more difficult to use with otters than with baboons, Tim admits, simply because so much of what otters do happens underwater. The actual amount of time he was able to spend observing one or two individual otters was very slight, but he was fortunate in finding a couple of good study sites in the islands.

The first was at Rosario Harbor on Orcas, where he lived for thirteen years. While working as a musician at Rosario Resort, Tim spent his spare time down at the resort's docks studying and photographing a pair of otters. Because the otters were living in an area frequented by people and thus were used to human activity, he could get close enough to see, right from the start: "I was able to go out and be with them almost every day in the winter. Eventually, I got to within 12 to 15 feet of them regularly." He observed the mother-daughter pair for over a year, noting behavior and trying to build his understanding enough to be able to anticipate the pair's actions.

Again, with baboons it was easier to get to know an individual and predict how it would respond in different situations. With otters, simply distinguishing between males and females is a difficult feat, and it's even harder to tell who's who among the same sex. But at Rosario, Tim was able to differentiate mother from child not only by size but also by behavior. For instance, if he saw the mother approach a part of the dock that held fish, rope, and boxes, he knew she'd beeline toward the fish, but the kit would focus on the boxes and rope, being much more inclined to play. At times, the kit and mother would play together, but "her mom had a very short fuse for that."

Playfulness is one of the first things to come to mind when thinking about otters, but though Tim was indeed able to observe some play behavior, he punctures a common belief regarding otter-style recreation.

"I have never seen an otter slide," he says. "Except on TV, and that was on snow. If you'd like to go out on that rocky hillside over there and slide down and tell me you enjoy it, I might buy it." He believes people find knolls and mud banks that otters regularly climb and where over time all the vegetation has been scratched away so that the bank becomes a muddy slick. "But it's coming up it that they do that. If you watch them go down, they *climb* down it," he insists. "I've heard so many slide stories, and when you talk to people long enough, they've never actually seen it in use; they've just seen what they've determined must be a slide."

Most of an otter's merrymaking occurs underwater, but Tim has seen otters nose feathers floating on the water and play with ropes and other items on docks. One stormy day, he watched the younger otter at Rosario swim out beyond the breakwater, roll over on her back, and surf the choppy waves for about five minutes. Tim laughs as he notes that one of the distinctions commonly made between river and sea otters is that the first "never float on their backs."

One of the wild's most acrobatic swimmers, the otter has a specially adapted nose that closes down when it dives and muscles that change the shape of the eye lens so it can see as well below water as above. A seal's eye, on the other hand, is unable to change shape, says Tim, thus leaving the seal relatively blind out of water.

An otter also differs from a seal in that it lacks the layer of subcutaneous fat that keeps seals and other water mammals warm in chilly waters. Instead, beneath the rich brown coat so coveted by trappers, otters depend on a dense underfur for insulation. This dependency leaves them more susceptible to oil spills. "They have to maintain a certain amount of air trapped in their fur, and they do that by grooming," explains Tim. "So probably the main problem is that if they get slicked, they'll ingest a lot of petroleum products."

One of Tim's favorite study sites was at American Camp, where he observed a female otter over the course of three years. She gave birth each March, stashed her blind and nearly hairless kits safely away, and then mated in April or May, not giving birth again until early spring of the following year. Otters experience what is known as "delayed implantation": fertilized eggs don't implant in the uterus wall immediately but rather remain free or "float around" within the uterus for eight months and then attach in December or January. The kits are born three months later. "It's to set up a timing of some kind, to get the kits out at a time that's especially beneficial for the species," explains Tim. "Certainly otters here aren't concerned too much with seasons; water temperatures don't change much, and there isn't any snow. But the species lives all the way up into Alaska, and it may be much more relevant for the Alaska subgroup than it is for the island otters to have their kits born during the spring so they have that full warm-weather time to develop."

Later in the summer, Tim saw the female bring her half-size kits down to the water to teach them to swim and hunt. By late fall, the males had grown so fast they were almost as big as their mother (adult female otters are about a third smaller than males) and were physically able to compete with her for food. Because the mother's hormones were by this time signaling her pregnancy to her, she probably chased the males out. "Something like this has been seen in other animals, so I'm borrowing from them to say she drives them away," says Tim. "It's likely she has to get more aggressive." There's evidence to suggest that sometimes the ousted males band together: "Periodically, out here in the islands, you'll see groups of fifteen to twenty otters passing through. I saw that maybe two or three times in all the years I was out there."

Tim estimates that there are hundreds of river otters in the islands, "because if you've got, at any one point in time, ten animals sitting on American Camp, and I know that the next female's area is only two or three miles to the north at most, the potential is vast."

The animals prefer grassy knolls, he says, places where they can climb up and catch the sun. Look for paths scratched out on knolls above the water and smaller-than-dog-size droppings with shells and very small bones in them, often in a single spot reserved as a latrine area.

One of his sites at American Camp was a logjam that the otters could enter from the water. Tim would sit on the hill above the small cove, waiting, and pretty soon "I'd hear these chuckles, a sort of happy, playful sound, under there."

One foggy day in late fall when the group numbered about a dozen (the mother otter plus her kits and older, returning juveniles), he saw one otter carry a large fish in under the logs. Another soon exited and swam off into the fog toward a point of land, returning in about ten minutes with a diving duck, which it hauled by the neck under the logs. Three minutes later, another otter swam out and headed off in the same direction, returning in under ten minutes with a cormorant. Much to Tim's delight, this one came back out of the logjam and began eating the cormorant on a rock just outside. Soon after, two other otters appeared, which he was able to distinguish as the first one's almost fully grown son and smaller daughter.

The mother otter feasted on the cormorant as her son sat close by, waiting. She defensively placed herself between the bird and the male, while her daughter stayed farther off, scrambling for tiny scraps that the others had no interest in.

"You could feel the tension between the mom and the male," says Tim. "She kept feeding for a while, and then almost in a blink, her attention dropped, and he was in and grabbed it and was gone. He swam out with it, and she went charging after him. Finally she stopped and came around and back. I had to read into that that she was just so angry but knew she couldn't go up against her big son anymore." Tim notes that in another month, when the female started feeling pregnant again, the balance would shift again in her favor.

Although river otters are often viewed as less than desirable neighbors with their tendency to nest under homes and leave scat and rotting fish on and under docks, most islanders take a soft-hearted view of this slippery mammal. It's a stony soul indeed who would wish the absence of an animal that perhaps more than any other suggests such a happy appetite for living.

Luckily for us, the otters seem here to stay. It is still legal to trap river otters, since they are neither a threatened species nor technically a marine mammal and so do not receive protection under the Endangered Species or Marine Mammal Protection acts. With the decreasing market for skins, however, Tim doesn't think trapping is much of a problem anymore. "The major problem is going to be continued loss of habitat," he says, but "I think in the islands they're going to be better off than most because they share space with people so well. Relatively well," he amends with a grin, "and it's going to be a long time before we really screw up a significant portion of the islands' shoreline.

"As long as they have a space to raise their kits, and as long as the islands don't suffer a major oil spill, I think they'll be okay for a long, long time."

# Chapter 3

# AUTUMN

AHH . . . TUMN. One can almost hear the sigh for September, when these tourist-weary isles start to edge out of summer's glare and sink into shorter days and shrouding mists. Summer fades like a departing ferry, and in its wake comes a time to pause, contemplate, and dream of drowsy woodstove days to come.

As we take to the woods, fields, and shores, however, we notice that the emphasis is not quite yet on peace but on preparation. Before the lullaby of late autumn, when the days turn gray, sodden, and still, another song stirs, a feverish tune of mounting restlessness. The islands reflect the bright vigor of days that often begin swallowed in fog but soon give way to crystal afternoons. Islanders gather and store harvests, chop kindling, tidy and tighten homes. Quail hoot in the early morning mist, hornets pester, thistledown rides the breeze, and ungainly craneflies seem to be everywhere.

Woollybears are on the move now, the fuzzy black-and-orange caterpillars of the Isabella tiger moth. Folklore has it that the width of the black bands foretells the winter's severity, and indeed, the bundled-up woollybear looks as though it might just know something about facing adversity.

The furry-coated creatures seem well prepared for cooler temperatures as they crawl along, perpetually crossing roads to somewhere. It's hibernation this animal so purposefully plods toward, seeking shelter until spring, when it will awaken, eat its fill, and finally spin a cocoon. (Some day when you cross its path, stop and consider for a moment why the woollybear shuns the caterpillar norm and chooses to spin its cocoon after, instead of before, the winter.) Should you find one already balled up for the duration, it's possible to "bring it to life" again in the warmth of your hand or sun. But why confuse the snugly curled creature? It's not, after all, a plaything but a fellow traveler that deserves your consideration.

Others are also preparing for the coming winter, though with a bit more panache than the stolid woollybear. Island folks' food gatherings are echoed in the woods by the spirited *Douglas squirrel*, or "chickaree," a hyperactive gray-and-tan bundle aptly called a furry mockingbird for the variety of its chatter. This small squirrel is probably our most visible woods mammal, especially in autumn as it scampers about to cache its winter food supply, and is the only creature that chal-lenges our presence in the woods; crows warn other crows with their squawks, but the chickaree seems to warn *us*. A heated burst of trills, squeaks, and squeals greets any intruder who disturbs its work, as I discovered during an eye-to-eye encounter with one that would simply not give way. Positioned head-down on a tree trunk and pinning me with its large dark eye, the squirrel fired a steady one-note fusillade, all the while holding an immature fir cone firmly in mouth.

I was bombarded in a different way, but from the same source, while spending some time on an early fall morning at a beaver pond. A curious crashing sound from up in the woods drew me off my perch to investigate. Soon crouched among the shrubbery and wishing for a hard hat, I was surprised by just how noisy falling cones could be as they bullet through branches. High up in a fir, not far from a soccer-ball-sized nest of twigs and leaves, a chickaree was cutting off the cones, which it would later pile into middens and tuck into holes.

Many times I'd have missed this critter had it not fearlessly called attention to itself with rapid-fire chatter, giving rise to the suspicion that it delights in razzing my rather bumbling dog. Instead of hiding in the underbrush until we pass, the chicka-ree explodes noisily out of shrubs well ahead and races up a fir. If you have some time to spend in the woods (sans dog) and would like to better observe a squirrel shimmying away up a tree, sit quietly for a spell, and then try making a few sucking squeaks on the back of your hand. Solomon's ring it may not be, but we lesser folk must make do with more prosaic communication methods, and this simple trick may bring a curious squirrel, as well as birds, in closer to investigate.

We also have chipmunks around (although, in the San Juans proper, only where introduced, such as on Lopez), so you may spot them now too at the busy task of stocking up nuts and seeds for the winter. The chipmunk's smaller size and black-and-white striping over the back easily distinguish it from the chickaree, but usually this agile little creature is more often heard than seen. Listen for a shrill *chip*.

Notice as you walk through the woods how many of the trees are alight in early autumn. The colors of summer once blended into a rich and mellow chorus; now they've become more distinct and startling, as if shouting one last fanfare for us to hold onto in the somber days to follow. Bright yellows of the *big-leaf maple* and *red alder* seem to catch and hold the sun's rays among the darker conifers. It's not old Jack Frost but mainly the decreasing hours of day-light cueing a tree's "inner clock" that causes leaves to change their color. Imagine autumn's dwindling daylight as a shadowy prospector

*Banana slug*

who travels these woods and chips away summer-green layers of chlorophyll to reveal the gold (carotene and xanthophyll) hidden below.

Other than the suddenly bright shades of leaves, few colors now startle us, used as we are to the subdued tones of mammals and nonbreeding birds that don't wish to advertise themselves. But there is still one bold shade to watch for, as striking a hue as a rufous hummer's blazing red throat: the cobalt-blue flash of a Steller's jay among the firs and cedars.

A dashing character that rivals the chickaree for feistiness, the Steller's jay is a year-round resident that favors the coniferous forest. It has a harsh squawk, along with a sweeter, rarely heard song, and a call that has fooled me time and again into looking skyward for a red-tailed hawk. Where this bird often errs in its mimicry is in overdoing the trick; a too-rapid repetition of the hawk's descending *scree* call soon clues one in. Also, don't fall into the common error of calling the Steller's a blue jay, which is an entirely different bird that inhabits the East Coast.

If the autumn forest sees some bold new colors in its trees, it also sees new color along its trails. When the days cool and the rains come, mushroom "flowers" suddenly seem to poke everywhere out of wet matted leaves. Look for the funnel-shaped, orange chanterelles in mossy areas under firs, hemlocks, and spruces. The white, stemless, fan-shaped angel's wings makes its home on rotting logs, and the thick-stemmed, broad-based boletes, with pores instead of gills, nestle under conifers. Those wonderful puffballs that "smoked" when you stepped on them as a kid are usually found in wet shady places, and in that smoke are actually hundreds of tiny spores. In the absence of children's feet, raindrops falling on this fungus prompt the puffs through a tiny opening in the balls, or they may become brittle enough to break open on their own.

Heavy clusters of bright red berries hang from the mountain ash and holly, and hips are huge now on the *Nootka rose* (a few frosts improve their flavor, so don't hurry to taste them). By early autumn, the orange-red berries of the *Pacific madrone* have also ripened, providing food for robins, pigeons, waxwings, quail, and small mammals. Cedar waxwings wait until summer's end to nest, not for the fluff of this-tle seed heads, beloved of late-breeding goldfinches, but for the ripe berries of madrone and mountain ash.

Perhaps no tree so boldly decorates the islands as the madrone. Autumn's russet glow is reflected in sunset-red trunks snaking out of windswept cliffs throughout the San Juans. This stunning island tree thrives on dry, rocky sites such as bluffs overlooking saltwater inlets. It was once used by coastal tribes, who brewed medicinal teas from the leaves and made dye from the bark and tools from the wood and roots. The madrone constantly renews itself, losing its glossy green leaves to a new crop in June and shedding its papery bark all summer, helped along by the legions who love to peel the bark like sunburned skin. Unlike the *Douglas-fir*, with its thick, corky armor, the madrone is a smooth and sinewy tree just begging to be stroked.

Look beyond the trees at dusk and you may find a deer or two feeding on the tender shoots of forest shrubs. Autumn's early urgings stir in our local buck, the

*Columbian black-tailed deer*, which snorts and paws the ground, clashing antlers with other bucks in the ritual of fall mating. Look for island deer grazing in open glades and fields; if you're lucky, you may even glimpse them swimming between shores. On one crisp October day several years ago, a state ferry passed what looked to be a tangle of floating branches, only to find that the "branches" sprouted from a huge buck. The deer was off Fidalgo Island and having a hard go of it, head plunging under, eyes heavy with exhaustion, when the ferry crew lowered a boat, grabbed him by the antlers, and towed him to the beach at Washington Park.

When autumn's early restlessness fills the forest, it also spills over into the skies, erupting into one of the greatest mysteries in the natural world. Migration is in full swing in September as the islands turn into a bustling Sea-Tac for avian arrivals and departures. Shorebirds that have summered over are scuttling south, and other summer residents, such as swallows, rufous hummingbirds, ospreys, and turkey vultures, leave the islands for warmer haunts.

Swans, geese, and waterfowl such as grebes, teals, *buffleheads,* and canvasbacks return from the north and fill the waters now. The country's largest flocks of wintering loons touch down in the islands, and heavy-billed *surf scoters* raft by the hundreds in protected bays. *Western grebes*, with their swanlike necks and black heads, congregate in large flocks in late September and early October. As you admire their grace on the water, remember that in years past others admired them a bit differently, slaughtering large numbers to harvest the plumage for ladies' hats. Now protected by law, western grebes are one of the most abundant diving birds wintering here, but it's not easy to approach this bird closely; perhaps memories of past persecution make the grebe an especially wary bird. An ungainly flyer, the grebe instead dives quickly to escape a perceived danger.

Thousands of *brant* return to Padilla and Samish bays in early October to feed on the *eelgrass* so basic to their diet. Each year the world's population of West Coast brant migrates from Alaska to Baja, stopping here to fatten up in the bays before continuing south, although a small number remain to winter over. A good time to see them is at low tide when the birds move closer in to access the gravel and grit needed to digest the eelgrass.

Watch for a wide variety of migrating raptors. Arriving from the north are rough-legged hawks and northern harriers, merlins, peregrine falcons, and snowy owls. Resident bald eagle numbers swell for a time as migrants fly down from Alaska and island eagles return home from mainland rivers in October. Watch for the passage of a cold front and northerly (often northwesterly) winds and then head for an open area with a view to the north and some elevation. This is also a fine time to observe hawks soaring on air currents; good viewing spots include Mount Erie on Fidalgo, Mount Constitution on Orcas, and Mount Young and Mount Finlayson on San Juan. Warm geysers of air, created when fall winds buffet the heated bluffs, are perfect for hawks that want to hitch rides.

Try keeping a calendar of the comings and goings of local birds; get to know their patterns from year to year much as you would the habits of a friend or family member. Become part of the family of birds. You can't go with them on their travels, of course, and perhaps you'll never really know what urges them onward, but there's much to gain from simply being aware of the flood and ebb of the sky. How much less our springs would be without the expectation of returning hummers, our summers without the hope of seeing whales, and our autumns without the honking farewells of the geese.

Keep an eye out, too, for unusual species, which may be spotted more at this time of year as storms, winds, or clouds force migrants off course and back to earth for refuge.

Migration is not only by air now but also by sea. Northern sea lions swim in and stay until spring, and if you're boating, you may catch sight of a few hauled out on Sucia Island. Another marine mammal, about twenty times as heavy as the harbor seal, may be seen feeding in island waters during its fall migration back to California and Mexico breeding grounds. This is the northern elephant seal, easily identified by its massive size and, in adult males, a wrinkled, trunklike snout. Usually it's males that are spotted here, since they range farther north than females to feed in the spring and summer.

It's unlikely you'll spot elephant seals anywhere but in the water now; during the summer, you may see them hauled out on island beaches for their annual molt, sometimes staying for several weeks until the molt is over. One male turned up on the beach at Bowman Bay on Fidalgo a few years ago. A popular spot with beach lovers, the area had to be cordoned off to protect both seal and people. A female turned up later, and because there was some concern over her condition, she was rolled up in tarps (all four hundred pounds of her), slid into a rowboat, and then lifted into a tub in the back of a truck and ferried to the Wolf Hollow Rehabilitation Center on San Juan.

Walk the beaches now and watch for treasures blown ashore in early storms. Although you're not likely to stumble across a massive elephant seal, you'll find the giant of the marine plant world, great tangled masses of *bull kelp*. The world's fastest-growing plant, this kelp thrives in island waters, forming large groves that shelter and feed marine animals. Its thick, hollow stem rises from a holdfast that attaches to rocks below the water's surface, and it ends in a bulb from which flow foot-long leaves, also known as the rippling hair of the Samish Indian princess Ko-kwal-alwoot, who wed a water spirit. After storms tear up the seaweed, it overwinters as an almost microscopic plant, growing again in the spring.

By mid- to late autumn, the crystal days are rarities, and autumn becomes the season of sighs, of a melancholy reflected in dark-dulled, rain-swept hours. Most of the leaves are down now, here and there lighting up the sodden trails like lingering embers in the mud. The bright berries of the *red huckleberry* are gone, long devoured by birds and mammals, but you can still identify this plant by its stiff, bright green stems. Dried wisps of *ocean spray* cling to clawlike branches, and even the birds have lost much of their color, for autumn is the time of their main molt.

Birds sing little now, and many forgo the isolation of the nesting season to flock together. Because breeding colors are no longer needed or displayed, many birds "dull down" and may look more alike. The mallard, for instance, loses wing feathers in the fall and for a time cannot fly, spending its time on secluded ponds until new feathers come in. The drakes also lose their bright colors and become muted like their mates. In trying to identify birds now, note three important things: size (big as a robin? bigger than a crow?); location (ground? under-story? tree-tops?); and behavior (soar-ing? darting? dab-bling? tree-clinging?). These simple, broad observations will help you narrow the field consid-erably without having to worry about color, so unreliable at this time of year.

Even if it should lose all its feathers, a bird impossible to mistake is the com-monly seen *great blue heron.* The heron's numbers peak here in September when the birds leave larger nesting colonies (heronries), such as those on Sidney Island and Samish Island, and wander back to the San Juans.

Known to the Nisqually Indians as the "grandfather" bird, this tall, spindly-legged heron does indeed seem to have the demeanor of a grumpy old man as it stands hunched and motionless in the

***Great blue heron***

shallow waters of marshes, bays, lakes, and tidal flats. This is another species that was once heavily hunted for its plumes; now it's the most widespread, as well as the largest, heron in North America.

Migratory across the rest of the country, the great blue remains here year-round, numbering several hundred strong in the islands. Eelgrass bays such as Samish and Padilla, which are full of juvenile fish, provide perfect dining grounds, and the herons will also catch small rodents such as voles in fields and even along highways.

A heron hunched over on a raft of kelp or staring into the dark waters of a for-est wetland is a familiar island sight. We will end our autumn rambles here, watch-ing the heron as the season draws to a close. The pond lilies curl up brown and dry now, bracken dies back, and the sun sinks a little sooner in the sky each day as wood smoke hangs over the valleys. Across the pond from us, the heron tenses with our presence, then rises with a squawking protest, neck curved into an S, broad wings beating slowly. Casting a misty reflection in the black waters below, the heron flaps heavily over the pond toward winter.

---

## AUTUMN WILDLIFE HAPPENINGS

- Brant return to Padilla and Samish bays.
- Canvasbacks, grebes, scaups, teals, wigeons, ring-necked ducks, ruddy ducks, goldeneyes, and buffleheads arrive from the north.
- Shorebirds migrate.
- Surf scoter numbers increase to flocks of hundreds.
- Rufous hummingbirds, turkey vultures, Canada geese, and ospreys head south.
- Northern and California sea lions arrive.
- Elephant seals may be seen feeding here on their southerly migration.
- Bald eagle numbers swell as migrants arrive from the north, and island eagles return from river salmon runs.
- Rough-legged hawks, northern harriers, merlins, peregrines, and snowy owls arrive from the north.
- Tundra and trumpeter swans head down south from Alaska.
- Heron numbers peak in early fall.
- Black-tailed deer mate.
- Flocks of loons fly through; many birds remain to winter over.
- Douglas squirrels and chipmunks actively gather and store food.
- Berries mature on madrone, holly, Oregon grape, kinnickinnick, and snowberry; wild rose hips ripen.
- Chanterelles and boletes fruit in the woods.
- Rough-skinned newts migrate out of breeding ponds.
- Cattail fruits turn to fluff and disperse.
- Bats migrate out of the area.

## BACKYARD WILDLIFE ACTIVITIES

- Collect nuts and fruits and store in a cool place for winter feeding.
- Clean out used nesting boxes and store hummingbird feeders.
- Sow native perennial wildflowers now. Don't pull up browned annuals, but let flowers such as marigolds and zinnias provide food for birds.
- Plant shrubs and trees for wildlife (root systems go dormant in late fall, so trees handle the stress of transplanting better then). Good choices: elderberry, huckleberry, vine maple, hawthorn, crabapple, serviceberry.
- Prepare winter bird-feeding stations. Wash feeders with a very diluted mild bleach solution and dry thoroughly. Check for mold and clean periodically through season to prevent disease.

# OSCAR GRAHAM
## *On the Wings of Wild Ducks*

William Butler Yeats's poem "The Wild Swans at Coole" is "the greatest waterfowl poem ever written," according to Oscar Graham, who, when he talks about waterfowl, seems far more comfortable keeping company with poets than with scientists.

"There's always more to the story than science gives us," he stresses. "I'd put any duck hunter or good bird-watcher on the line with the wildlife biologist (unless he or she has really been in the field a lot), and I think we'll all come out about even in terms of what we really know about the birds."

Oscar lives on Samish Island, along the Pacific Flyway, where he's a regular and appreciative witness to a wonder science has not yet been able to fully explain: migration. Though it's still early in September, this morning he heard the honking of geese on their southward course. "I never get tired of their calls," he says. "Migration punctuates something significant not only for the avian world but for us. It gives us an idea that we're part of something big."

Science can guess at the causes of migration, such as glandular response to the number of daylight hours, but much still remains shrouded in mystery—for instance, the birds' incredible sense of direction. Oscar describes how brant fly from Izembek Lagoon in Alaska all the way to Baja California, a journey of more than 3,000 miles.

"What a flight," he muses. "I just look at going from Burlington to Mount Vernon with one lane of traffic closed across the Skagit River bridge. By the time I get to town I'm frustrated. You put these feats of migration into perspective with our daily movements and, really, they stack up pretty favorably."

Oscar's love for waterfowl goes back to a duck-hunting boyhood in Tacoma, when he'd awaken on stormy "duck weather" mornings and skip school to head out hunting with his dad. In his later teens, he gave up the hunting (he has since come back to it), and over the next twenty years he didn't pay much attention to ducks until moving here in 1983.

"I got up here and saw a large flight of mallards come over and thought, This is something that still excites me." Oscar worked with the Padilla Bay Reserve for four years and with the state Department of Ecology, and he is now a senior planner with the Skagit County Planning Department, a job that has allowed him to stay in an area he loves.

"I don't want to move on at all," he said, reflecting on the riches of a place that hosts one of the largest and most varied concentrations of waterfowl on the West Coast. "The great thing about Padilla, Skagit, and Samish bays is that we have an intact system of estuaries that continues to attract literally thousands of waterfowl annually." He explains that some of the old pilings placed years ago along the shoreline to protect the dikes have been gradually undermined by wave action, and now the areas behind those pilings have turned back into salt marshes, real "hot spots" for birds. "If you drive by, look down through the trees into those salt marsh areas. You'll see sometimes as many as thirty to forty thousand ducks."

What you'll see there are the puddle ducks, which prefer a shallow water environment, "tipping up" to forage for food along the bottom. They all have bright patches of color, or speculums, on their wings, and unlike diving ducks, which need to run along the water's surface to take off, puddle ducks can burst straight up out of the water on their larger wings and more forward-positioned legs. The most common puddle duck species in our shallow bays, ponds, and flooded fields are the mallard, pintail, teal, and wigeon.

Pelagic species—the diving ducks of the deeper waters—include oldsquaw, our deepest diver, capable of plummeting to 300 feet. Listen sometime for its yodel, which Oscar describes as an "incredible, haunting call." Other divers in our waters are the scaup, scoter, bufflehead, merganser, and harlequin duck, salt water's answer to the flashy, freshwater wood duck. Look for these stunning birds near the base of rocky shoreside cliffs. To get a close-up view of a goldeneye, another diving duck, Oscar suggests a walk in February along the Stanley Park sea wall in Vancouver, British Columbia: "I've never been to a better spot."

Today, he focuses on the puddle ducks. Teal are a favorite. "The three species we have here in the Northwest are all just spectacular-looking birds. The green-winged teal, which is the most common, has this russet head with a green eye patch. They're the earliest duck to migrate down and one of the last ducks to migrate back in the spring," he says. "We also have the cinnamon teal in the spring migrating north, and that's a great time to see them in full plumage. You often see cinnamon teal in the sloughs or even in agricultural drainage ditches, and they're just such a beautiful bird." Blue-winged teal make up our third, equally handsome species.

He notes that wigeons, hardy ducks once called "baldpates" because of their white crowns, seem to be on the increase in western Washington's favorable habitat, namely grassy fields by the bays, where the ducks are often seen pulling up entire plants to get at the roots. (If you see a large flock of ducks with a good deal of white on their wings coming into a field, says Oscar, they're invariably wigeons.) One extremely cold winter, he had close to a thousand ducks in his backyard over the course of a day. Stressed out by the weather and a lack of food, wigeons and pintails descended in large numbers, sat on the frozen ground to thaw it with their body heat, and then finally grazed on the defrosted grass.

As we walk along the shore of Padilla Bay this sunny September afternoon, Oscar points out a small flock of pintails, early migrants from the north. Here in Washington, he says, the pintail is "the most graceful duck in flight. There's nothing more beautiful than a flock of pintails coming in. They'll come in high and will circle and circle before setting down."

He notes that certain birds have become symbols of different flyways: the mallard for the Central Flyway, the black duck for the Eastern. The pintail has always been identified with our own Pacific Flyway. But he and many others are concerned that this status may be affected if conditions don't change soon in the bird's nesting area up in Canada. For the past ten years, the pintail population has steadily decreased, thanks to an extended drought in the prairie provinces, the bird's prime nesting ground.

Oscar remains optimistic, however. "If you look at waterfowl populations, they tend to evolve through periods of scarcity and abundance. It's not to say that we don't need to pay attention and watch out that a habitat isn't decimated, but we do see that pattern, and it's happened for over fifty years. So I hope it's not a final problem, and I don't think it is."

He is more concerned with the preservation of local waterfowl habitat. "Over the next ten years, we're going to be able to gauge the effectiveness of our commitment to preserve some of these resources. We've got the commitment in writing from the legislature. Let's see if we have the commitment in our hearts." He sounds a warning note as he compares the local area to Pierce County, where he's from, and where a vast estuary now tops the Superfund list for cleanup. "Commencement Bay's one of the worst examples of environmental degradation that we have to look at."

For Oscar, protecting the habitat of waterfowl also secures the survival of important values. "I think what waterfowl have to offer us is a source of inspiration and a source of beauty, which may equate across the board with inspiration." He encourages people to get out into the field, adding that it takes a lot of time to become really adept at identifying ducks. But it doesn't have to be a big deal, he stresses; a simple walk along a bay will bring real pleasure in a region awash in waterfowl.

"The opportunities for those who want to take advantage of them are here," says Oscar. "It doesn't take a diehard to enjoy it. Any time you drive along a coastal area, you're going to see diving ducks, and in the winter, you're going to see puddle ducks if you're in an agricultural area or a marshy area." A confessed diehard himself with a "twisted look on things," he prefers going out in extreme weather, when 50-mile-per-hour winds and driving rains force the ducks in for closer viewing.

Field identification of waterfowl is based on general color, calls, habitat, and flocking behavior. Color may be hard to discern from a distance, so Oscar suggests looking for general shadings such as a light underside or a dark head. Calls are another help when distance reduces flocks to mere blobs on the water. Many people think ducks do nothing but quack, but oldsquaws, for instance, make a distinct yodeling call, whereas pintails use three high whistles, with variations.

Calls identify birds not only by species but sometimes also by sex. Mallard hens are the ones who make the loud quacking noise; the drakes are much more subdued. When the ducks start to pair off during the mating season, you may hear an unattached female give the "lonesome hen call"—a long, loud, mournful quack. Often, her plaintive cry works; a drake will come in and give a few short *jeeps,* and she'll answer with a quieter, more conversational quack. If all goes well, the hen shows up a few weeks later with a brood.

Habitat is fairly simple: look for puddle ducks out in the fields, ponds, and shallow bays, diving ducks in deeper waters. Probably the best time of the year to observe waterfowl begins in early February, when the ducks are no longer being harassed by hunters, the concentrations are high, and breeding colors make identification easier.

Flocking behavior is often distinctive, says Oscar. Teals, for instance, fly in compact units of ten to thirty-five ("There's not a more spectacular bird in flight"). Pintails and mallards have loose flock groupings, whereas canvasbacks fly in a wavery V, and brant travel in long lines, sometimes balling up and stringing out again.

When Oscar picked out the pintail over the bay, he focused mostly on its body shape, which is long and slender, with long wings. "That's the main thing in the fall because they're still in eclipse plumage, so you can't go on color so much. They all look like hens," he says. "You can get hints from flocking behavior; that gives you a first-cut determination. If they were geese, they'd fly in V formation. If they were some type of diving duck, they'd fly in a more regimented formation. If they were teals, they'd fly in random formation, if you can call random a formation."

Binoculars are great, he notes, but "good optics only take you so far." More important is spending time out among the birds and becoming aware of the differences. As for field guides, the simpler the better. One of his favorites is a small, thin paperback called *Ducks at a Distance*. It's easy to pop in a pocket and includes some information not usually given in other guides, such as notes on flocking behavior and the comparative sizes of different species. The booklet was originally produced for hunters and is free upon request from the U.S. Fish and Wildlife Service, (206) 553-5543.

A great way for the land-bound to observe waterfowl is simply to drive past the fields. "You'll always see mallards and pintails and, to a lesser degree, teals, and a lot of wigeons, as well as swans and geese in the fields eating," says Oscar. "You can drive by a large flock of wigeons, for example, and if you do have binoculars or a spotting scope, if you have a flock of about 500 wigeons in a field, you can scan that flock quickly and pick out the Eurasian wigeons." This Siberian fugitive has a reddish head that distinguishes it from the American wigeon's green-masked face.

"It's a treat when you start to recognize the different birds. When you do have a fairly rare sighting, it makes you feel like you've been observant enough to at least know that you've seen something special." He hastens to add that each and every one of the birds is special. "The most common mallard is a beautiful bird."

Even with the mallard, you can get an unusual sighting or two. Oscar says he has seen some strange things, such as a mallard landing on a fencepost. "They're not built for that kind of thing. They're not a perching bird, they're a water bird. They don't *do* that." Another time he was driving home and saw thousands of mallards simply pouring into a barley field, an unusual and heady sight.

Oscar also likes to watch the swans coming into the pastures. "You go in and see them just whirling down into these fields, flock after flock," he says, voice full of wonder. "It's like there's a magnet in the field. You can see them coming toward it." One of the best blinds for waterfowl watching is simply your car. "If you roll down the window and turn off the engine, you'll hear this huge uproar in the field when they're feeding as hard as they can. It's amazing."

Yeats's poem ends with a wistful reflection that one day the swans will fly away and something more than their presence will be lost in the going. Oscar understands the poet's lament. "What would life be like if we didn't have the swans, if we didn't have the migrating waterfowl every autumn and spring to inspire us?" he asks.

"It would be a whole different world."

*Chapter 4*

# WINTER

Winter in the islands is not often a roaring, heavy-footed intruder who flattens plant life and sends wildlife scurrying for shelter. Thick, blanketing snows are rare here; wind and rain are what lull the islands into a seasonal rest, which is more of a slowing down than a stop. The world is raw and muffled now, but you can still hear the tenacious chirp of the winter wren in the dripping woods, still find the unassuming slug at your feet. Among alders and maples stripped to their bones, you can still see the deep greens of trees and shrubs that bridge the seasons to make a mockery of winter's efforts here.

Nonetheless, I have snowbird friends for whom the dampness is too spirit-dampening, and indeed, island winters are perhaps welcomed only by those of a melancholic disposition. But these days can have their magic as much as a languid summer afternoon and a noisy spring dawn have theirs.

For Northwest Native Americans, winter is a time to retreat into the longhouse and themselves, a sacred time for ceremonies, storytelling by firelight, and visits from the spirits. Those of us who lack a longhouse can hunker down by the woodstove or else bundle up and take to the forest and fields for both reflection and renewal. There is much to see in a stripped-down woods and much to admire from wildlife that have a whole new range of coping skills in these cold days. So go forth and find out how a brisk walk, a keen eye, and a little knowledge of our wildlife can rout the winter blahs, and perhaps, in this stiller, slower-paced time, the spirits will whisper their secrets to you in the wind.

All around, rain-slicked greens such as sword fern, Oregon grape, and salal keep our islands lush in the grayest days. Fir, cedar, hemlock, spruce, yew, and madrone all provide an evergreen background, their softening effect too often taken for granted. Let's look more closely at a few of these trees; we depend on them more than we know, if only for their ever-present, soul-heartening shades of green.

Three of the largest conifers in local woods are called firs, although only two of them truly belong to that family. Our most common Northwest tree, the *Douglas-fir*, actually resembles a yew or spruce more closely and can be easily told from the true firs by its branches and cones. The needles of Doug-fir branches burst from all sides like a bottlebrush as spruce needles do, whereas *grand fir* needles lie flat and feathery like those of true firs. (We have another fir, the Pacific silver, which is less common but which might confuse you because its branches also have flattened needles like the grand's. But the silver's branch is more of a cross between grand and Doug-fir branches, with needles that extend out to the sides and around the upper part of the branch.)

You won't find grand or silver cones hanging from fir branches; they grow only at the tops of those trees, upright, instead of dangling down. Doug-fir cones, on the other hand, are easily accessible. They're well loved by squirrels, and many other animals such as shrews, mice, and winter wrens enjoy their seeds. Crossbills, chunky finches that are fairly common island residents, pry the seeds out of these cones with their bizarre but useful beaks.

The cones themselves are easy to distinguish from others; look for three-pointed, "pitchfork" bracts poking out from between the scales. I've heard several versions of a rather whimsical way of remembering how to identify the Doug-fir cone, and I share one of them here without being able to credit a source. A very long time ago, a lively bunch of field mice were playing in the woods when they heard a fearsome noise and scrambled to safety in the fir cones. But the mice weren't very adept at hiding themselves, and if you look today, you'll see the two tiny back legs and tails (the three-pointed bracts) of each jittery mouse protruding from the scales.

Crush a Doug-fir's needles between your fingers and you'll get a lemony scent (grand fir smells like oranges). Follow the method of Northwest natives: collect a handful of the fresher needles, pour two cups of boiling water over them, and let the mixture steep for a midwinter brew high in vitamin C. The Swinomish Indians also used Doug-fir boughs in their sweat lodges and broke off buds to chew much as we use throat lozenges.

You may wonder at finding some tan, papery cones with scales that look a bit like bran flakes along a trailside. The trees that bear them are *Sitka spruce*. Grasp one of the tree's bristly-needled branches firmly; its prickliness will identify this spruce, which rarely grows far from saltwater shores.

Two other common conifers of our evergreen woods are the *western hemlock* and *Pacific yew*. Both do well in the shady understory and are often hard to distinguish from each other. Yew needles are of fairly equal length, paired, pointed but not sharp, and narrow at the base. Northwest tribes once dried these needles and pounded them into a substitute for tobacco; they also used the strong yew wood for bows, arrows, and harpoon shafts.

Hemlock needles differ in that they vary in length and are blunt-tipped. Hemlocks are often recognized by the drooping ends of their branches, and they also have small, soft cones. Female yew trees don't have cones but instead sport thick seeds surrounded by cups that ripen to red in the fall. The flaming cups are a come-on to birds, which aid in the yew's propagation by scattering the seeds after demolishing the juicy cups.

The *western redcedar* is perhaps one of our most readily recognized evergreens, with its stringy red bark and flat, scaly leaf sprays, which smell like pineapple when crushed. The tree was highly prized by Northwest tribes, who used the cedar's fibrous bark for clothing and blankets and its trunks for totems and canoes.

As you're walking through the winter woods and trying to get to know the trees better, begin with the conifers and evergreen shrubs that are easily recognized year-round. Then, for a bit more of a challenge, focus in on the bare-limbed trees and shrubs such as the alder, ocean spray, cottonwood, maple, and willow. *Ocean spray* usually has a few fluffy-looking seed pods clinging to its branches that will help you to identify it.

A stubborn leaf or two still holding fast to the tree is often a better clue in winter identification than a pile of dried leaves or cones that may have blown around its base from some other tree. Tree shapes, locations, and the color and texture of barks will also help your sleuthing. For instance, bitter cherry, a fairly common local tree, has a reddish gray bark with 2-inch horizontal welts on it. Alder boughs burn red against the sky when the sun highlights them.

Winter is the best time of year to peer into those bare branches for exposed bird nests. Birds have a way of constantly leaving us open-mouthed, as when we see a peregrine's rocketing stoop or a hummer's whirring wings or hear of a tern's 20,000-mile migration. Those are the obvious dazzlers, but we shouldn't overlook the less obvious. A bird nest is no less a mouth-opener than is bird migration.

Look carefully at the nests you find and try to discover who the clever architect was. As you examine the structure itself, note what building materials were used (sticks? feathers? hair? from whom and where?) and how they're held together (plastered? woven?). Note the diameter and depth of the nest and also its shape (cup? bowl? gourd?). Then make sure to consider where the nest was found (tree? shrub? building? ground?) and how it may have been protected from both rain and casual observation. Studying a nest and trying to guess its former occupants and their situation and objectives create added respect and understanding of the birds that brighten our days.

Unlike larger birds such as hawks and great horned owls, which avoid building huge nests annually, songbirds don't reuse their nests from year to year. So collecting a few in the winter to look at thoroughly won't make a difference to returning birds, although be aware that nests may contain parasites such as lice.

You might hear the hooting of the *great horned owl* in the winter woods more than at any other time of year because it's already mating time for these birds. They may be on the nest here as early as February, which makes them perhaps the earliest nesters in the islands.

The bird you're most likely to hear in the woods, however, is a tough little troubadour called the *winter wren*. A mighty singer at mating time, piping out a melodic tune of over a hundred notes, the winter wren now most often chirps a *chip-chip* call in the forest understory as it searches out dormant insects. Dark brown to blend in with the forest floor and brush, and with a short, uptilted tail, this species is one of the few songbirds to remain here through the winter and a constant reassurance that even the dreariest winter days can be met with equanimity.

If you're craving a closer sight of this fairly secretive bird, make a squeaking sound and you may be able to call him out to within a few feet to see who else is crazy enough to be taking in the dismal, drenching grays of winter. It's usually enough for me, however, to simply hear the companionable chirping and catch a quick glimpse now and then.

As you walk the woods, ask yourself how the winter wren and, for that matter, our other winter birds, such as the chickadee, junco, towhee, kinglet, and varied thrush, survive the freezing times, bundled as they are in only summer-weight feathers. Why haven't they joined the flocks that headed south? What special gift makes them a hardier breed?

It's not necessarily that our winter birds are any hardier than those who've flown hundreds of miles to warmer retreats. One reason they remain where others don't is that these winter residents often have a more varied diet, gleaning sustenance not only from seeds but also from hibernating insects or their eggs.

*Winter wren*
*and yew branch*

Constantly searching for food to heat their insides, winter birds may huddle together at night in communal roosts for warmth or essentially shut down their systems. During the night and through prolonged cold spells, winter wrens and others may enter a hibernationlike torpor. (Some birds can even restrict the blood flow to their legs, centering the warmth where most needed.) Crossbills have a sort of pocket halfway down their necks where they can store extra food and so reduce foraging time in bad weather. And despite the lightness of their feather cover, winter birds can tense the muscles in their skin to fluff those feathers out until the bird's size is nearly tripled, trapping a large amount of insulating warm air against the body.

You may see noisy flocks of birds foraging in the treetops during the winter; these are likely to be kinglets, chickadees, and nuthatches. The nuthatches are looking for insects tucked away in the trunk bark while the chickadees comb the branches and twigs for insect eggs, oftentimes hanging upside down on cones as they tirelessly prod for food. It's truly a treat to walk through a quiet wood and come upon a chittering roar somewhere above, as if one tree suddenly shook itself alive from its slumbering neighbors and burst into brilliant, springlike song.

Although many birds and also slugs, squirrels, deer, muskrats, and rabbits are meeting the winter head on, others are not. A *red fox* may simply cozy up for the night with its tail wrapped snugly around its nose, but that would hardly do for those without a fur coat. Worms and ants huddle deep in the ground, and *garter snakes* curl up together into balls in rock dens, hollow logs, or underground burrows. Pull a strip of bark away from a rotting stump and you'll find snoozing creatures such as spiders, beetles, and perhaps a mourning cloak. All winter long, I capture yellow jacket queens that have hibernated in our woodpile and have prematurely revived next to the warmth of the woodstove.

For clues to which animals are out foraging these cold days, look for tracks and other signs such as chewed branches. Check the branch cut: if clean, the muncher may be a rabbit; if torn or shredded, a deer.

I often see *banana slugs* plodding stoically along even on frosty midwinter mornings, but I assume that in a truly intense cold snap they find refuge beneath the warm layers of forest leaf mold. Newts become more or less inactive, whereas *red-legged frogs* may become torpid (not fully in a state of hibernation) in holes or under logs. But I've also heard the croaking of *chorus frogs* consistently through the winter, and I once found one among some snow-covered ferns during a February walk, where it alerted me by squealing twice, though I could discover no cause for its alarm. Perhaps the unexpected snow drove it to its shrill response.

In the estuary, when the eelgrass dies back and exposes the flats to colder temperatures, animals dig deep into the mud to survive. Ponds at this time, sometimes thinly coated with ice or steaming in frigid temperatures, appear lifeless as water striders and other wetland insects hibernate in and under plants along the water's edge. Skunk cabbage, cattails, rushes, and pond lilies have all died back, and duckweed has mostly sunk to the bottom of the pond, coating the mud until the spring, when it will once again rise to the surface. Snails have sealed off their shells to preserve moisture and are hibernating under plant debris, but otters, beavers, muskrats, and great blue herons remain active in the wetland. Ducks such as mallards and mergansers are seen as long as the waters remain open. Subcutaneous fat layers, along with watertight feathers, help insulate these birds from the cold.

One morning after a light snowfall, I walked along the edge of a beaver pond where nature had drawn a memorable winter's image. Sitting atop a large gray snag in the middle of the pond's shadowy waters was a magnificent adult bald eagle, its black-and-white coloring a perfect blend of the snowy dusting and dark waters below.

Now is the best time of the year to get out and look at raptors. The islands have a healthy hawk population, and the Samish flats are recognized as one of the country's prime hawk-watching areas, according to raptor biologist Bud Anderson (see "Wrapped Up in Raptors").

The rough-legged hawk comes down into our area from the arctic and winters here October through March. Watch for it now in the fields and meadows hunting for voles. To distinguish it from the *red-tailed hawk,* with which it's often confused, focus on the head. Red-tails have a smooth profile, whereas rough-legs, as Bud says, have heads that look "like tennis balls with little beaks glued on." The rough-leg's vole-catching feet are also not as large as the red-tail's; sometimes you'll see this hawk's huge, bulky shape perched on branches seemingly too small and thin to support it. Feathered to the toes (as opposed to the bare tarsus of the red-tail), the rough-leg may also be identified by white at the base of its tail (not a white rump patch like that of the harrier).

Yet another sizable bird visits our area in the winter. Looking sculpted from some arctic snowfield, the *trumpeter swan* is the largest waterfowl in the world. Our state has the greatest number of wintering trumpeters outside of Alaska, with some of the biggest concentrations in the Skagit Valley farmlands.

When a 35-acre meadow was bulldozed and made into a marsh on San Juan Island, a pair of trumpeters flew in to visit in 1976. The following year, four swans were spotted, and today trumpeters can be found all over the island, most notably at Three Meadows Marsh, a prime feeding ground. Other seasonal wetlands on San Juan also see swans, and some flocks winter on Lopez and on Orcas (the winter of 1993–94 saw sixteen trumpeters on Cascade Lake).

Two other swans are visible here: the tundra and the mute swan, which one expert calls the "starling of our ecosystem." The mute is an introduced Eurasian bird easily distinguished from the other two swans by a bright orange bill with a black knob at the base. It's a highly aggressive bird, not at all docile like our native birds, and it will take on other swans or even humans when roused, furiously hissing its displeasure. The mute swan has totally displaced native species in areas like Chesapeake Bay and is classified by our state Department of Fish and Wildlife as a "deleterious" species harmful to native waterfowl. They're not a common bird in either the islands or the valley, but you may spot them when looking for our black-billed natives.

Tundras and trumpeters both breed in Alaska and fly into our area in mid- to late October. The tundra swan (formerly the whistling swan) is a smaller bird with a yellow spot right in front of its eye and a dish-shaped bill profile. Adult trumpeters weigh up to 30 pounds and have a wingspan between 8 and 9 feet. Their heavy, straight bills have a red "grin" line (which may also be present in some tundras. To further challenge birders, the tundra's yellow spot may be absent about 15 percent of

**Above and left:** *Mute swan*
**Right:** *Trumpeter and tundra swans; full trumpeter swan*

the time). If bills and body size still leave you confused, listen for the bird's call. The trumpeter has a deep two-note call, while the tundra has a higher-pitched, quavering *whoo-whoo*.

Sometimes you'll see flocks of large white birds flying overhead that look like swans but are actually snow geese migrating in from Russia's Wrangell Island. Black-tipped wings distinguish this species, which, unlike swans, can still legally be hunted.

You may also notice a rust coloring on swans or snow geese; the staining is from a heavy iron content in some of the northern soils and water that discolors the bird's feathers while it feeds. If you also see sooty gray swans among the flocks in fields or marshes, these are not birds that haven't bathed recently but young swans, or cygnets.

It's interesting to note that swans, like other waterfowl, aren't born waterproof. Aquatic birds preen themselves with the oil from a gland at the base of the tail, but very young birds don't preen. How then do they follow the mother duck or swan out into the water without sinking? Presumably, as the chicks snuggle into their parent's feathers, they become well coated with the adult's waterproofing oil.

Watch the swans in the fields as they feed. They're curious, social birds and engage in a lot of interaction, such as wing waggling, chasing, and head bobbing. They feed on corn and vegetables such as potatoes and carrots in the fields and aquatic plants and small crustaceans in the marshes. It may not appear to be so, but that stiff-looking bill of theirs is actually very flexible; a swan can peel corn off an ear or even pinch a person's arm with its beak.

Watch also as the birds get ready to leave the feeding grounds. Notice that they don't just burst into flight but run a good 50 feet or so to become airborne. Until you

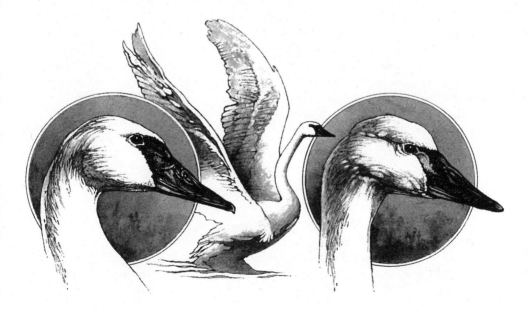

consider this taxiing run, it may seem odd that despite its huge wings, a swan that injures its legs loses its capacity to fly.

When you do come across a flock of swans feeding in fields or wetlands, keep a respectful distance to avoid scaring the birds. Photo "hunters" who repeatedly flush swans to get that one great shot are damaging the birds' wintering capability, for the swans are in the fields and marshes now trying to feed and build body reserves. Swans have a good memory, and too much disturbance may cause them to forsake a feeding ground for good.

Before we leave the winter scene, let's take a quick trip shoreside and look at another large bird that is not as big as the swan nor white and bugle-throated but black and nearly voiceless. Flying low over wind-whipped waters, its heavy body perhaps shadowing a small group of buffleheads riding the waves, the *cormorant* is a familiar sight here, well represented by three different species. Commonly called "shags" or "sea crows," cormorants are all goose-sized with long beaks hooked at the tip.

Superb underwater swimmers, cormorants use their wings to help propel themselves through the water. The bird's nostrils close off as it grows, so that the adult breathes only through the mouth, and its heavy body can reach depths of over 100 feet. Oriental fishermen take advantage of the cormorant's diving and fishing skills by forcing it to hunt at the end of a long leash. A ring around the bird's neck prevents it from swallowing its catch; after several catches, the fisherman removes the ring and the bird is finally allowed to feed for itself.

Because the cormorant's plumage is not entirely waterproof, presumably so the bird can dive deeply and quickly, a common sight in the islands is a large black figure perched on a piling with wings outstretched to dry. (Were it not for the head and neck shape, the spread-winged cormorant would look exactly like a huge black bat.) Watch for cormorants also as they make their way back and forth across the water from their evening roosts in V formation or in long, strung-out lines.

It's time to leave the cormorant and the swan, black and white reflections of a winter landscape drained of color in these cloudy, damp days. Even the enveloping greens can lose their power in drizzle times, but then the clouds part, the sun makes the greens glisten, and the winter wren sings a trembling overture to its nesting days. Then we exhale the blahs with our misty breath and trudge on to find what nature reveals only to the faithful.

---

## WINTER WILDLIFE HAPPENINGS

- ◆ Trumpeter and tundra swans feed now in fields and wetlands.
- ◆ High population of winter raptors: rough-legs, gyrfalcons, and prairie falcons fly in, while migrating balds, red-tails, and harriers swell local populations.
- ◆ Hibernating or torpid now are snails, snakes, frogs, hornet and bumblebee queens, honeybees, and mourning cloaks. Raccoons, squirrels, and newts are less active.

- Deer shed antlers in late winter.
- Bull kelp dies off and tears from rocks in winter storms.
- Great horned owls mate in late winter.
- Flocks of chestnut-backed chickadees, nuthatches, and golden-crowned kinglets may be seen foraging in treetops.

## BACKYARD WILDLIFE ACTIVITIES

- Build nest boxes and bat houses now for the spring nesting season.
- Put out suet for insect-loving birds. Raw beef suet is fine, or melt it and combine with bread crumbs, sunflower seeds, and popcorn. Let harden slightly, form into balls, and hang in netted bags.
- Trim a tree for the birds with popcorn, pretzels, doughnuts, or scooped-out orange halves filled with seed or melted suet.
- Mix small seeds or cornmeal with peanut butter and coat pine cones to hang.
- Provide fresh water when other sources have frozen.
- Prune trees and shrubs and collect prunings into a brush pile about 4 to 5 feet high as a winter shelter for birds, insects, rodents, and small mammals.
- Cleaned-out nesting boxes may come in useful as sheltered roosting spots during severe weather.

# BUD ANDERSON

## *Wrapped Up in Raptors*

Bud Anderson describes his twenty-year search for a black merlin nest as "looking for the holy grail." Although peregrines are his specialty, he stresses that he loves all raptors, speaking about them with a fervor some folks find unsettling.

Hawks inspire not only admiration but hatred. Back in the mid-1980s, when Bud displayed wounded hawks at fairs for educational purposes, he says, "At least once a day we'd get someone who'd come up and say, 'What do you have *these* here for? I shoot these!'" Taken aback, he tried to discover the reasons for the shootings. "I said, 'Gee, that's interesting. I'm doing a study—could you tell me why you shoot these particular birds?'" The most common response was that hawks were hated for killing chickens.

"If you introduce a prey source into a natural environment, it'll be preyed upon," he told them, adding, "If you want to see the most effective predator on earth, look in the mirror." Anyone who provides a prey base, whether it be chickens, quail, or a fish hatchery, will find it exploited by the natural predators. "Put your chickens in a chicken coop," he says with some exasperation.

Outside Bud's home, Tyee, a beautiful mature golden eagle, sits tethered to a stump. Tyee's right wing was crippled in a shooting on San Juan Island. People still shoot hawks illegally, and much of Bud's effort as founder of the Falcon Research Group in Bow is devoted to education "to teach people how neat hawks are." He does hawk-watching classes in Seattle, Tacoma, Olympia, and locally at the Padilla Bay Interpretive Center, as well as field projects where people can have hands-on experience with hawks.

Bud holds state and federal permits that allow him to keep unreleasable birds. Before bringing one of these birds into the classroom, he advises his students not to stare but to act as inconspicuously as possible and walk up to the hawk in a slow, zigzag style.

He lets me hold one of his birds, a young kestrel that goes by a variety of names including "Rambo" and "Godzilla" because of his fearless venture into the woods one day while still unable to fly. A beautiful bird not much bigger than a jay, this smallest of the falcons is strikingly colored with blue-gray wings, rufous back, and black striping. He fairly glows in the sun as he constantly cocks his head and vocalizes, taking in everything with a piercing dark eye. The bird's intensity is almost palpable, even a bit unnerving. There's no woolgathering here because a wild bird can't afford that luxury; it must be present, as Bud says, 100 percent in the moment.

We sit beside an old cattle pond on his property one summer morning as he talks about how his interest in hawks began. Before he gets too far, however, he points out other raptors zipping across the water, the mosquito hawks of the pond. "That's a male dragonfly patrolling territory and driving out another male," he says. "They're looking for females to come in; they'll mate with them, and the females will oviposit in these soft rushes here."

Born and raised in Seattle, Bud never had much chance to see hawks but somehow remained interested in them through boyhood. It was at the University of Washington that he picked up a book on falconry. "It was like somebody actually grabbing me," he recalls. He began what was to be his life's calling by studying and learning how to catch hawks, and he finally became a falconer himself, "although never a very good one." He spent several years trapping, banding, and releasing hawks; then came more schooling and finally his own fieldwork contracts and the creation of the Falcon Research Group in 1985.

The organization has about six hundred members in Washington and a few other places. "I'm sort of the last of the low-key conservation groups," he says, noting that the best way to get involved with hawks is through his free introductory class at the Padilla Bay Center. Those who want to study further can move on to his advanced raptor class and possible involvement in one of the research group's field projects or "join other organizations involved with raptors—rehab clinics, the Raptor Research Foundation, the local Audubon group. Go to a university for more education on wildlife biology," he urges. "I strongly recommend that." Bud's involvement with raptors, especially peregrines, has taken him all over the world: Greenland, Peru, Ecuador, Chile, Israel, Argentina, and Fiji. "That's what I really love doing, going into new areas, finding out new stuff about how birds fit in."

But for many of us who relish the sight of raptors, there's no place like home. The islands have one of the largest populations of breeding bald eagles in the Lower Forty-eight, and the Samish flats are one of the best places in North America to watch for wintering hawks, especially if you're a falcon lover. According to Bud, "It's the only place that we know of in the U.S. where you can see all five species of North American falcons in a single day."

Why are the flats rolling in raptors? For several reasons, the first being the maritime climate, which is "like the tropics for an arctic bird. It seldom freezes here, so the waters are open, and there's a high population of shorebirds that are fed on by just about everything. They're sort of the plankton of the flats." Also, a wide agricultural area provides an abundance of ground prey such as voles, white-footed deer mice, and shrews.

One red-tailed hawk figured out the relationship between the start-up of a tractor-loader that was cleaning out a ditch and the sudden availability of rodents. He flew in from the nearby woods whenever the machine roared to life, once even boldly grabbing a vole from the bucket. "Red-tails exploit any food source, and they learn very quickly," says Bud. The most commonly observed raptor in this area, red-tails are the "one-dollar bills of the hawk world." Not only do we have a healthy population of resident red-tails here, but we also get the migrants that come down from Alaska in the winter.

An adult red-tailed hawk can always be identified by its distinctive red tail and big, bulky body. Bud compares the different-sized hawks to vehicles on a freeway. The eagle is the semi of the bird world, red-tails and rough-legs are the pickups, and accipiters and falcons the sports cars. Although the red-tail is one of the largest of the group, it weighs in at only about 2 1/2 pounds. "They've evolved a very light airframe," says Bud, pointing out that a bird's bones are hollow and that the feathers of a golden eagle weigh more than its whole skeletal system. "They do naturally what Boeing engineers get paid for."

We hear the high scream of a red-tail as we sit by the pond, but Bud is skeptical of its authenticity. "There's a Steller's jay that's been bugging me recently," he says, referring to the jay's ability to mimic the red-tail. Sure enough, we soon spot the blue flash of a jay among the distant trees.

When asked why the jay would mimic a hawk, Bud confesses he doesn't know but calls the jay, which is part of the same family (Corvidae) as crows and ravens, a most intelligent bird. On the matter of intelligence, he shakes his head. "You know, there was male chauvinism in the seventies. I think now we suffer from intelligence chauvinism, believing we're the chosen species." He describes how a peregrine that hatches out in July and fledges in August on the north slope of Alaska can be in Santiago, Chile, by October. "Now, how many human beings could do that even as adults?"

His voice becomes reverent when he dwells upon the right-on-the-edge lives of raptors. "If you're a hawk and you mess up, you die. Most of us are very removed from the natural world now. We live in warm, dry houses year-round, so we don't have to contend with the weather. We don't have to find and catch our own food. If we're sick or want some time off, we just rest up on a weekend, watch some TV, knit, play with the kids. It's not that way out in the wild," he stresses. "The birds that live out there and handle the pressures have to be the equivalent of our Olympic athletes. They're the epitome of wild animals. They're tough, and they're out there making it, and for me that engenders a lot of respect for these birds."

To keep track of just how the birds are doing, the Falcon Research Group conducts a winter hawk count every year. Bald eagles are increasing exponentially—"there are more now than ever." Peregrines have come back in big numbers. "It used to be, back in the early seventies, if you saw a peregrine, it was a red-letter day of the year. Now they're seen quite often, because they've come back so well from the DDT problem."

Raptors face many threats to their lives, including starvation, collisions with cars, electrocution, shootings, and, in the past, pesticide poisoning. Bud describes cases of great horned owls flying through wire fences, getting their wingtips caught on the barbs, and then spinning over the wire and hanging there until dead.

A few days earlier, he helped a red-tail that had taken a bath in a sewage lagoon: "It was just coated with green manure. We held it under the shower a couple of times, washed it off, and released it and it was fine." He notes that birds have flown down smokestacks and then died when they couldn't get back out. "It's just a very strange group of mortality factors."

Weather also takes its toll. Although our winter climate is moderate most of the time, the winter of 1992–93 saw a lot of snow and a prolonged freeze. Nearly seventy barn owls in the area starved to death, the crusted snow preventing them from reaching food such as voles. Nonetheless, Bud points out that a huge productivity in barn owl young the previous summer allowed the population to recover from the winter's loss. "People have to realize that, as sad as it may be, natural mortality is a part of life."

Simply being young and inexperienced is also a liability; 50 to 90 percent of raptors die in their first year. An immature hawk often takes all day to make a successful hunt, whereas an adult might polish off its dunlin or vole before the morning's half over. "First-year hawks are always messing up," says Bud. "They're here, there, everywhere. They're like teenagers; they gotta try it out and see if it works. The adults, they've done that. They've made it though their first year, and they just get smarter and smarter until finally, when you've got an adult five to ten years old, man, everything it does is *art*."

Spend some time in the field with these birds and see for yourself what life on the edge is all about. There are four seasons to hawk-watching here, with November to March offering prime-time viewing. Spring sees the northern birds move back to breeding grounds in Alaska and Canada, while the local population starts courting. "The breeding species people can expect to see around here are somewhat limited, actually. They're balds, red-tails, Cooper's hawks, kestrels, and that's about it—anything else is somewhat rare." Those are the species to look for in the summer, when nesting and rearing are under way; otherwise, it's a relatively "dead" season.

Autumn brings the southerly migration from the north, and it's also the time young hawks start fledging. In the winter, the population really swells as the migrants fly in to enjoy a more temperate climate and abundant prey. The most commonly seen species in winter—the "big four," according to Bud—will be in this order: red-tails and bald eagles (they trade off depending on the time of year), northern harriers (marsh hawks), and rough-legged hawks. "About 90 to 95 percent of all raptors that you see on the flats in the winter will be those four species."

Focus on the bird's size and shape and scan constantly when looking for raptors: "Good hawk-watchers won't talk with you face to face, because they're always look- ing for birds." Especially check out the ecotones, edges where two habitats come together, since there are more prey there and, thus, likely more raptors. Drive around, and if the hawks are perched nearby, stay in your car so as not to disturb them.

Use whatever binoculars you have, although the best for hawk-watching are 10 x 40s: "Ten-power because a lot of hawks are way out there, but they're not very good binoculars for up-close passerines." If you're a serious hawk-watcher who isn't counting pennies, you should "do yourself a favor and get the most expensive pair you can. When you look at a bird, you'll see them in such fine detail that it's a real pleasure. And that's what you're out there for." He's fond of the quote "Binoculars are to birders what instruments are to musicians" and suggests Leica, Zeiss, and Bausch and Lomb Elites as the top-drawer brands.

For identification, he recommends the Peterson Field Guide *Hawks*, by Bill Clark. *Birds of Prey* (Ian Newton, ed.) is an excellent, accessible introduction to the basic biology of birds, "not so densely technical you fall asleep after the first three pages," and the two-volume *Handbook of North American Birds*, by Ralph Palmer, is another good work on bird biology. *Hawks, Owls, and Wildlife*, by Frank and John Craighead, is also strongly recommended as "the book that started raptor biology," and another wonderful read is Fran Hammerstrom's *Harrier: Hawk of the Marshes*. "It's one of those books you just can't put down."

To really begin to understand a hawk and its daily cycle, lectures and books are important, but they are no substitutes for time in the field; the map, as Bud sternly points out, is *not* the territory. He tends to divide birding into two different types: checklisting, where the focus is primarily on finding and crossing off species ("I'm not into that at all. I don't even have a life list"), and field biology, which is observ- ing the behavior of a bird to really learn something about it.

Pick a favorite hawk, he suggests, one that "really turns you on," and then go spend a day with it. Choose a buteo or eagle so you can keep up with it and a wide- open area so that you can see the hawk as it flies and follow it by car. Bring your binos, a scope, a field guide, and a notebook. If a full day is just not possible, then spend an hour or so watching a hawk on its perch and note what it does. Does it preen or leave the perch to bathe? ("I get a lot of calls: 'Do something! There's a bald eagle in the middle of my pond and the water's up to its wings!' Well, it's taking a bath; they do that all the time.") If the hawk's around a nest, does it leave to defend its territory? Does it have an obvious bulge in its throat sack, or crop, indi- cating a recent meal? If the weather suddenly changes from soggy to sunny, does it take off to soar on the thermals? How does the hawk behave when it spots a distant dinner—what's its hunting technique?

A flock of robins suddenly rises out of the trees beyond the pond. "See how they're all weaving? There's a hawk around." Bud describes what he feels is the greatest sight for any hawk-watcher: a merlin hunting a shorebird flock. "That's the most dramatic thing going. What you'll see is a compact flock of shorebirds in the sky turning very rapidly and erratically. It's not a slow movement but very quick and jerky. Whenever you see that, it means they're being attacked by a predator, usually a falcon. The flights can sometimes go on for more than a minute, and in my opinion they're the greatest, most spectacular thing in bird-watching in western Washington." Perhaps with the exception of a 1000-foot vertical peregrine stoop, he adds, but definitely top of the list to be watched for. "You see this flock twisting and turning, like a louver effect, where they flash white, brown, white, brown. You can see that on a sunny day from over 3 miles away. Whenever you see it, stop what you're doing, look in that cloud, and try to find the falcon above it, or in it, or behind it."

"Once you see it, you'll never forget it."

---

Sixteen species of diurnal (daytime) hawks are found in western Washington, and Bud teaches a special mnemonic for remembering them: 2-2-3-4-5—two eagles (bald, golden), two buteos (red-tailed and rough-legged hawks), three accipiters (sharp-shinned and Cooper's hawks, northern goshawk), four of a kind (turkey vulture, northern harrier, white-tailed kite, osprey), five falcons (kestrel, merlin, prairie and peregrine falcons, gyrfalcon).

Hawks are categorized according to wing shape and flight pattern. Buteos are the soaring hawks, with broad wings and short broad tails. Accipiters are the sprinters, with short wings and long tails. Falcons have long, pointed wings and short tails.

# PART 2

# Invited Home

## A Guide to
## Wildlife Habitats

*"There is a pleasure in the pathless woods;
There is a rapture on the lonely shore. . . ."*

—*George Gordon, Lord Byron*

# Chapter 5

# WETLANDS

SWAMPS, BOGS. THE HUMBLE WORDS LIE THERE, flat and uninviting. Wastelands. Breeding grounds for mosquitoes. Eyesores that mar the countryside. Smelly, moss-hung, mud-sucking pestholes. Such has been the popular perception of wetlands for so long that the U.S. Fish and Wildlife Service estimates that in our march to conquer and redesign, we plow under or pave over about 450,000 acres of wetlands a year in this country.

Those who enjoy wildlife don't sneer at swamps. They know that wetlands are some of the most biologically rich habitats on earth, providing food, cover, and nesting areas for a variety of birds, amphibians, reptiles, insects, and mammals.

Just what *is* a wetland? Counties are struggling to come up with a definition that will please developers and wildlife lovers alike, but simply, a wetland is an area covered by water or having waterlogged soil for part or all of the year and characterized by specific types of vegetation and soils. There are both freshwater and saltwater wetlands in the archipelago: bogs thick with undecomposed plant residues; swamps dominated by cottonwood, alder, hawthorn, and willow; and both fresh- and saltwater marshes, which are treeless and populated by grasslike plants such as rushes, sedges, and cattails.

To better understand the differences among freshwater wetlands, look at what happens to a pond over many years' time. Slowly, the pond fills in with sediments and pieces of plants washed in from the land. As the edges around the pond build up, grasses and sedges gradually move in and spread until the pond becomes a marsh. As more years go by, the trees along the marsh edge are able to get a foothold in the built-up soil and push farther in until the marsh becomes a swamp, and the swamp eventually becomes a woodland as the trees dominate. Should the pond have very poor drainage or none at all, it may escape this progression and become a bog. A mat of floating sphagnum moss forms along the sides of the pond and gradually pushes inward. After many years, the bog may become a swamp and then the swamp a forest.

Wetlands are vital resources. Drinking water in the islands comes only from rain (not snowpack melt), which soaks into the soil of wetland areas such as Beaverton Valley and Crow Valley to build up groundwater storage. Wetlands are thus also crucial for flood control (they retain and gradually release large amounts of water), as well as pollution control (dense vegetation traps and filters sediments and pollutants out of the water). Finally, wetlands provide educational, scenic, and wildlife values.

Our focus is on wildlife, so let's head into an island wetland and see who visits these swampy spots and what plants grow there. Because the soil is so saturated with water, we'll find only plants that can survive with low oxygen levels.

*Red alder,* our fastest-growing tree, and Scouler's *willow,* the eagerly welcomed pussy willow of springtime, are a couple of common local trees that don't mind soggy roots. The tall Pacific willow is also very common around island ponds and lakes, streaming with long yellow catkins in the spring.

Around ponds and creating inpenetrable thickets in wet areas is the shrubby *hardhack,* a favorite nesting spot for warblers called yellowthroats. In the summer, this plant puts on a show with fluffy plumes of tiny pink flowers. *Swamp gooseberry* is another somewhat unfriendly shrub that likes wet soil. Look for tall, weak, spine-covered stems, black, bitter berries, and small, maple-shaped leaves.

What's the difference between two grasslike plants you'll find in wet soils and standing water, sedges and rushes? A sedge has a triangular stem, whereas the stem of a rush is cylindrical. (The simple mnemonic "Sedges have edges; rushes are round" will help you remember the difference.) *Cattail* are neither sedge nor rush but belong to an entirely different family. Their leaves feel spongy when touched because of tiny air sacs in the tissue filled with gases such as oxygen, a commodity that can be especially hard to obtain in waterlogged soils. Cattail leaves are easily made into baskets or seats; Northwest natives wove them into mats that covered frames to provide temporary and mobile summer shelters.

The cattails clustered around ponds and marshes are incredibly useful plants. Adapted to places where the soil is wet but not constantly under water, cattails have spreading root systems that help stabilize soggy areas, and their dense vegetation provides prime nesting areas for many species such as the red-winged blackbird. The plant is also savored by muskrats, which eat the early spring shoots, leaves, and stems in summer and the roots through the fall and winter.

Muskrats munching on cattails seems natural enough, but we might balk a bit about ourselves doing the same. Nonetheless, the plant has seemingly endless possibilities as a food source for people. I once listened to a naturalist rave about cattails; if we raised the plant commercially, he said, we could feed the world.

Almost the entire plant is edible. Cattail cuisine might include cutting off the roots to use in place of bean sprouts in a stir-fry. The best time to get the shoots from the rhizome is before they break the surface. You might boil them with a little curry powder and eat as you would asparagus. Another option is to peel or scour the rhizome, which is full of starch, boil five to ten minutes, push through a strainer, and use as mashed potatoes or as a soup thickener. Or dry the rhizome and grind it into flour.

Pick the bulbous top part of the cattail when it's green and firm, like a thin hot dog on a stick, and before the pollen gets heavy on the stem above, and eat like corn on the cob. When the pollen comes in, it can be collected and mixed with flour.

Let's move now from the tails of cats to those of horses. Make a mental trip back to about three hundred million years ago and you'll see the tree-tall ancestor of some of today's most common and primitive water-loving plants, the *horsetails*. The hollow, jointed stems that populate wet fields and woods in early summer hold tiny silica crystals that make the stems abrasive enough for scrubbing camp pots. Later in the season, the plant opens up into the wiry spreading branches that give it its colorful name.

Cotton grass is a sedge you'll see in swampy areas and wet meadows; look for tall grassy stems topped with cottony fluffs. You may also notice sunny splashes of color among the grasses and sedges from May to September. These belong to our common monkeyflower, a 2-foot-tall plant with yellow, snapdragonlike flowers that supposedly resemble monkey faces.

Look for the little broad-leaved sundew in the more acidic soils. This carnivorous bog plant traps insects such as gnats and mosquitoes by luring them to the sweet, sticky globules of "sun dew" at the tip of its leaf hairs. In the sun, the plant lights up invitingly; when the unwitting insect lands, the plant's hairs bend around it like tentacles to force it against the leaf. The leaf then curls around the insect, and digestive juices dissolve the prey to extract the nitrogen necessary for its survival in the acidic bog. Finally, the leaf expands again to produce a new blob of sticky bait, the last step in a cycle that may take several days. The sundew blooms here from May to August (try the floating logs on the north side of Mountain Lake on Orcas or the bog islands of Cranberry Lake). Look for tiny stems rising out of a tuft of red, spoon-shaped leaves.

Scan the surface waters of a pond and notice the green dots of duckweed, a favorite, high-nutrient food of ducks, geese, and muskrats. In the fall, this free-floating aquatic plant sinks waterlogged to the bottom of the wetland; in the spring, the plant grows new air sacs, which fill with gas and float it again to the surface. A stem extends downward from the waxy green globule but doesn't root, contrary to pondweed, which has several leaves attached to a rooted stem. Also unlike the non-blooming duckweed, pondweed sends up a green flower spike in midsummer.

One summer's day, I watched a small girl splashing in the water at an edge of Heart Lake, thick with duckweed, grasses, and lilies. It was the *Indian* (or yellow) *pond lily* that most interested the child, who, after getting her father to name this wonderful plant, pressed him further. "But what do they *do*, Daddy?" "Well," he fumbled, "they make flowers and then just lie there the rest of the year."

Well, true, but hardly an inspiring account of this striking water plant. Sitting atop large, heart-shaped leaves, this small sun of the wetland is firmly anchored in the mud by means of a long stalk enclosing an air-filled tube. The leaves, or lily pads, are so large because they need to catch as much light as possible to process enough food for the plant. As they "lie there," these leaves are convenient landing strips for dragonflies, springtails, frogs, and other animals that rest, feed, and lay their eggs. Turn a leaf over and note the life clinging to the slimy underside: tiny snails and their eggs, whirligig beetle eggs, water mites, and more. Inside the bright yellow bowl of the flower is a thick knob, which holds more insects as well as the petals and seeds of the plant. Northwest natives ground the seeds to make flour and even roasted them like popcorn, a point that probably would have fascinated our young swimmer.

Water lilies are also seen on island ponds; their sweet-smelling flowers open in the early morning and close in the afternoon. Usually, the flowers are white, but I have seen some beautiful deep blush varieties along the roadside edge of Heart Lake.

The rich vegetation of island wetlands provides food, nesting areas, and cover for an equally rich variety of wildlife. Waterfowl such as *Canada geese* migrating along the Pacific Flyway use the wetlands as stopover spots. Marsh grasses both shield and feed the birds that need to rest and fatten up before flying on.

Other resident birds such as mallards and wood ducks, herons, coots, and rails depend on wetlands for shelter and sustenance. The *mallard* is the most commonly observed dabbling duck of the marsh, and much can be learned as well as enjoyed from watching this ubiquitous bird. The drake is a truly handsome fellow with his glossy green head, white neck ring, brown breast, and curled tail feathers. The brown hen may be more subdued in color but not in voice. It's she who makes the loud quacks, fitting for one with full charge of a brood that can number over a dozen.

Although wild mallards are wary, the fact that they are so easy to find makes them a prime candidate for quiet, patient observation. Look for on-the-water courting displays in February, nests carefully concealed in tall reeds or under low-hanging branches, and mother-duckling interaction in spring and summer. The ducklings hatch about four weeks after the eggs are laid, and soon after hatching the brood dutifully follows their mother into the water.

Virginia rails and the shy sora are often hard to catch sight of in island wetlands, but one bird is brazenly nonsecretive. The *belted kingfisher* is a rascally bird in both sound and appearance, if not in behavior. Its wildly feathered crest gives it a sort of bristling bravado; one friend commented that the kingfisher looks "as if it just jumped off a Harley." I always think of it as the feathered counterpart of the Douglas squirrel, that choleric critter of the woods. Indeed, it's not hard to mistake the rattling call of the kingfisher for that of the scolding chickaree.

The kingfisher's pugnacious look is carried through in its disproportionately large, thick bill and stocky, stub-tailed body. Males are belted with a blue chest band, whereas females have an additional chestnut breast band; thus, the kingfisher is one of the very few species of North American birds with the female more variously colored than the male. (The female osprey, another superb fish hunter, is also distinguished from the male by an added brown necklace.) It's easy to come up with reasons for the usual flashy male–dull female scenario, but the opposite case is puzzling. As you watch the kingfisher, ask yourself why this species reverses the norm.

Calls are made to declare territory and often while diving for fish. Many times you'll hear the loud, chattering cry before spotting the bird; once you've located it, watch for its next hunting attempt. Some experts believe the kingfisher has the keenest sight of any bird, for it can spot a 2-inch fish as it flies by 50 feet overhead. When it spots its prey, the bird jerks to a stop, hovers momentarily, and then dives.

If it makes a successful catch, the kingfisher subdues the fish or frog by beating it
against its perch; then it shifts the prey so
it's swallowed headfirst to ease the
passage of prickly fins. Later, the
fisher king regurgitates pellets of
indigestible bones and body parts.

Mammals such as river otters, beavers,
and muskrats also call the ponds and marshes
home. Although *beavers*, also aptly called
"slaptails," are not present in the San Juans
proper except in isolated cases such as Moran Park
on Orcas, they flourish on Fidalgo Island. Cranberry
Lake alone has three active lodges on its south bog
island. When you visit their homes, remember that
the beaver is one of the only creatures besides ourselves that creates its own habitat.

To produce its building materials, a beaver holds
onto a trunk with its large upper teeth and chews with
its lower, making the distinctive chisel marks found on
so many toppled trees. The beaver is the largest of the
rodents, and, as is true of all rodents, its teeth never stop
growing. Two folds of skin behind the teeth seal off the

*Belted
kingfisher*

beaver's mouth underwater, so that it can pursue its chews without choking on
water. Other special adaptations for underwater living include nose and ear valves,
which shut out the water, and transparent eyelids.

Both the beaver and the *muskrat* are largely nocturnal creatures, but you can
catch sight of them busily finishing up their work in the early morning hours, and
I've seen muskrats much later in the day. The beaver can be easily distinguished
from the muskrat by its larger size and the flat, scaly tail that slaps those warnings on
the water's surface. The muskrat, on the contrary, has a long, hairless tail like that of
a huge, well, rat.

You might spot another animal swimming in the wetland that may give you a
moment's surprise. Many people don't think of *raccoons* as swimmers; in their mind's
eye, these animals are usually perched in a tree or toppling park trash cans. But raccoons are fine swimmers. One day at an island wetland, I watched one swim among
a thick cover of lily pads, blithely ignoring a passing merganser hen, to a snag,
which it rapidly climbed. The coon's goal was a wood duck nesting box, where it
hitched itself, head pointing skyward over the top of the box, while it plunged one
paw in as far as it could reach in a hopeful search for eggs.

Some of the most intriguing wetland denizens are those we may not have paid
much attention to since our early days mucking about in places humming with mosquitoes and crawling with slimy creatures. Those mosquitoes biting your neck are
the females; blood helps their eggs develop. Male mosquitoes can't pierce the skin as

females do and so are restricted to sipping nectar and other plant fluids. If you become so besieged by buzzing bloodsuckers that you wonder what on earth could be their purpose other than your undeserved torment, think of all the meals mosquitoes provide for fish, frogs, dragonflies, bats, nighthawks, and songbirds.

Look for a tiny black beetle called the whirligig that lives on the surface of pond waters. Such a small, homely creature might not seem worthy of much attention other than as an amusement for children captivated by its whirling movements, but let's look a little closer. The beetle is not only an acrobatic surface swimmer but a good diver and flier as well, a combination of skills not many can claim. Its remarkable eyes are adapted to both air and water environments; it can simultaneously see above water with the upper halves of its eyes and below with the lower halves.

If you pick up a whirligig, it may give off a milky fluid, which gives rise to another name: "vanilla bug." You'll usually find this insect in groups; dozens whirling around like tiny bumper cars on inevitable collision courses will in fact not crash into each other, thanks to a special sense organ that picks up water vibrations. Why do they whirl so? Some think it's to confuse or escape predators, but the question remains unsettled. Watch them and see if you can enlighten the rest of us.

Along with the whirligigs, you may catch sight of water striders airily skimming the waters of the wetlands, zipping over a film of water much like the surface tension that holds a drop of water momentarily at a faucet. Sometimes called "pond skaters" or "Jesus bugs" for their seemingly uncanny water-walking ability, the striders can break this water film and sink below the surface for food or protection. Once out again, they need to be completely dry to regain their water-walking skills.

Although we don't often pay much attention to the antics of insects (except when they annoy us), we might want to adjust our focus a bit and take time to marvel. Water striders, for instance, have a unique mating ritual: the male gathers a tiny bit of wood, sits by it, sends out a pulsating signal with his foot in the water, and waits for a willing female to appear. When she does, the two will mate and the female will then deposit her eggs on the wood.

Caddis flies in their larval stage live at the bottom of shallow pools, where they build protective cases about themselves of bits of sticks or plants or of pebbles held together by the creature's gluelike secretions. If you see what looks like a bit of stick or plant stem at the bottom of a quiet pool and it starts to move, you'll know you've chanced upon the caddis fly larva.

Early morning and late afternoon are the best times to visit a shallow wetland because those are the times of most activity. The warmed-up water of midday can't hold as many dissolved gases as cold water, and so pond animals slow down because of oxygen depletion. When you visit, bring a hand lens with you as your passport into this marvelous microcosm. Scoop up some water and a bit of mud and see what wonders you can find.

On to the slimy, or to wetland creatures unfairly perceived as such: the reptiles and amphibians. (Snakes are by no means slimy, covered as they are with dry scales.) We have at least five *garter snakes* here, but the double-striped common garter is the snake you'll commonly find sunning itself on wetland paths. Don't be unnerved by the forked tongue flicking in and out; it's not a sinister or threatening movement but simply a way for the snake to sense its surroundings.

The northern *red-legged frog* breeds in local wetlands, laying its gelatinous mass of eggs in January or February. The undersides of this frog's hind legs are a pale red, and the head usually sports a dark mask. The skin is smooth and moist, unlike the warty skin of a toad. Dr. Eugene Kozloff, in his *Plants and Animals of the Pacific Northwest*, describes the red-legged frog as having a unique odor comparable to that of a "wet rubber balloon." The red-leg is larger than our other common species, the *Pacific chorus frog*, but much less vocal. If you hear croaking in the wetlands, it likely belongs to the chorus frog; the red-leg doesn't croak, but it sometimes makes a frightened squeak.

I always feel especially rewarded when I chance upon a *rough-skinned newt* in the moist woods or wetlands. This is the salamander you are most likely to see because it's the only one openly active during the day; don't look for it during hot weather, however, for its skin needs to remain moist. Warty-skinned and dark brown or gray above, the newt has a rich orange underside, which it displays as a warning to predators. Glands on that bright belly produce enough poison, it is said, to kill twenty-five thousand mice, although our wetland snake, the common garter, preys on newts to no ill effect.

The poison seems a surprising weapon in an animal so apparently passive. The newt is quite docile when picked up and causes no harm to its handler, although washing up afterwards is recommended. I always enjoy picking up a newt, staring into its hooded, sleepy-looking eye, and watching its tiny limbs, which move as if the creature were walking through molasses. Only the bright orange throat pulses quickly until I gently set it down again among the leaf litter.

The sleepy newt knows what so many of us don't; wetlands are wastelands only to the uninitiated. Pull on your boots, grab the mosquito repellent, and go soar with the dragons, spin with the beetles, or simply idle a while in a muck full of magic.

## SITE GUIDE

The following is a list of representative wetland areas open to the public. The San Juan Preservation Trust and San Juan Audubon Society also have permission to lead hikes in private areas such as San Juan's Three Meadows Marsh and the Gilson Marsh on Shaw; contact these groups for further information.

### San Juan Island

**Egg Lake:** Good birding at this 6¹/₂-acre lake. Look for red-wings, buffleheads, scaups, cormorants, mallards, swallows. Yellow pond lilies, cattails, elderberry, thimbleberry, and salmonberry thickets edge the sides.
ACCESS: From the ferry, turn right off Spring Street onto Second Street, which soon becomes Guard Street. Turn right off Guard onto Tucker, which becomes Roche Harbor Road. Follow Roche Harbor Road about 4 miles and turn left onto Egg Lake Road. Lake is another ¹/₂ mile down the road to the left. (As you head up

Roche Harbor Road to Egg Lake Road, you'll see Sportsmans Lake on your left, another good bird-watching spot.)

**Jakle's Lagoon:** Located in the American Camp area and bordered by forest to the south and Griffin Bay to the north, the lagoon is used by the UW biological lab as a study area and collecting site. Look for puddle ducks, great blue herons, kingfishers, swallows, buffleheads, hooded mergansers, and shorebirds such as killdeers and yellowlegs. Check out the shoreside cliff banks for nest holes of kingfishers and swallows. Offshore, loons, grebes, scaups, scoters, otters, and seals frequent the area. ACCESS: Follow directions to Jakle's Nature Trail (see "Forest"). After you reach the beach, turn right and walk the cobble shore to the lagoon.

## Orcas Island

**Frank Richardson Wildfowl Preserve:** Also known as the Deer Harbor Marsh, this extensive freshwater marsh is one of the islands' prime birding areas. Look for hooded mergansers, wood ducks, Canada geese, wigeons, scaups, buffies, mallards, marsh wrens, yellowthroats, teals, coots, rails, and ring-necks, among others. The red-winged blackbirds really set this spot humming on an early spring morning, and rough-skinned newts can be seen migrating to the marsh in that season. Vegetation includes common mare's tail, reed canary grass, and salmonberry.
ACCESS: From the ferry, take the Horseshoe Highway 2¹/₂ miles to the intersection with Deer Harbor Road. Turn left and go approximately 4¹/₂ miles to an unmarked road on the right just after the Deer Harbor Inn and just before the village of Deer Harbor. Turn right and cross bridge. Bear left after the bridge and head uphill about ³/₄ mile to a marsh on the right side of the road. Small turnouts off the road provide scant parking.

## Lopez Island

**Spencer Spit Lagoon:** This is a saltwater marsh lagoon formed when two sandspits joined into one, providing habitat for herons, kingfishers, puddle ducks, brant, otters, and migrating Canada geese. Stay on trails and walk along the spit or on the west side of the marsh, where you can watch from a cover of wild roses and flowering currant. Goldfinches like the rosebushes, and you're bound to see rabbits and possibly black-tailed deer.
ACCESS: Take the ferry road to the first intersection (about 1 mile) and turn left onto Port Stanley Road. Follow the road 2¹/₂ miles to Baker View Road and turn left. Continue straight about ¹/₂ mile to park entrance. Drive down to the parking areas by the rest rooms and take the Beach Access trail down to the wetland.

## Fidalgo Island

**Beaver Ponds:** Watch for newts, snails, and garter snakes on trails and for frogs in the small ponds. On the big beaver pond, you may see wood ducks (nesting boxes have been put out for their use), hooded mergansers, mallards, swallows, kingfishers, and herons. Look also for bald eagles, ospreys, and muskrats. Beavers and river otters may be seen in the early hours at the south end of Cranberry Lake; late risers will at least see plenty of beaver-chewed trees and the animals' lodges. Look for skunk cabbage, pond lilies, duckweed, and, on the bog islands, cotton grass, shore pine, and wild cranberry.

ACCESS: Coming into Anacortes from Highway 20, turn right onto Commercial Avenue and proceed to 32d Street. Turn left and follow 32d to D Avenue. Turn left and go 1 1/2 miles to the parking area on the right marked "ACFL Mitten Pond Loop/Beaver Trail." Walk in on the road and take the right-hand trail (No. 108). Stay on the main trail—through the trees to your right, you'll see the cattails of the 32d Street swamp and hear the red-wing chorus. Farther up the trail, note all the skunk cabbage on the right; puddle ducks are often seen in this spot. Cross the bridge and note the beaver dam to your left and, in the bridge area, frogs, duckweed, huckleberry, elderberry, salmonberry, sword fern, and lady fern. Across the bridge, turn left onto No. 108-B and follow to the shore of the big beaver pond; then take the trail out to where it connects with No. 107, turn left, and head down to Cranberry Lake. Turn left again, cross a bridge, and follow a somewhat challenging rocky trail around the south end of the lake until you're across from the large bog island. Look for the beaver lodge nestled in a small cove of the island.

**Sharpe Park:** This area has a large cattail marsh surrounded by woods. Look for red-wings, wood ducks, pileated woodpeckers, mallards, swallows, horsetails, alders, red currant, and elderberry. The ringing whinny of the sora can often be heard on an early spring morning.

ACCESS: Coming into Anacortes from Highway 20, turn right on Commercial Avenue and go to 32d Street. Turn left on 32d, proceed to D Avenue, and turn left again. Travel just over 5 miles to Sharpe Park on your right. Park in the lot and take the trail in about 500 feet to wetland on your right.

**Toot Swamp:** This little jewel at the south end of Whistle Lake often has wood ducks, mergansers, mallards, and great blue herons. Frogs sing in the waters, and flickers call from the surrounding woods. Vegetation includes pond lilies, duckweed, cattails, osoberry, salmonberry, serviceberry, huckleberry, water parsley, alder, big-leaf maple, wild cherry, cascara, willow, and hardhack.

ACCESS: See directions to Whistle Lake in "Forest."

*Broad-leaved sundew*

85

# JUDY GILSON MOODY
## *Wooing the Wood Ducks*

When Betty Gilson of Shaw Island began restoring 10 acres of a wetland on property she and her husband, John, had just purchased, her family shook their heads. Over the years, the marsh had gradually filled in, and Betty's desire to bring it back to life created what daughter Judy Gilson Moody unsentimentally describes as a "bombing practice area. It was 10 acres of dirt and devastation," recalls Judy, "and I thought, It's hopeless."

The wetland was part of a 26-acre parcel bought in the fall of 1975 from a logger who had drained the area and subdivided the surrounding property. Some of the upland acreage had been logged, and the area near the drained wetland had been used as a log landing. Betty Gilson bought the land with the stipulation that the former owner would restore the old dike, install a new culvert, and recontour the wet areas so that there would be numerous channels and three islands.

Judy shakes her head and grins. "She was literally out here with her Audubon magazine article 'How to Restore a Wetland' in one hand and directing the bulldozer with the other." A lifelong birder who also owned property on Squaw Bay and loved watching the shorebirds, Betty was equally interested in a wetland area where she could enjoy freshwater species such as mallards, red-wings, and, most of all, wood ducks.

"We immediately put in wood duck nesting boxes as soon as the marsh was filling up and they didn't come and didn't come. . . ." Judy talks about the frustration of not being able to attract wood ducks to a wetland that had seemingly bloomed into a wood duck's Waldorf.

Three years earlier, after digging the channels and building the islands, the Gilsons did no reseeding but simply set out a few trees—a 5-foot maple, a birch, some firs—and waited for Nature to do her work. The following spring, water started to collect and the marsh slowly greened, although patches on the bottoms and sides of the channels were still bare. Because it had originally been a wet area, Judy thinks, all the "right seeds" were there. Marsh grasses, hardhack, and alders sprouted, setting the stage for frogs, muskrats, and a parade of birds that still lacked the most prized member. A common breeder in the islands and one of the world's most beautiful birds, the male wood duck with his sweeping crest and showy plumage seems as hopelessly fastidious as he is flamboyant.

Finally, ten years after the nest boxes went up, the wood ducks came. Why so long? Judy feels it was "just a matter of getting the right atmosphere." It wasn't until alder branches shaded the water that the ducks showed up and stayed. For several years, the marsh had been an open, grassy area with no large trees, but now she points to a tall clump of alders. "As soon as the trees started to overhang the water and shade it a little bit, the ducks started hanging out under there."

So that their mother could more fully enjoy the wood ducks that now frequent the marsh, Judy and her brother built a wooden observation tower in 1991. From the tower, it's possible to see over the tops of the tall grasses and spot the ducks hanging out under the branches. When they first bred successfully, "we felt like, well, new parents. It was *so* exciting. Because it really was the whole reason for doing this. We wanted to provide habitat—build a duck factory."

Red-winged blackbirds also enjoy the tower and defend it during nesting season, so marsh-watchers may risk being attacked by males claiming the tower territory as their own. But in March, when the wood ducks show up to nest, Judy and Betty brave the blackbirds and take their binos to the tower ("We never go into the marsh in nesting season"). One wood duck box is especially visible from the tower, and Judy has often watched females flying into it: "Most of them fly in fast, and then they put on the brakes about 15 feet from the house and put out their toes and just sort of catch the edge and tip in. But one day I was sitting here watching, and a wood duck flew in fast. She didn't slow down at all, no braking, nothing. She just folded her wings and went in headfirst, just shot into the hole." Smashed wood duck seemed the likely outcome, but in the next moment, the duck popped out the opening, hooked herself up to the top of the box and started preening. Judy laughs. "What an entrance!"

What she is really waiting to see, however, and the main reason the one box was left so visible, is the emergence of the chicks from their nest. Wood duck chicks leap out of the box soon after hatching and follow their mother to water. "They hatch precocially," explains Judy. "They're not naked like some little hatchlings; they're ready to go out. Within 24 hours of hatching, they hook their way up. Those houses have little hardware cloth ladders to help them get up to the hole, and then they just hurl themselves out and fall. They can nest as high as 65 feet, so their first taste of the world can be a 65-foot drop," she marvels. "But they know what they're supposed to do—their little wings are flapping wildly as they go down. I desperately want to see this."

Until that great day, there's no dearth of wildlife happenings to enjoy in the wetland. Mallards nest in the wet, weedy southern area, and the marsh has also been visited by cinnamon teals, hawks, kingfishers, an occasional ringneck, and gadwalls, owls, woodpeckers, ravens, and scores of swallows, mostly violet-greens. Hooded mergansers, with their startling crests, are a special treat, rivaling even the wood ducks ("By now we joke, oh ho hum, another wood duck.").

An old road that wound along the marsh area was moved farther away when Judy found she was startling nesting mallards on her walks. She enjoys the new trail even though it provides no real view of the marsh, "because you can sneak up on the marsh and hear who's home." It may be a mallard quacking or a rail (the marsh hosts both soras and Virginia rails. "They're very shy—if they know you're around, they won't make their calls."). Sometimes she'll spot an alligator lizard sunning on a stump. Muskrats swim by with bundles of reeds, and garter snakes slither through the water past planted trout.

She loves the marsh in winter best of all because the islands are quieter. ("The airplanes just drive me nuts in the spring and summer.") In winter, the little year-round birds are there, the towhees, song sparrows, and winter wrens, and the bigger hawks, especially red-tails and northern harriers. "Mother saw a harrier that was quartering the marsh the way they do, and now with the tower here, we're high enough so you can actually see the flash of white on the rump."

At least two pairs of pileated woodpeckers reside on the property. Judy pointed out a rectangular hole nearly a foot long and half a foot deep in a cedar tree near the marsh. A pileated pair had gone at it day after day until "one day we arrived and ants were just *pouring* out of the tree. They must have dug into the nest and disrupted it. And that was it, they left, that was the last of the excavating, they were getting to the ants." Judy's interest was piqued, and her investigations revealed that pileateds are useful to other cavity-nesting birds. Because part of their pair-bonding ritual in early spring includes digging together, pileateds will often dig extra nests, which other birds take over.

Two cans under the cedars were full of fish food and cracked corn. The wood ducks go through a lot of corn in the springtime, and the treat is also dear to a pair of Canada geese that for the past two years have stopped to rest up at the marsh for a couple of weeks. Judy laughs again, recalling a less than restful moment in this pair's life. One spring day, the geese committed the folly of falling asleep below the tower when the red-wings were in full defense posture. "This blackbird was in the alder nearby getting more and more upset, making his territorial calls and shrieks," says Judy, "and all of a sudden he dive-bombed the tail of one of the geese. It was a kamikaze attack; he slammed right into the tail of the goose, *goosed* the goose." She pauses, still chuckling. "You see all kinds of wonderful things."

What would she say to those who would also like to expand their wildlife viewing and enjoyment by creating a wetland on their property, be it a small pool or a several-acre marsh? "I want to encourage anybody who has a wet area on their property to keep it," she says. "If you have an area where you think you might be able to put in a pond, don't think so much *pond* as a variegated water feature with deep areas and shallow edges and a slow transition from the dry areas around it into the wetland area. The more you can slow that transition, the more life you'll have, the less maintenance you'll have, and the more beautiful a wetland feature you'll have."

Judy sees a lot of ponds that have been dug to provide water reservoirs for fire protection (especially important in the islands) and that the owners hope will also serve as wildlife habitat. Deep holes are dug, with steep sides, and the owners end up mowing clear to the edges of the pond to keep it free of thistles. "You can have a deep area for fire protection or water storage, " says Judy, "but you also need those shallow places, areas that are seasonally dry but where there's enough water that the reeds and sedges and wetland plants grow. You won't have thistles; you won't have to mow around your pond, which will ruin the edges as habitat. The edges are critical, because that's where the frogs are and so many things that feed on frogs." Not to mention the things that feed the frogs: "Insects like that warm muddy edge."

She notes that great strides have been made in designing wetlands and feels people can find excellent help at the soil conservation service "if they're *clear* on what they want. If they say, 'Not only do we want a reservoir, we want wildlife habitat.'"

The Gilson wetland area is virtually maintenance-free, although the dike must be kept clear of trees (roots create passages for water) and the access road is mowed. Underbrush is left for wildlife ("I think there's one thing people need to hear: shrubbery is *good*; resist that urge to clean up!").

One other maintenance chore comes along with the wood ducks. More than one female will lay eggs in the same box, so a single box may hold up to thirty eggs. The behavior is called "dumping," and Judy isn't sure why it occurs, although her research has revealed that it's a normal behavior. Only the top eggs get incubated, leaving a sometimes smelly mess below. "We go in every year and drop those boxes down. They're built so that they can be lowered, and they'll open up, and then I just take out all the stuff, sometimes lots of rotten eggs. It's a great job," she groans, adding that they take along a little picnic with "absurdly elegant and fattening hors d'oeuvres to reward ourselves for a dirty task well done."

The wetland and surrounding woods, a total of 26 acres, belong to Judy and her brother now and have been put into the county's open space program, a tax abatement program for property owners who agree not to further develop their land and to preserve its natural resources. Prior to that arrangement, however, Judy's parents put a conservation easement on it with The San Juan Preservation Trust, deeding over the rights to conserve the marsh to the Trust and thus insuring its protection in perpetuity.

The marsh is a popular place with groups such as Audubon and the Shaw Island school, who come equipped with spotting scopes to look at ducks or microscopes to examine water drops. The more spectacular birds, such as the wood ducks, are the biggest cause of excitement, although when the kids get a look at the smaller ones through a spotting scope and see how dramatic a common yellowthroat can look, that's almost as exciting. "They had no idea there was stuff like *that* in the bushes."

Stuff like that and more, all combining to create the special magic of a wetland saved, thanks to the vision of Betty Gilson. Her daughter looks over the marsh and says quietly, "I love the progression of things. It's nice to see, each year, the ducks come, see their mating displays, watch them going in and out of the houses, and then the ducklings." She reiterates her hope to one day see the wood duck chicks make their stunning descent from the nest boxes.

"It would make my *life* to see that."

# Chapter 6

# SHORELINE

WALK DOWN TO THE WATER'S EDGE NOW and become a child again. Let the salt air cleanse your mind and draw your thoughts out with the tide and return them to settle in the rocky pools. There are 375 miles of saltwater shore in San Juan County, more than in any other county in the U.S., and although much of it is privately owned or restricted to wildlife, there are still miles of beach that await your footsteps.

San Juan waters are home to a huge diversity of wildlife. They nurture plants from rockweed to the giant bull kelp; several hundred species of invertebrates, including the world's largest chiton, the gumboot; over two hundred species of fish; and a variety of marine mammals such as harbor seals, river otters, and three pods of orca whales. The island shores are also a vital wintering and nesting area for seabirds of the Pacific Flyway. Let's stroll down to this colorful ecosystem to get an overview of wildlife at the water's edge, first letting our eyes scan the rocks and sands of the intertidal zone and then looking seaward.

The lives and activities of shore creatures are largely determined by the rhythm of the tides, two highs and two lows daily. The greatest number of sea creatures inhabit the low tide zone, and your best chance to see sponges, hydroids, tube worms, sea cucumbers, anemones, and sea stars is when this zone is most fully exposed—during a low spring tide, which occurs every two weeks near the times of either a full or a new moon.

Island shorelines include both sandy beaches (Bowman Bay, Spencer Spit) and rocky shores (Rosario Beach, San Juan County Park). Other beaches exist, such as cobblestone and mudflat, but, for simplicity's sake, we'll limit our visits to the sandy shore, so popular among beach walkers, and the rocky shore, which hosts the most varied wildlife.

Along the high tide mark of a sandy beach stretches the strand line, a weedy, meandering strip made up of crab shells, dead jellyfish, seaweed, fish bones, empty skate and dogfish egg cases (mermaid purses), remnant chiton plates (butterfly shells), and usually a surprise or two, all of which make this area an excellent one for beachcombing. Bouncing about in the wrack are tiny, shrimplike sand hoppers (beach fleas), which use their tails and last three pairs of legs to spring through the seaweed like fleas (to which they bear no other resemblance). By day, these small crustaceans usually burrow into the weed to keep their gills moist, becoming active again at dusk as they scavenge for food.

Between the strand line and water you'll find the cockles and clams that burrow in the sand until the waters cover them and they emerge to siphon-feed. Lugworms, fat wrigglers up to a foot long that are prized for bait, create U-shaped burrows that allow both the worm's head and its tail to reach the surface. Look for neat coils, which are fecal castings of undigested sand, at one end of the burrow.

Another creature also leaves sand-sculpted clues to its presence. Keep an eye out for "sand collars" (also known as "clergymen's collars," each somewhat resembling the base of a rubber plunger), which the huge-footed moon snail makes by mixing its eggs with fine sand and mucus. As the eggs hatch, the collar nest disintegrates. Should you find a clam shell with a hole near its hinge, you've probably stumbled across yet another sign of the moon snail. The snail burrows after a clam in the sand and devours it by drilling a small hole through the hinge of its victim's shell.

Look along the beach and you'll see a variety of shorebirds, from sandpipers to plovers to herons. The distinctive bill shapes and sizes of these wading birds are clues to how they feed at different depths on crustaceans, mollusks, and worms and are a good identifying mark. Identifying shorebirds is an exasperating business, but the birds' behavior, as well as their silhouettes, will often help you recognize them at a distance.

For instance, spotted sandpipers constantly bob their tails (and thus are also known as "teeterers"); sanderlings searching for worms and amphipods run along the wave's edge in a line or in small groups; dowitchers stab the mud with extremely long, straight bills for clams and crustaceans; plovers run along the beach in starts and stops and are small, chubby birds, with shorter bills than other shorebirds'. Dunlins are often seen in large flocks, their white bellies flashing as the flock flies and turns in perfect unison.

You may also spot a *hermit crab* scuttling over the sand, searching perhaps for a larger snail or whelk shell to call its own. An efficient scavenger of the shore, the hermit consumes dead and decaying organisms and recycles empty shells for its own use as it grows. Hermits explore a potential shell to make sure it's free and clear, then hastily back into it and clamp onto the shell with the rear pair of legs.

Dungeness crabs are also often found along the beach; unlike hermits, they deal with growth not by house hunting but by regularly molting their shells. Flip one over to tell if you have a male or female. In the earliest stages of their development, crabs swim about and have tails somewhat like lobsters', but as they grow, the tail folds under the body and embeds in the belly. In males, this tail or abdominal flap is narrow, whereas females have wider flaps for carrying eggs.

Dungeness crabs feed on small clams such as cockles, siphon-feeding creatures that draw in water through one siphon tube, filter out the food, and expel wastes via a second tube. When the tide is out or the clam is threatened by a predator such as the crab or a sunflower star, its muscular foot digs rapidly into the sandy depths.

At times the sandy shore may look as though it's studded with large, lingering drops of water, and indeed, jellyfish are almost 98 percent water. Most are small, umbrella-shaped globules equipped with stinging cells on their tentacles with which to stun creatures unfortunate enough to become caught in their drifting webs. These ephemeral beings live only one season and may light up a beach after dark with their luminescence. Though most can be handled without harm, there's one species in local waters that is poisonous to people. Variously called the sea nettle, sea blubber, or lion's mane, *Cyanea capillata* is the largest jellyfish in the world (up to 8 feet across, though locally only about 2 feet) and may be found tangled in fishing nets or washed up on beaches during the summer. At the other extreme, tiny, two-tentacled, transparent balls dotting the shore are sea gooseberries (comb jellies, not jellyfish) and are fun to pick up and examine.

Rocky shores make up the bulk of the archipelago coastline and offer perhaps the richest wildlife experience. During low tide, the rocks are a lunch counter for marine birds such as oystercatchers, gulls, and black turnstones, which feed on the exposed crabs, limpets, mussels, chitons, and periwinkles. These last four are particularly suited to their environment, clinging tenaciously to rock faces in their bid to withstand the push and pull of the tides. *Mussels* and *barnacles* fasten for life; the first anchors itself with plasticlike strings, and the latter cements its head to a rock. *Limpets* scrape out scars to which they meld after foraging over the rocks for algae while the tide's in, and *chitons* and periwinkles also graze the rocks and then use their fleshy feet to hold on tight when the water recedes.

It might surprise you to know that the shell of that rock-clinging chiton is not solid like a mussel's but is built with eight leathery plates that give the animal flexibility. Should you or an oystercatcher pry the creature off its rock, it can curl those overlapping plates into a defensive posture until it resembles a "sea cradle," the name by which it's commonly known.

Plants on the rocky shore include brown rockweed, which everyone enjoys stepping on to pop the two-eared bulbs; leafy brown sea cabbage; and ruffled green sea lettuce, which the Quileutes used to cool the sting of sunburned lips. Kelps include the showy *bull kelp*, with its long leathery stem and hollow bulb (once used by coastal Indians to carry water and fish oil; Makah children also cut rounds of the kelp's stem for toy wagon wheels). All of the above have holdfasts at the end of their stems, rootlike anchors that secure the plants to the rocks.

Some of the greatest treasures of our rocky shores are their tidepools, formed where the curve of rock catches and holds tidal waters, and in which marine creatures stay until swept out to sea again. Although at first glance a pool may appear to hold only seaweed, be patient and soon things will come into focus.

Look for *sea anemones* waving their tentacles to capture food; tiny shrimp; red and green *sea urchins*, like pincushions; *mussels* opening their shells to feed; perhaps even a *sea star*. Our most commonly observed star is the five-rayed, rough-skinned purple star (which may be orange or brown instead). Blood stars are bright orange, with five comparatively skinny rays, and the wolfish sunflower star (fastest star in the west and a voracious predator) may have as many as twenty-four thick rays. A sea star can regenerate itself; when oyster farmers realized they would get two for the slice of one, the predatory creatures were no longer hacked in two but boiled to death.

Anemones and urchins are two of the most often seen and most eagerly looked for tidepool tenants. Anemones resemble flowers but are actually related to jellyfish, with whom they share the trait of possessing tentacles studded with stinging cells that poison prey. When out of the water, they retract these tentacles and look like drab, unimpresssive jelly blobs.

Porcupines of the tidepool, urchins are related to sea stars. The spines that immediately identify an urchin are used both for protection and for movement, acting as stilts to lift the body as it walks over rocks in search of food. The spines cover the urchin's shell, or test; its body is inside. If you turn one over, you'll find the mouth, which consists of five teeth on bony plates that project to scrape algae off the rocks.

While you watch these fragile-looking creatures (and you may have to stay very still and wait for the return of those that have scurried off

*Urchin, sculpin, and anemone*

at your approach), contemplate the shifting conditions to which they've had to adapt. Temperatures may heat up and cool down rapidly in the small pools. Waves threaten to pull those that don't buckle down back out to sea. Sometimes, too, the pool goes dry, and then inhabitants must either dig down into the mud until the tide returns or retain water inside tightly closed shells.

Don't be afraid to gently touch the animals in the pool; an urchin's prickly look may put you off, but place your finger deep between its spines and see if you feel a tingle as the pedicellariae (tiny pincers) nip at you. Or run your finger along the anemone's tentacles and feel their sticky pull.

It's necessary to note here that care and consideration must be part of your shoreside behavior. When you remove a shell-less creature from a pool (briefly!), handle it with damp hands to avoid damaging its protective slime coating. Animals can also be removed and viewed in a jar filled with seawater, but be sure to return them before the water gets too warm, since most are adapted to cold water and may die from heat and oxygen depletion.

Look under rocks that are large enough to resist being moved by winter storms and that allow some water to circulate underneath, and you'll likely find more wildlife, such as chitons and crabs. Be sure, though, to gently return the rocks to their original position. Leaving them overturned will suffocate the animals formerly on top while the bottom animals die of exposure to sun and predators. Hundreds of visitors carelessly flipping hundreds of rocks a year can easily create a major drain on certain populations.

It is up to us to become knowledgeable about the shores we walk and to govern ourselves the way early coastal peoples did. The traditional Samish, for instance, revered their relation to water, remembering to be grateful for what was given and to care for the source of those gifts. They did not overuse the water animals, such as the clam, believing that such carelessness would destroy the seed, and they returned oyster and mussel shells to the water in the belief that this practice would fertilize succeeding generations. The Samish followed rules that insured the life of beings wherever they were found, not wasting the animals they called their brothers and sisters but instead practicing both consideration and gratitude.

We must do no less. San Juan waters have been nominated for sanctuary status to protect and restore their rich marine life. Whether or not that designation becomes official, beach walkers must do their part now by observing the above attitude and by familiarizing themselves with the marine restrictions now in force.

For instance, it's a state law that all clam holes must be refilled; on most beaches here, wave action is not strong enough to level out the piles, and small clams may suffocate under them. State law also prohibits the gathering of marine organisms in the San Juans proper (including Cypress Island) not intended for food, except by permission of the director of the biological station on San Juan Island. Tidelands may be permanent biological preserves, privately owned, or closed to clamming and other collecting because of red tides or as a temporary means of encouraging recovery of certain populations. If in doubt regarding the status of an area, ask. Better yet, remove nothing living from rocky shores, and observe limits elsewhere on the taking of edible species.

You can also help preserve sea life by picking up and packing out human-made shore debris. Plastics and other trash may be mistaken by wildlife for food. Seabirds ingest bottle caps and pad nests with plastics that make home a hazard to their off-spring. Birds can also strangle in six-pack rings, and both birds and seals die tangled in nets and lines. Boaters should observe a policy that no trash is dumped overboard (since 1989, it's illegal to dump plastics overboard in all U.S. waters) and reduce the amount of plastics on board.

Boaters are seeing another side of the marine scene, much of which can also be experienced by the shore walker. Looking out from the sand and rocks, we're rewarded with a wonderful variety of waterfowl, especially during the winter, when the bays are filled with grebes, scoters, oldsquaws, and loons back from the north.

In riptide areas and near kelp reefs, watch for gatherings of gulls, terns, and alcids (chunky, short-winged, black-and-white seabirds). You may also spot a *great blue heron* standing single-legged on a kelp bed to survey the scene or a *cormorant* perched on a piling with wings spread wide to dry.

*Belted kingfishers* wheel chattering along the shore, and *bald eagles* swoop down from the firs to pick off young seabirds (always scan the tall firs and cedars along the shoreline for the white head of an eagle). *River otters* swim in rocky coves or lumber along the driftwood, and the glistening smooth heads of *harbor seals* poke above the water to reflect the shore in the clear, dark pools of their eyes. Farther off, whales—orcas, minkes, even a humpback—feed and breed; *Dall porpoises* play in the bow waves of boats; exposed rocks host colonies of *black oystercatchers* and *pigeon guillemots*; and perhaps even an elephant seal hauls out to begin its molt.

Beach time is one of the special blessings of the San Juans. Here we can soak up shore life from lugworms to sandpipers to orcas and know again why we're grateful to call these islands home.

## SITE GUIDE

The following is a listing of representative beaches easily accessed by car. It is by no means all-inclusive and is provided here only as a solid starting point. For the purposes of simplicity and brevity, boat-access-only beaches are not included; a good listing may be found in the Muellers' *The San Juan Islands: Afoot and Afloat* or in the DNR guide *The San Juan Islands: Your Public Beaches* (call (360) 753-2400, or write the DNR, Division of Private Forestry and Recreation, Olympia, WA 98504).

### San Juan Island

**Cattle Point:** Good viewing of black oystercatchers, harlequin ducks, surf scoters, mergansers, and common loons along this rocky shoreline. Don't forget the tidepools in the headlands. The oystercatchers pry chitons, limpets, and mussels off the rocks, and you'll also see anemones, periwinkles, and sculpin in the pools. Watch for raptors, which are common here, and check out the offshore islets, which have breeding colonies of gulls.
ACCESS: Follow South Beach directions to American Camp, but instead of turning off at Pickett's Lane, follow the road about 2 more miles to Cattle Point Lighthouse Recreation Site. The DNR oversees the 10-acre area from which the Cattle Point beach can be accessed.

**False Bay:** This shallow bay on the southern end of the island is sheltered from heavy wave action and is an excellent study area for marine populations such as chitons and crabs, especially at low tide when the entire bay is exposed. Also known for the "best shorebird habitat in the archipelago" (*Birding in the San Juan Islands*). Observe, but tread softly and do not collect specimens, since this area is a University of Washington biological preserve.

ACCESS: Drive west out of Friday Harbor on Spring Street to the San Juan Valley Road and Douglas Road intersection. Go south on Douglas Road 1³/4 miles to Bailor Hill Road. Turn right, travel about ¹/2 mile to False Bay Road (gravel), and turn left. Follow the road just under a mile to the bay.

**Lime Kiln State Park:** Look for orcas, minkes, and Dall porpoises offshore. Orca pods pass through here in the summer to feed on salmon migrating to spawn in freshwater streams. You may also spot river otters and harbor porpoises. Stay on the trails—the vegetation is fragile.

ACCESS: Follow directions to San Juan County Park. From the park, continue 2¹/2 miles along West Side Road until you come around a curve and are suddenly looking at salt water. The road to the park takes a sharp turn right; parking is about ¹/2 mile farther down. A trail leads from the parking lot to the lighthouse and point.

**San Juan County Park:** Looking out on Smallpox Bay, this popular park has a good rocky shore for tidepool tripping. It also commands a view of the Low Island Wildlife Refuge, which has a nesting colony of black oystercatchers. Watch also for Canada geese, as well as seals offshore and on the rocks.

ACCESS: Take Beaverton Valley Road out of Friday Harbor to West Valley Road. Turn left at the Mitchell Bay Road intersection, then left again in 1¹/4 miles on West Side Road. Head south about 2 miles to the park.

**South Beach:** The longest public beach in the islands, this 2-mile stretch of gravel and driftwood takes some heavy wave action from the Strait of Juan de Fuca. Shore life consequently does not thrive here, but scan for offshore birds such as terns, common mergansers, gulls, and plovers and also possibly for a pod of whales. Shorebirds such as yellowlegs may be evident, as well as bald and golden eagles and plenty of flotsam and jetsam. Low tide exposes large rocks to the west with good tidepooling. Above the beach, look for yellow sand verbena, Japanese beach pea, and silver bursage.

ACCESS: Take Spring Street out of Friday Harbor to the San Juan Valley Road and Douglas Road intersection. Head south on Douglas for about 1¹/2 miles; then turn left on Little Road to the Cattle Point Road intersection.

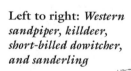

**Left to right:** *Western sandpiper, killdeer, short-billed dowitcher, and sanderling*

Follow Cattle Point Road south into American Camp, and take American Camp Road to Pickett's Lane. Turn right and travel ¹/₂ mile to the parking lot.

## Orcas Island

**Obstruction Pass:** Hike in to the DNR campground along a pebble and sand beach with 400 feet of public tidelands. Explore tidepools in the rocks on either side of the bay. Look for seals and otters and for marbled murrelets, pigeon guillemots, and other alcids.

ACCESS: From the ferry landing, follow the Horseshoe Highway north through East Sound and then south to Olga. Head east out of Olga onto a road signed to Doe Bay. In 1¹/₂ miles, turn right onto Obstruction Pass Road until you reach a gravel road branching to the Obstruction Pass DNR Recreation Site. Turn onto the road and follow it 1 mile to the parking area at the trailhead. A half-mile trail winds through woods to the walk-in camp and beach.

## Lopez Island

**Upright Channel/Odlin Park Trail:** After you hike down to the beach and pass through big-leaf maple and a riot of horsetails, turn right and walk the cobble shore 1¹/₄ miles to the sandy beach at Odlin Park. Stay below the driftwood line; the uplands are private. Look for seals, loons, surf scoters, bald eagles, turkey vultures, cockles, crabs, gulls, shorebirds, and nest holes in the high sandy banks. Otters like this beach; if you don't see them, scan for tracks and scat in the sand by the driftwood.

ACCESS: Take the ferry road about 2¹/₂ miles to where Military Road cuts off to the right. Stay on Military Road until it forks right again. Continue about ¹/₂ mile farther to the park entrance on your right. This 20-acre DNR site is open 8 A.M. to dusk, May 1 to September 30. Park in the lot and walk the road down to where a

gravel trail cuts off to the left. Follow the trail through what was once an old homestead; you'll see among the alders and big-leaf maples some old fruit trees and laburnums (golden chain trees).

**Spencer Spit:** The spit is a popular spot with over 7,800 feet of shoreline. Clamming is allowed during the summer low tides. Sandy beach with lots of driftwood—look for pieces pocked with holes by wood-boring clams called shipworms or by tiny gribbles, which work closer to the surface. The spit also encloses a saltwater lagoon, which hosts a variety of birds during migration, such as ducks, brant, and Canada geese. Watch for kingfishers and great blues here year-round, and note the many rabbits on the hillside by the spit. Raccoons and deer forage along the beach at night.
ACCESS: See "Spencer Spit Lagoon" in "Wetlands."

## Fidalgo Island

**Bowman Bay:** This long, curved sandy beach is open to swells from Rosario Strait. There's good viewing from a long pier that stretches out into the bay; look for seals and shorebirds such as buffleheads, grebes, mergansers, and pigeon guillemots. Cormorants are often seen on the offshore rocks and kingfishers and bald eagles along the shoreline. Small wetlands near the south end of the beach often host great blue herons. Also at the south end, a sandy neck connects Reservation Head with Fidalgo—two elephant seals once hauled out there. Mudflats are exposed at low tide south of the sandy neck—look for intertidal plants and animals. Note the yellow blooms of Puget Sound gumweed along the salt marsh.
ACCESS: Follow Highway 20 south to the intersection with Rosario Road, just beyond Pass Lake. Turn right at the intersection and left almost immediately at Bowman Bay Road. Follow the road to the parking area.

**Padilla Bay Estuary:** This freshwater and saltwater soup creates one of the most productive ecosystems in the world. Thirty times more fertile than the open sea, the estuary nurtures millions of baby fish. Look for the waterfowl that feed on them: herons, gulls, and puddle ducks. Large populations of brant can be seen during the winter months, as well as seals and river otters, bald eagles, and red-tailed hawks. There is exceptional bird-watching along the $2^1/_2$-mile dike trail with farmland on one side (watch for raptors) and mudflat on the other. At low tide, wade out through the mud to investigate eelgrass and the creatures it shelters (the slender pipefish, eel-like gunnels, mud snails, clams, and crabs).
ACCESS: Take Highway 20 east from Anacortes to the Farmhouse Restaurant intersection. Turn left and follow Bayview-Edison Road to the state park entrance at Bayview. The dike trail access is south of the park.

**Rosario Beach:** This area features an underwater park famous among divers and marine biologists. Look for some of this lush underwater life in the tidepools along the rocky shoreline, and keep an eye out for herons, harlequin ducks, and river otters playing in the coves. (For more on Rosario Beach, see the following section.)
ACCESS: Take Highway 20 south to the intersection with Rosario Road, just after

Pass Lake. Turn right and proceed north to the intersection with Rosario Beach Road. The road leads down to the parking area.

**Washington Park:** This 200-acre park has extensive shoreline, including two beaches (West Beach and Sunset) and several overlooks into Rosario Strait and Burrows Bay. Look for oystercatchers and harlequin ducks along the rocky areas. Buffleheads, seals, and bald eagles are also common.
ACCESS: See directions to Washington Park in "Forest."

# JUDY FRIESEM
### *Rocky Shoreline High (and Low)*

She has walked this shore hundreds of times before, yet when she shows the beach to newcomers, her enthusiasm is as fresh as theirs. Scrambling over the rocks and slippery weed of Rosario Beach on a bright summer morning, Judy Friesem spurs on a trio of grade-school explorers with tantalizing descriptions of the local crab community: a decorator crab dressed to "party" and a porcelain-shelled creature she half-apologetically dubs the "toilet-seat crab," much to her young listeners' delight. But there is a shading to her appreciation that her audience, as yet, lacks: a shading of concern.

"Let's comb the sea grass back, because that's the roof of the shrimp's house," she tells the kids. Later, she picks up a red gunnel from a small pool and shows how to handle the tiny eel-like body with wet hands so as not to destroy its protective coating. Then she's off again to respond to another excited cry of discovery. The wonder comes first, she knows; she hopes the caring will follow.

Raised in the "canyons of steel of New York City with parents who thought the outside world was nice but something you look at in picture books," Judy largely missed the type of experience she now shares with others as a marine educator. Being sent off to camp helped get her away from the city and outside, "where, I realized, I'm happiest." Later, she enrolled in a college in upstate New York and eventually put together her own environmental education degree. Her first job out of college took her even farther into the wilds: to a nature center in the Thousand Islands.

"I got up there and it was pouring down rain," she recalls. The woman who was to become her closest friend "took me out on a boat to her island, and I was, I guess, standing in the bow just *drinking* in the rain. She laughed and said, 'Judy, most people go for cover.' But I was in my element."

Marine teaching started for her when she landed at the Padilla Bay Interpretive Center, at that time not much more than a handsome building. Told that programs were needed for the upcoming weekend and asked, "What can you do about it?" she plunged in and created the Junior Ecologist workshops. During her seven years teaching about the estuary ("where the beauty is more subtle"), she became fascinated with another world, a star-studded landscape of bizarre water beings tethered to the tides—the world of the rocky shore.

In the next tidepool, Judy shows the children a pinkish green anemone and encourages them to draw their fingers across its waving tentacles. There are many tiny barbs on each tentacle with which it poisons its prey, but she reassures the children that their tough skin won't be bothered by the poison. Soon empathizing with the mute creature, she adds not to waste its energy by making it close up repeatedly to engulf a counterfeit prey. The kids are intrigued by a pull on their fingers like that of Scotch tape. "What does it feel like to the anemone?" Judy wonders.

Not all of the kids are willing to get down, get dirty, and touch strange or slimy-looking creatures, but Judy doesn't push. In her estuary days, she saw people come down to the mudflats for a learning session who "got up to their necks in mud" and others who arrived in high heels or white boots. She shakes her head and grins. "But at least they were there."

A child slips and scrapes herself, so Judy breaks open a rockweed (*Fucus distichus*) bladder and squeezes out a substance like soothing aloe. "Fucus mucus" she calls it, adding that she has seen it dry up many a tear. The rocks are slippery thick with weed, and though the effect is that of a lush sea garden, the heavy growth is more insidious than healthy, a sign that all is not quite right at Rosario.

One of the most popular state parks in Washington, Rosario Beach is literally being loved to death. "I used to find octopus, and big sea stars, and more urchins, and lots and lots more chitons," says Judy. "It was easier to walk, and there was less seaweed. Over the years, I noticed a change, and I remember a couple of times capturing a state parks person and saying, 'Look, I'm concerned.'" So were the parks people, but a lack of funds and staff back-burnered their concern.

Judy tells the kids about the realities of life on the shore: "Everyone spends their brief days out here trying to be *diners* instead of *dinners*." People, coming in at the top of the food chain, have collected for their own consumption many of the shore grazers, such as chitons, limpets, and snails, which feed on the seaweed.

Judy believes it makes sense to suppose that if you remove the creatures from one part of the food chain, the balance of the whole becomes upset; in this case, there's no natural check on the seaweed, and it spreads at a prolific rate. "Not only is it hard to walk, which is a minor problem, but it blocks out the light for the other organisms," resulting in the decline and even disappearance of species that once flourished here. A case in point is a telling letter she once received from the director of a marine biological station, who wrote that where he once was able to find twenty-two species of crab at Rosario, he could now find only *five*. On an earlier trip over these rocks with Judy, we found no sea stars, and she compared this pitiful showing to the experience of a friend who years ago used to "pile up" sea stars.

Judy's concern led her in 1990 to apply for funds from the Puget Sound Water Quality Authority to try to protect the site. Surprised but delighted to receive her first grant ($21,700), she decided to target visitors to the beach, divers, and middle-school children. (Regarding this last group, she points out that school buses drive up and unload students with little or no supervision, adding, "There are fewer programs for that age because they're typically more energetic and sometimes harder to reach. I thought they'd be a good challenge.") So she wrote a curriculum and did teacher workshops on site, spending half a day tidepooling with the teachers and working up games and activities that could be brought back to the classroom.

Divers frequent an offshore area rich in underwater treasures such as nudibranchs, sponges, and sea urchins. A certified diver herself, Judy worked with dive shops in Anacortes and Oak Harbor to make the divers more familiar with the marine world. "They knew the fishes, because that's what they were spearing, but they didn't know the little things," she says. "It opened their eyes. Some of them had never seen plankton before and were just astounded." Topping the list of her own favorite creatures below are the nudibranchs, or sea slugs—an admittedly poor name for creatures so ornate and diaphanous. A chance encounter with a *Dirona* is especially to be savored, particularly the one that "looks like she wears a petticoat with fringes of white light. When I find her when I'm diving, I squeal, she's just so beautiful."

Another problem Judy targeted in her dive presentations was overharvesting, and after the session, one of her questions was "If you saw your buddy taking more than his or her share of abalone, what would you do?" The response was gratifying from people who previously had little or no concern for their impact. "Well, I wouldn't cut the air off underwater, but when they came up . . . !"

Overharvesting is less an underwater problem at Rosario, where fortunately the waters are still very rich, especially around Urchin Rocks, than it is a shoreside problem. "I've come out here on sunny low-tide weekends and seen people collect all kinds of things. People take buckets of things with the best intentions, caring about them, wanting to put everything back, and they *do*," she emphasizes with a sad smile. "They put everything back in the *high tide* zone." Shore creatures have specific niches on the beach and cannot survive for long out of their proper habitat. The problem is not that beachcombers don't care, Judy stresses, but that they don't *know*.

She did programs on the site for park visitors, and while they were learning from her, she also tried to learn from them. One time she came across a woman gathering gumboot chitons. When asked why she was collecting them, the woman replied that her family came out to gather chitons once a year for a big gumboot barbecue. Judy then asked the woman if she'd noticed any changes over the years, immediately putting her on the defensive, although, Judy says, "I was doing my very best to ask questions to understand and not to blame, just to learn from her."

Her soft voice reflects that kindliness that extends to all, from a crab carefully returned to its hiding space to beachcombers who don't know any better. If she had a chance to rule the world at Rosario, this gentle spirit wouldn't set up any barricades to keep the people out. "I think that what's most important here is that we learn to care, start to talk, respect each other, and learn how to take care of the area. I would rather educate and have people understand why this place is so valuable, even if it means they come out here and kill inadvertently or pick things because they don't know better yet. I'd rather do that than close the beach off and hope that it'll come back to its close-to-pristine state."

Instead of a barricade, something far more worthwhile in Judy's eyes has gone up at Rosario, the first sight of which brought her to tears. Thanks in part to her efforts, a sign was finally erected to inform walkers of the fragility of the shore environment and the need to treat its creatures with respect. Judy urges people to get out there and explore: "Look closely. The closer you look, the more you'll see." But she echoes the sign's injunction to "do it with respect and a sense of humility that we are visitors here."

Later, I walked back along the shore, now filled with folks scrambling over rocks and peering into tidepools on this sun-baked afternoon. As I headed past the sign that stands with the carved Samish maiden like two guardians above the beach—one a symbol of a people who knew how to care for the water's gifts, the other a guide for a people still learning—I heard a small voice yell from the recesses of the rocks, "Hey, Justin, come here! I've found some *sea stuff!*"

---

Want to know what a marine educator takes along on a beach walk in this area? Judy's preference is for Steve Yates's *Marine Wildlife* because it's succinct yet comprehensive and targets the local area. She also carries *Tidepool and Reef,* by Rick Harbo, because of its color pictures and "amazing amount of info." Back at the ranch, her extensive reference collection includes two good books she recommends for avid beach walkers, although they are a little bulkier to pack along: Eugene Kozloff's *Seashore Life of the Northern Pacific Coast* and Gloria Snively's *Exploring the Seashore.*

# Chapter 7

# FOREST

WALK INTO THE WOODLANDS NOW, and discover for yourself why Thoreau believed a town is saved as much by its trees as by its citizens. You may wonder, as I once did, just exactly what he meant by this odd claim. Trees *serve* people, yes; that's easy to see. But *save* them? Perhaps you find that a little harder to swallow.

Walk regularly through island forests of fir and cedar, salal and sword fern, and you'll puzzle no longer. Stay with them long enough, and trees will bring a steadying calm to a spent mind. Rub shoulders for a time with beings remote from human foolishness, and soon your focus returns more composedly to the familiar. Trees can inspire poets and create philosophers, and all that they provide in mental health is equaled by their contributions to our environmental health.

Trees have a center-stage role in regulating oxygen and carbon dioxide ratios, controlling the earth's temperature and water cycles, and producing and preserving soil. During photosynthesis, trees absorb carbon dioxide, splitting the molecule and using the carbon for growth while releasing the oxygen. Planting trees and preserving forests helps control the buildup of carbon dioxide, which traps the sun's rays in our atmosphere and promotes the rise of temperature known as the "greenhouse effect."

Trees also regulate water cycles. Roots draw up water deep below the surface, circulating it through the tree and into the leaves, where it's eventually released as water vapor. Without deep-rooted trees, rainfall would decrease and droughts would become more common. Those roots also produce topsoil by breaking down bedrock and help bind the soil together to reduce erosion.

Tragically, both the mental and environmental benefits of trees are not always apparent, and forests are razed to provide more tangible benefits. But the trees have their defenders; here in the islands, groups sprang up to prevent the logging of special areas such as Chadwick Hill on Lopez, Madrona Point on Orcas, and the community forestlands on Fidalgo.

This last area was threatened in a particularly interesting way. If one were to suggest that the best way to keep a cake intact for an upcoming dinner is to eat a few chunks out of it here and there, one might expect a heated inquiry into one's sanity. Yet a similar situation existed in the Anacortes Community Forest Lands, where *clearcutting* was the method of choice to fund management and preservation of the nearly 2,200-acre forestlands.

Friends of the Forest in Anacortes was originally formed to nudge more folks into the woods but became politically active in 1989 with their successful attempt to prove you can't have your forest and cut it, too. Alternative funding methods and increased volunteer efforts support the forest today, and hikers, horseback riders, mountain bikers, and groups of schoolchildren share the twenty miles of trails through acres of largely undisturbed wildlife habitat.

It's well to remember the hard-fought battles as you seek out your special place of peace. Remember also that when you walk into the woodlands, you're entering someone else's home, and act with consideration, a dictum too seldom followed by those who view the forest as an escape from restraints imposed in human neighborhoods. Pack along a bag, and pick up the bottles and cans left in nature's living quarters by more ill-mannered folk than yourself.

In the woods, you are a guest; try not to be an unwelcome one. Stay on the paths, and don't trample plants or break off branches when picking berries. Furthermore, don't pick orchid plants, such as the calypso, which associate with fungi. Attempts to transplant the fragile calypso fail because the vital link between plant and fungus is broken, and even simply picking the flower may disturb its connection enough to kill the plant.

Since we're down on the forest floor with the exquisite calypso, let's focus on this part of the woods as we begin our walk. Numerous white-flowered plants spread a delicate beauty among thick roots and rough-grained trunks. Look for the frothy white cups of foamflower (also less charmingly described as false mitrewort), which bloom well into summer. The genus name of this tall perennial herb (*Tiarella*) comes from the Greek word for tiara; its flowers look like tiny dazzling crowns and were exchanged as love gifts among the Greeks.

Six-petaled white stars (sometimes pink or with fewer or more petals) shine amid large glossy-green leaves of the starflower, or Indian potato as it's also called because of its small tuber. The paired drooping white bells of twinflower rise above evergreen leaf mats (bend down and breathe their aroma), while white-blossomed woodland strawberries offer up succulent berries in June. Candyflower (which, like foamflower, also carries a stuffier title, Siberian miner's lettuce) graces the trailsides from spring through early fall, wearing white petals etched with candy-cane striping. Look also for the hairy stems of fringecup arching well up out of bases of leaves and covered with frilled white flowers.

Poke farther along the forest paths and perhaps you'll find mushrooms such as the honeycombed morels on the forest floor. Mushrooms lack chlorophyll to produce their own food and instead feed on decaying and dead plants. They secrete enzymes that help break down this dead material into soil; without these fungi, our forests would be drowning in wood.

You'll also notice bracket fungi growing on logs and dead or living trees. Especially striking is the large artist's fungus, which hangs like a huge brown-and-white mouth on the side of a tree. Scrape a picture with your fingernail onto the white underside of the fungus, and your initials or drawing will grow along with it.

Also growing on trunks and even on bare rock is lichen, a combination of a fungus and an alga. One of the most seemingly inconsequential of plants, the humble lichen has fed hungry arctic explorers and is a major producer of nitrogen for forest plants and animals. As the only plant able to live on bare rocks (especially colorful in the spring when it's growing), lichen is a principal player in breaking down those rocks and turning them into soil. The symbiotic partnership is described in an uncredited saying that is a good mnemonic for defining a lichen: "Annie Alga took a lichen to Freddy Fungus and now their marriage is on the rocks."

One woodland plant that somewhat resembles a mushroom and always makes a hiker stop and stare is the *Indian pipe*. Skulking in the shadows of moist woods, this strange plant has little need for the sunlight since, like fungi, it produces no chlorophyll. But it is not a fungus itself; instead, it takes its food from fungi. The flower atop the spindly white stem droops over to mimic an Indian peace pipe, but the sight of this weird plant so intrigues that one name hardly suffices. Wonderfully ghoulish labels like "ghost flower" and "corpse plant" brand this benign plant with an undeserved malevolence. Be kinder to it with your actions and don't pick it, for the plant will blacken and die when its connection to the fungus is destroyed.

The forest floor gives up rich evidence of animals all too often hidden. Look for pellets disgorged by owls and other birds such as hawks and crows; I've found many golf-ball-sized rounds of downy feathers and matchstick bones in what was obviously a roost area. Other pellets are more sausage-shaped. Raptors swallow their food whole or in large chunks nearly whole and regurgitate the indigestible bones, fur, and feathers in matted pellets. Pull them apart to discover tiny skulls and other animal parts; trying to identify the prey species will give you clues to the predator's identity.

Although the animals themselves may not always be easy to find in a forest, learning to "read the woods," as by watching for raptor pellets, will assure you you're not alone. Prints of tiny "hands" tell you a raccoon has been in the area; a cloven hoofprint points to deer. Bird whitewash on the understory may indicate an overhead nest or roosting site. Droppings or scats also give clues to the presence and feeding habits of animals. Otter scat can often be identified by the presence of crayfish shells, whereas porcupine scats are round, tapered, cellulose pellets usually deposited near the animal's den.

Some of the creatures crawling about on the forest floor take no pains to hide from you, and though these simpler sorts may not be as sought after as the furred or feathered, don't be too quick to eschew the forest "lowlifes." Spend a little time sharpening your observation skills with the beetles and sowbugs, centipedes and millipedes, slugs and snails.

Land snails (different from freshwater snails in that they have four retractile tentacles or "horns" instead of two) developed about four hundred million years ago and are well represented in our woods. At the end of their longest horns is a tiny pair of eyes; the shorter horns are used to smell and taste. When threatened, the snail withdraws into its shell, spreading a mucous shield across the opening to prevent evaporation of the moisture it requires. Snails are especially evident in the spring; walk the wooded trails around Fidalgo's Heart Lake then, and you won't be able to take your eyes off the trail for fear of squashing one among the multitudes.

Slugs are snails that evolved without shells, and the ubiquitous representative of our island woods is the *banana slug*. Our most maligned Northwesterner, this slug suffers from unfair association with those garden-gobbling nonnative species such as the spotted grays and heavily ridged browns and blacks. Nonetheless, even when we recognize the banana slug's benevolence, we may find it difficult to summon up esteem for a creature whose name ends in "ug." So let's look more closely at this fellow sojourner in the hope that familiarity will breed appreciation and not its opposite.

Dubious? How many of you can pull your eyes into your head, claim your mother is also a father, regrow your wasted teeth, and make slime? So unwrinkle that nose and show a bit of respect for the remarkable slug.

The largest land mollusk in the Northwest, the banana slug grows up to 10 inches long in some disconcerting instances. An olive-colored (sometimes spotted) woodland creature, it helps keep the forest floor clean by devouring decaying plants, roots, seeds, fungi, animal droppings, and carcasses. Slugs have mouths but don't chew; they use a ribbonlike structure covered with teeth, called a radula, for rasping away at their food. Like shark's teeth, the slug's can be replaced when worn through. One local, while sleeping out in a meadow on Lopez, was "stabbed" in the chin by a slug that used its radula on what it took for a novel treat—a rather unique experience, I believe, and one that shouldn't be taken as a warning against camping in the islands.

Look closely at the slug's wonderful body. Those sets of tentacles can retract like glove fingers pulled inwards, drawing deeply into the safety of the head. Should a tentacle break off, it too can regenerate itself. The loose flap of tissue on the upper forward part of the body is called the mantle; the hole on the mantle's right side brings air into the underlying lung.

Crawling is done by means of muscular waves passing along a large fleshy foot. Slugs secrete a transparent film, better known as slime, over the body and beneath the foot while traveling, to prevent abrasion. This slime is so protective that the creatures can pass unharmed over a razor's sharp edge, and it also discourages all but the hungriest from making a meal of them.

Truly, the banana slug is a creature not to be scorned. Welcome its company on your woods walks, for this is one of the few wild animals that won't bristle at or run from your approach; stop a few moments and learn from its tolerance.

Let's move up into the understory now. You'll see rotting stumps and "nurse logs" giving life to hemlock seedlings, ferns, mosses, fungi, and the green-branched, delicate-leaved *red huckleberry*.

Berry bushes are well represented in the understory. Look for *red elderberry* with its soft pithy stems (hollowed out, they make children's whistles), white pyramid

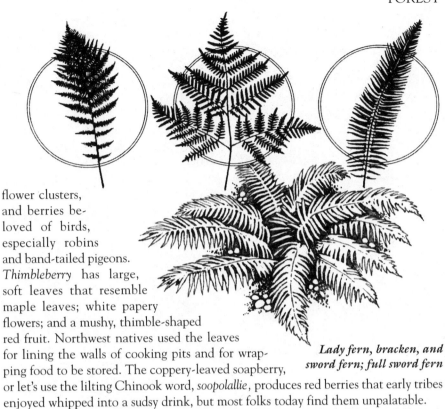

flower clusters,
and berries be-
loved of birds,
especially robins
and band-tailed pigeons.
*Thimbleberry* has large,
soft leaves that resemble
maple leaves; white papery
flowers; and a mushy, thimble-shaped
red fruit. Northwest natives used the leaves
for lining the walls of cooking pits and for wrap-
ping food to be stored. The coppery-leaved soapberry,

*Lady fern, bracken, and sword fern; full sword fern*

or let's use the lilting Chinook word, *soopolallie*, produces red berries that early tribes enjoyed whipped into a sudsy drink, but most folks today find them unpalatable.

The tall, curving, thorn-covered stems found in tangled thickets sheltering nesting birds and small animals belong to *salmonberry* shrubs. Showy, dark pink flowers are later replaced by raspberrylike fruit savored by both birds and people. A berry that is shunned as much as the salmonberry is enjoyed is the *snowberry*, whose fruit unfortunately is bitter and unappetizing. Well into winter, the tiny snowball fruits tremble on spindly shrubs that will rarely know a real snow.

You'll also find two types of *Oregon grape* in the understory; the tall variety has shiny, hollylike leaves, whereas the leaves of the lower type are dullish and lack the prickly points. Although the tall variety may sometimes be confused with the non-native holly, which pops up here and there in the woods, one way to easily tell them apart is by the leaflets; those of the Oregon grape grow opposite each other, whereas holly leaflets alternate. The shrub's blue berries ripen in the fall and are quite sour but can be mixed with salal berries or apples to make jam; the Samish ate them raw and also brewed a tonic from the plant's roots.

Certainly a prime contender for the title of most common shrub must be the *salal*. The Samish made a tea from this plant's glossy green leaves to cure coughs and mashed and dried its blue-black berries into cakes. Salal's pinkish white bells flower from May to July and are often humming with bees; its berries ripen by mid-August and can be very flavorful if the plants have had enough water and light. Dried, the berries can be eaten as raisins.

Another common berry largely responsible for August's purple-stained hands is the *blackberry*, of which we have three distinct types. Our native species is the dewberry, which has a small berry prized for island pies and cobblers, and a vine often found trailing across woodland paths and over stumps. The two nonnative species, Himalayan and evergreen, are more typical of disturbed areas.

Two types of wild roses brighten our understory, and they are quite easy to distinguish by stems and flowers. The stem of the *Nootka rose* is studded with large, scattered thorns, and its blush-pink flower is comparatively large, up to three inches or more across; the baldhip rose has a far smaller blossom and a completely bristled stem. Smell the Nootkas sometime after a spring shower for a special perfume.

Before we leave the understory, let's look for a moment at the ferns that keep our forests so lush. *Sword fern* is by far the most familiar due to its large size and common presence; look for a small triangular projection at the base of each bladelike leaf. Sword fern can sometimes be confused with the licorice fern usually found growing among rocks. The fronds of the latter are smaller, however, and although its leaf is bladelike, it lacks the triangular projection at the base.

Two other fairly common ferns are the feathery lady fern of moist soils and bracken (a contraction of brake-fern, so don't say "bracken fern"). Our tallest fern, bracken has wide triangular fronds that turn bronze when the plant dies back in the fall. It grows from rhizomes, which Northwest natives roasted, peeled, and ate. One of the few ferns that doesn't need dampness or shade, bracken is found in many places throughout the world, and legends abound regarding it. One superstition says that if you capture the bracken's spores on a white napkin at midnight, you will possess the power to become invisible.

Ferns reproduce by spores, not seeds; flip over a leaf and you'll see dozens of round, evenly paired spore cases. When the spores finally ripen, the cases burst to release them, and new ferns develop from their growth. Fronds of the new fern are tightly spiraled in the popularly named fiddleheads.

*Orange honeysuckle* vines twist up and around tree trunks and along branches, their tubular blossoms a compelling come-on to hungry hummingbirds. Taller shrubs that may almost qualify as small trees are the osoberry, *ocean spray*, and *Western serviceberry*. The osoberry, or *Indian plum*, is one of our earliest bloomers, a welcome harbinger of the island spring. Its drooping white blossoms produce orange fruits through the summer that people usually choose to admire from a distance but that birds relish. Crush the leaves of this shrub for a pleasant cucumber smell; the blossoms have an off-putting odor.

Columbian black-tailed deer, Douglas squirrels, red foxes, raccoons, porcupines, skunks, chipmunks, and coyotes are some of the mammals that make their homes here in the woods, although only the first four live in the San Juans proper.

Move quietly if you hope to see mammals and birds slipping in and out among the trees. In the summer woods especially, use your ears to detect wildlife hidden in the thick foliage. Listen for the long whistle of the varied thrush or the chipping of the tiny winter wren, the scratching of a towhee in the brush, the drum of a downy woodpecker or the squabbling of a squirrel.

Walking through the woods around Fidalgo's Cranberry Lake, I was followed by a loud croaking high above and then a series of sounds—*tick, tock, tick, tock, tick, tock, tock, tock*—and then what sounded like the drumming of a woodpecker, only produced by a voice. Even the dog was unnerved, staring up into the treetops to spy out this strange sky spirit. Later I watched the garrulous *raven* fly over the lake uttering a swallowing sound, like a loud *gu-lulp*, and yet another call: *cruk cruk CRUK, cruk cruk CRUK*.

Such a wonderfully varied vocabulary comes from a bird that possesses the largest brain relative to its body size. That impressive voice and attendant intelligence has inspired a good deal of admiration. The Irish have a saying, "raven's knowledge," which means the equivalent of "all-knowing," and the Vikings believed ravens brought messages from the gods. Northwest natives revered the raven as the bringer of light, the creator, the "One Whose Voice Is to Be Obeyed." Indeed, I always stop when I hear the ravens, somehow impelled to listen.

Voice is one way to tell the raven from its smaller cousin, the *crow*. Body size and tail shape are other distinguishing traits. The largest of our perching birds, the raven, with its 4-foot wingspan, rivals our raptors in size. Its tail is wedge-shaped, contrary to the crow's squared-off tail.

Another woodland bird considered wise, or at least mysterious and somewhat otherworldly, is the owl. These nocturnal birds are not likely to be noticed by the average woods walker; during the day they usually sleep next to the trunks of conifers. Look for 2-inch-long disgorged pellets of small bones and feathers, or X tracks, which signal the presence of the *great horned owl*.

This owl will feed on crows, so if you see a group of crows making a racket up in the trees, suspect them of mobbing an owl. You may also hear their hooting in the early mornings or as you're hiking home at dusk. The great horned (popularly known as the hoot owl) utters a deep *hoo, hoo*; the smaller screech owl has a higher call, like a series of bouncing whistles.

You may also hear a woodpecker call, and if the sound is fairly sustained, it may be time for the umbrella. Many people around the world believe that when a woodpecker increases its calls, wet weather is bound to follow. One legend goes that when God finished creating the earth, He commanded the birds to peck out hollows for lakes, rivers, and seas. The woodpecker, however, refused, and as its punishment, it must forever peck wood and drink only rain. We have a few different woodpeckers in the islands, but the king of the conifers is the dashing *pileated woodpecker*, called the Rain Bird by Vancouver Island natives. Large as a crow and boldly marked with a flaming red crest, the pileated's presence is more often detected by the large rectangular holes it drills in dead (and living) conifers.

Two other woodpeckers are difficult to distinguish from each other. The downy, our smallest, has a comparatively inconsequential-looking beak and spotted white outer tail feathers. The hairy is a third larger but warier, with a heavier beak, a harsher call, and unspotted tail feathers. The *northern flicker* is our most common woodpecker and is easily told from the others. It's the oddball of the group since it's usually seen feeding on the ground and is by far the most vocal; the spring woods fairly rings with its rapid-fire *wait-wait-wait-wait-wait!* A beautiful bird with a barred cinnamon back and a black-spotted breast, the flicker also has a white rump patch like the marsh hawk's, which quickly identifies it in flight.

Right now, though, don't concern yourself with matters of who's who. Concentrate instead on how wonderfully adapted to its woodworking this beaver of the bird world is when you finally spot one drumming away. The sharp opposing claws easily grip a tree trunk, while stiff tail feathers function as a third leg propped against the bark. The bill, which takes such a beating chiseling nest holes and digging under the bark for burrowing insects, continues to grow and renew itself. And though most of us would find such head-bashing activity a real headache, woodpecker skulls are exceptionally thick, with shock-absorbent spongy tissue between the beak and the cranium so the bird's brains don't scramble while hammering.

How, though, does the woodpecker reach grubs and ants deep in the heartwood of a tree? The narrow hole tunnels it drills don't allow much room for a beak to open and pinch its prey. The answer lies in one of the woodpecker's most wonderful adaptations: its tongue, so long that it wraps around the skull to anchor at the base of the bill. A woodpecker can extend this amazing tongue, which is barbed and coated with a sticky saliva, far beyond the end of its beak to spear a meal.

We come at last to the trees the owls are roosting in and the woodpeckers beating upon. Dominated by conifers, climaxing in *Douglas-fir,* island woodlands also include *western redcedar, red alder, western hemlock* (our state tree), *Pacific madrone, big-leaf maple, grand fir, Pacific yew, juniper,* and *shore pine.* As you get to know the individual characteristics of the trees (see the "Winter" and "Reference List" sections of this book), remember that these often huge wellsprings of life are in fact mostly dead; only about 1 percent of a tree's trunk is alive. Yet nowhere else does Nature reveal herself so vigorously. Spend some time among the trees, lean on

*Raven*

110

them, and they will sustain beyond your imagining. Listen for the steady beat of the raven's wings, watch the slug inch its way among the roots, and relax into the age-old rhythms of the woods.

## SITE GUIDE

The following suggests a few representative areas in the islands where you can easily observe many common woodland plants and animals. Tips on what to look for are only that—the mere tips of huge icebergs waiting to be explored. What you'll see will depend on the season, the time of day, and your own tenacity.

### *San Juan Island*

**British Camp:** As you follow the trail from the parking lot out and up to Mount Young, notice thimbleberry, big-leaf maple, wild roses, starflower, ferns, madrone, huckleberry, fringecup, red-flowering currant, ocean spray, serviceberry, and honeysuckle. Chocolate and fawn lilies, as well as a patch of shooting stars, grow on the mossy right side of the trail as you head up Mount Young. Listen for chickadees, nuthatches, and woodpeckers, and watch for deer.

ACCESS: From the ferry, take Spring Street to Second Street. Turn right and follow Second as it turns into Guard. Turn right again onto Tucker off Guard, and continue onto Roche Harbor Road. Take Roche Harbor Road to West Valley Road and turn right. Proceed just over a mile to the entrance of British Camp. Park in the

***Crow and raven***

lot and follow signs to Mount Young. The trail crosses the West Valley Road and is a wide, easy grade, with Mount Young itself not too much steeper.

**Jakle's Farm Nature Trail:** Follow this wide, easy trail down through mixed conifer-broadleaf woods and you'll find fir, cedar, hemlock, ocean spray, big-leaf maple, salmonberry, thimbleberry, wild roses, Oregon grape, spotted coralroot, ferns, foamflower, and starflower. Watch for red-tailed hawks, woodpeckers, crossbills, towhees, robins, nuthatches, and other woodland birds.

ACCESS: From the ferry, take Spring Street out of Friday Harbor to the San Juan Valley Road and Douglas Road intersection. Head south on Douglas for about 1 1/2 miles; then turn left on Little Road to the Cattle Point intersection. Go south on Cattle Point for about 3 1/2 miles to the Pickett Lane intersection in the American Camp area. A few hundred feet east of the intersection a side road branches north, ending at a gate beyond which vehicles are prohibited. Hike the wide trail down to the first intersection and take the left fork; follow the trail down to the water. See the map at the trailhead if you wish to complete the entire loop.

## Orcas Island

**Madrona Point:** For a different type of forest, follow the trail to lovely Madrona Point, a place sacred to the Lummis and once slated for logging. At the trailhead, note the western crabapple bushes to your right. Lose yourself in the riot of madrones, and look also for baldhip roses, snowberry, ocean spray, honeysuckle, yerba buena, and woodland flowers. The trail ends at a meadow known for its camas and shooting stars, but until a trail has been marked for use, wandering through this fragile area is discouraged.

ACCESS: From the ferry, follow the Horseshoe Highway about 8 miles to Eastsound. Proceed through town to the sign for Prune Valley Road, and turn right to the Oddfellows Hall, just beyond the sign. Head past the Oddfellows Hall to the point's parking area.

**Moran State Park:** Dozens of trails in this park of over 4,900 acres will lead you into and through the forest. The trail around Mountain Lake is only one example. This nearly 4-mile loop, called the Bonnie Sligar Memorial Trail, is a wide, well-packed trail, level except where it swings uphill away from the lake for a short distance. Several small bridges cross streams that feed into the lake. Look for the fir-cedar-hemlock triumvirate, along with ocean spray, shore pine, baldhip roses, gooseberry, and woodland strawberry. A grove of large alders lies at the north end of the lake, and tall snags line the shore. Listen for woods birds such as the winter wren and flicker; you're also apt to hear the scolding chickaree. Look for bald eagles in the shoreline trees and for ospreys during the summer. Scan the lake for scaups, common mergansers, and other waterfowl.

ACCESS: From the ferry, follow the Horseshoe Highway toward Eastsound and watch for signs to Moran, about 12 1/2 miles from the ferry. Go 1 1/2 miles from the park entrance to Mount Constitution Road. Head 1 mile up the road and turn right at the sign for Mountain Lake. (In the spring, as you head in to the lake, check out the skunk cabbage city on your left). Park at the Mountain Lake landing; the loop begins at the signed trailhead south of the campground. A bonus to this trail is a fork on the north end that heads up 3/4 mile to Twin Lakes for added woods walking.

## *Fidalgo Island*

**Heart Lake:** The trail that follows the circumference of the lake is state park land; ACFL trails traverse 80 acres of moist woodland north of the lake. Wood ducks, buffleheads, scaups, ringnecks, coots, and hooded mergansers are among the ducks that use the lake; listen and look also for ravens, ospreys, and bald eagles. Cormorants often perch on the old lake pilings, and otters may leave their scat along the shore. Watch for rough-skinned newts, snakes, and snails along the trail, and listen for squirrels and woodpeckers (note the excavations of pileateds in the trees). Vegetation includes black cottonwood, alder, honeysuckle, salmonberry, thimbleberry, osoberry, wild rose, huckleberry, gooseberry, water parsley, calypso, foamflower, fringecup, twinflower, ocean spray, red elderberry, hemlock, fir, cedar, big-leaf maple, and lush stands of sword fern. Lots of nurse logs and stumps.
ACCESS: Coming into Anacortes from Highway 20, turn right on Commercial Avenue to 32d Street. Turn left and head up 32d to H Avenue, which soon becomes Heart Lake Road. Turn left and proceed 1 1/2 miles to the park entrance. Take the shore trail, No. 210, in to where it intersects with No. 23 and turn left. Walk a short distance and cross Ace of Hearts Creek; then take your first right, No. 209, which winds through the forest. When you meet a T intersection, head right and continue to follow No. 209, always bearing right at the forks, until the trail crosses the creek again. Proceed through dense sword fern uphill and back to No. 23, then turn right and follow to where No. 23 rejoins the shore trail.

**Washington Park:** This 200-acre park is a treasure of mixed habitats: shore, meadow, and woods. Follow any of the several well-marked trails into fir-cedar-hemlock stands and the typical understory of salal, Oregon grape, wild roses, berry plants, wildflowers such as starflower, and orchid plants such as spotted coralroot. Bald eagles nest in the park; watch also for black-tailed deer and Douglas squirrels. Look for gnarled old Rocky Mountain junipers on the cliffsides and also dwarf and Douglas maples, trees usually found only east of the Cascades.
ACCESS: In Anacortes, take Commercial Avenue to 12th Street. Turn left at the light, and travel about 3 miles to the light at the intersection with the road to the ferry landing. Continue straight for approximately 1 more mile to the park.

**Whistle Lake:** Several different trails exist in the lake area—ACFL maps are available at local bookstores for those who want to explore more thoroughly. The lake loop described here takes you past Indian paintbrush, orange honeysuckle, foamflower, fringecup, starflower, twinflower, woodland strawberry, spotted coralroot, stonecrop, ocean spray, thimbleberry, huckleberry, wild rose, Indian plum, cedars, firs, hemlocks, alders, and Pacific madrone, to name just a few. Fawn lilies sprout from moss-covered rocks. Listen for flickers, squirrels, and woodland birds and check out the lake for buffleheads, wood ducks, and common and hooded mergansers—and the snags along the shore for bald eagles. Ospreys nest on the east shore of the lake in summer, and owl pellets can be regularly found on the east-side trail.

ACCESS: Coming into Anacortes from Highway 20, turn left on Commercial Avenue and proceed up the hill to the street's end. Turn right on Fidalgo Avenue and follow it around to the left to "O" Avenue. Take "O" to the first left, Haddon Road, and follow it to Whistle Lake Road. Turn right and continue straight to a sign pointing to Whistle Lake Terrace. Turn left and follow the road as it curves around to the right. Take the first right and proceed up a potholed dirt road to the lake. Park in the lot and take the Gerry Walrath trail to the lake. When you reach the lake, take trail No. 204 to the right and follow it along the lakeshore until the trail comes to a T intersection. Turn right, and go uphill on No. 204 until you reach the next fork. Turn left onto trail No. 21. Follow No. 21 until the next fork and turn left onto No. 22. Take No. 22 around the south end of the lake, and at the next fork, turn left onto No. 205. Stay on No. 205 around Toot Swamp, across the old dam, and back to the lake. There is some steep climbing on No. 205 heading around to the east side of the lake; stay to the right when the trail branches, and follow No. 205 through roosting areas (look for pellets) and back to the lake's edge. The trail travels around the north end of the lake to complete the loop.

# DENISE CROWE

### *How You Gonna Keep 'Em Down in the Woods (after They've Seen Nintendo)?*

When she first visited Anacortes, Denise Crowe had a surprise in store. As she drove through the tunnel of trees that shades Heart Lake Road, she demanded of her husband, "What *is* this place? How can there be all this forest?" When told that the trees pressing up against the roadsides were part of the city's community woodlands, "I was astounded when I found out the extent of the forest," she recalls. "And so happy."

These are feelings the "forest lady," as she's known today, hopes to inspire in the scores of youngsters she takes with her into the woods. Many have never experienced the forest and sometimes find the subtle, often secretive world of nature a tame substitute for the television.

A case in point is a ten-year-old on one of her hikes who never stopped muttering a Nintendo soundtrack. "He was just obsessed," says Denise, who tries hard to compete with the rapid-fire stimulation of an electronic world. "It *is* hard to hold kids' attention. They're used to this quick switching, and they have to change their internal rhythm to be present in the woods." To ease the transition, she uses plenty of hands-on activities, encouraging the kids to explore and get muddy. "They need to *feel* it," she says. "They need to touch and smell the place."

The free Forest Discovery programs were started in Anacortes in 1984. Organized into three half-day sessions, they focus on the forest one day, wetlands another, meadow and mountain the third. Children explore duckweed-covered ponds for beaver signs and dragonflies, scoop bottom mud with strainers, pick berries, make up songs, and play games. (A special mountain biking program is also available to encourage minimum impact on the trails, and 1994 saw the start of a curriculum for seventh-grade students that explores the connection between the forestlands watershed and Puget Sound.)

To help the kids tune in at the start and adjust their perceptions, Denise often picks a section of trail and lays out items that don't belong in the forest, such as a spoon, a thimble, or a piece of plywood. The children walk the trail and quietly count all alien objects spotted. It's a fairly standard activity, she says, adding that there was only one time a child proceeded slowly enough to notice every misplaced piece.

Denise is not above using what she calls "titillation" to capture and hold the attention of kids who may have been pressured into joining the hikes by parents. "One girl who really did not want to come ended up being the most enthusiastic," she says. "I take that as a challenge. If a kid's got a spark, I court it."

It's definitely a courtship tailored to the gum-chewing crowd. Older kids giggle over the sex lives of slugs, and everyone gets into scat analysis. "It's one of the first things I say—Do you know what scat is?" In a conspiratorial whisper, she adds, "It's the word for *poop* in the woods." She feels strongly about idealizing nature, cringing over the Bambi-among-the-flowers scenario. "I work hard to overcome both the fear of the swamp, on one end of the spectrum, and Bambi glorified, on the other end," she says. "Neither one of them is the reality of the woods."

The kids got a good dose of reality one summer when hornets tormented the hikers. "Every single session, I had a group encounter a ground hive," says Denise. That summer cemented her desire to carry a cellular phone on the trips, especially after one child had a severe allergic reaction to a sting.

Sometimes rain provides another reality hit, though not necessarily an unwelcome one. "I end up really hiking kids on those days and they love it." Although somewhat taken aback at the enthusiasm for wet-weather walks, Denise says the response to the Forest Discovery programs is usually very positive. Many times children come to the end of their three days eager to continue through the week.

Groups are small, generally eight to ten, and as "social barriers between the kids break down, they become this kind of gang in the forest." When stimuli no longer bombard, those barriers sometimes break down so much that by the last day, on Sugarloaf Mountain, kids "consistently become very emotional and say things like 'My mom died, I miss my mom,' and go into this deep place. I had a girl a year ago express suicidal feelings, a seven-year-old girl talking about how she didn't want to live." Denise feels that slowing down in nature has a lot to do with letting emotions come to the surface: "I think many kids' lives are very busy, filled with organized activities and a lot of television," she says. "Given just three afternoons in the woods with the same small group of people, the stuff that comes out is really amazing. It's a time for reflection, a time to say, 'Here I am in the forest—*who am I?*'"

She shares with the youngsters how she has come to learn what she knows about the woods, hoping to inspire them enough to follow their own paths of wonder and inquiry. Distressed by a prevalent "Feed me!" attitude, she struggles with how to turn that around. "It's just a completely different way of coming at learning," she says, frowning. "I balk at handing out spoonfuls. It's not my style at all. The main thing I demand is that they take the steps on their own. They have to be present. They have to start thinking and feeling about the place."

More and more children are doing just that as they head out into the woods, not only on summer Forest Discovery hikes but also on school field trips. The school trips started with just a few several years ago but have since grown to include all the first, second, and third grades and some younger and older students as well. Funding for the program (through the Friends of the Forest, which, "in reality, doesn't have enough money to fund a program like this, but I'm doing it") has increased, as have Denise's efforts to become more involved with curriculum development. She feels the program suffers from a lack of support in the classroom and believes teacher education is a large part of her job.

"Environmental education was not part of a lot of teachers' experience," she says. "Many don't place much value on it. That's something I'm constantly surprised by. I have such a passion for this stuff, and to be in certain social or work situations where I'm the only one who feels this way . . . I just have to laugh at myself. I think, well, there's a lot of work to do!"

Denise's "passion for this stuff" started while exploring neighborhood woods as a child and on family backpacking trips. In college, she took community studies and art until her last year, when she noticed that it was the science classes who were having all the fun in the field. A course called "Forests and Salmon" soon came up, and she signed on.

"We studied old-growth forests, the salmon, their history and their interactions with each other, and it was wonderful," she says. "It was a big step for me in demystifying science. I discovered that I had a real affinity for it and that because I came at the study with more of a community-based view, I was fascinated with traditional uses of plants and salmon and with Native American communities. It just got something rolling in me in a big way." When the forest position in Anacortes opened up, "it was perfect for me."

In a two-hour chunk of time, she takes about thirty schoolchildren, their teacher, and three or four parents into selected parts of Anacortes's 2,200 acres of forest. She visits each class for at least fifteen minutes beforehand to let them know what to expect, and, if asked, she may tailor-make a session to fit a group's current studies. Her main goal and biggest challenge is to enable this many children, in that short amount of time, to see the forest "through their own eyes." Noting that she's working for a group, Friends of the Forest, that is politically active in the community, she tries to avoid anything that resembles a lecture or the urging of her own agenda. "I focus instead on my relationship to the forest and try my best to have all the kids feel theirs for themselves. Because I think that's really the power of nature for us, especially in these times. The rest comes later."

Her resolve can be severely tested, however, as when deformed frogs were discovered during two different trips in a wetland near the old city dump.

"A little boy found the first one on a field trip, and I said, 'What did you *do* to it?!' You know, I'm trying to get them to be gentle with the frogs, and here I blurt this out because I see something's horribly wrong. And he said, 'Nothing, it was like this!'" She shakes her head and describes how the frog's right eye, enlarged and clouded over, was drawn back onto the side of its body. A second frog, with one leg that was just a stump with deformed toes, was found a month later in the same area.

Although Denise's policy is never to remove anything from the forest, she took the frogs to have them photographed, returning them later to the woods, where it's hoped they resumed their active, if impaired, lives. To add further to the alarm, a great blue heron was found dead in the same area a week after the discovery of the first deformed frog. Herons in wetlands feed on frogs.

"It's one of my biggest fears, that contaminants from the old dump are leaching right down in," says Denise, who once wrote a position statement about a soil remediation project at the dump and its possible effects on nearby wildlife. She adds softly, "I love frogs. Frogs are amazing creatures. They're so smart and so vulnerable. Their skin is this living, breathing organ, and they live in the water and on the land, so they're exposed to every part of the environment in the course of their lives." She points out that although there is something akin to a worldwide amphibian crisis right now, deformations haven't been part of it, and she hopes that someday a sediment study can be done in the wetland. "Here was this frog, through no fault of its own, so severely altered."

When you have thirty pairs of young eyes looking at you for an explanation, eyes that have so far been mostly entranced by what they've seen, it becomes necessary to carefully weigh your response. "The second time I actually did swear under my breath," she says regretfully. "It was one of those horrible moments when one little boy heard me." She discussed the dump with the children, being careful to say there was no way to know for sure if the deformations were connected to the dump without doing tests. "But," she was forced to add, "the dump is up there and icky stuff has been buried there for years and years." She felt justified in suggesting a connection after having talked with ecology and wildlife officials who echoed her suspicions.

It's disheartening to come across neglect and destruction when trying to foster just the opposite in beginning woods walkers, children who are in a "place they *do* care about. I'm always surprised and excited by the energy and understanding children bring to the woods, the things they already know or the things they feel an affinity with."

Some exhibit a real fear of the forest, but usually by the end of the field trip, such feelings have changed. One child ends up fascinated with crayfish, another with a kingfisher, another with the rotten stumps at the south end of Cranberry Lake, and still another with whirligig beetles sprinting over the water's surface.

Many become thrilled to know that people lived here long before them. "I try to provide that history," says Denise. "That this place has been inhabited for thousands of years and that the people who have lived here before us had a deeper understanding of home and took care of the place better than we have. How people were able to live here without cars, grocery stores, running water, *television,* without all these things, and lived very well, from what's in this forest around us."

"Kids are fascinated by that."

---

For information on the Forest Discovery programs and other nature hikes on Fidalgo Island, contact the Friends of the ACFL, 619 Commercial Avenue, #32, Anacortes, WA 98221, or call (360) 293-3725.

# Chapter 8

# MEADOW

THERE IS SOMETHING ABOUT A MEADOW. Woods tend to make one introspective. Old trees inspire thoughts more natural to an older, wiser age, but a summer meadow turns one into a child again. Is it the unbroken space stretching around and before one like the undiscovered, inviting years spread before a youngster? Even when we can't find a meadow to physically ramble in, we can park our bikes alongside an island pasture and send our minds forth to play and tumble and expand once more.

Meadows are basically filled-in ponds or areas once cleared from woodlands for farming but now left for pasture. The most interesting to the nature lover are those meadows left undisturbed for several years, no longer grazed or plowed under but relatively abandoned and slowly returning to their former woodland vegetation. Grasses are still the dominant feature here, but wildflowers and shrubby plants are starting to make inroads.

In the islands, the most common meadows—and the most wildly beautiful— are those on the south slopes, naturally formed when glaciers spread a thin layer of sand and silt on top of rock. The plants that grow in these meadows are specially adapted to surviving thin, dry soils and being sun-baked in the summer and wind-whipped in the winter. Some, like the gnarly *Rocky Mountain juniper*, usually grow east of the Cascades but find the similar harsh conditions here well suited to their needs.

Let's take a look at some of these roadside pastures and mountainside meadows. Usually the first thing that comes to mind when we think of a meadow or pasture is grass, one of the world's most successful and widespread flowering plants.

Grasses flower? Yes, although their flowers are minuscule compared to the showier blooms of plants that attract insect pollinators. Grasses are wind-pollinated and so have no need for extravagance. They consequently tend to suffer in our esteem, for who pays any attention to the grass surrounding a chocolate lily or shooting star? Nevertheless, grasses don't deserve the disdain they usually prompt. Watch a breeze moving over meadow grass and you'll see the shape of the wind pass like a hand as it strokes the plant tops and scatters pollen.

Take a hand lens and really look at the flower heads of grasses as the bees and butterflies see them. (A lot of people don't really know how to use a hand lens. Bring the lens as close to your eye as possible. Maneuver the plant so that sunlight falls on it, and then bring it toward the lens instead of bringing the lens down to it, a common mistake.) You'll see a wonderful variety of shapes and colors in the blossoms and anthers of grasses. Perhaps the most attractive common grass here is the feathery-topped red fescue, its reddish brown sheath giving a rosy tint to many island meadows.

Don't confuse grasses with sedges or rushes. Grasses have hollow, segmented stems. Grass stems are also round, whereas sedges have triangular, solid stems. Rush stems are round like those of grasses but are smooth (unsegmented) and solid.

Don't forget to examine grasses for the tiny creatures that may be attached to them. In spring, frothy spit masses stick to grass blades, not because spring inspires excessively juicy mouths but because a tiny insect called the froghopper or spittlebug lays its eggs in the plant tissue. When the froghopper nymph, which looks a bit like a tiny frog, emerges from its egg, it surrounds itself with the protective foam.

Leafhoppers and grasshoppers may also be found clinging to the meadow grasses on which they feed. Children, closer to the earth than adults in both size and inclination, enjoy the incredible jumps of grasshoppers, and perhaps we too can reclaim our early sense of admiration. The world is not all whale and eagle, nor should it need to be to capture our attention and astound us.

Poke among the humble grasses, then, and give a moment to the grasshopper. Did you know it has five eyes and its ears are under its wings? Did you know the back legs work like a steel spring to launch their owner high into the air? Or that the insect clings to those grass blades by means of a sticky fluid secreted from hairs on its toe pads? I could go on, but this isn't the place for a treatise on the grasshopper. Let these few observations spur you on to your own discoveries.

An examination of grass stems may also turn up the caterpillars of moths and butterflies. How do you tell the difference between the winged adults? Usually, butterflies are out by day, moths by night. (Although some moths do fly by day, most spend the day sleeping in the cooler depths of the grasses.) If you're unsure, watch for the creature to land on a blossom, and note its wing position. Butterflies hold their four wings together up over their backs, making themselves more inconspicuous to birds, whereas moths spread their wings. This rule also has its exceptions, so note the antennae: a butterfly's antennae are long and slender, with knobs at the tips, whereas a moth's are short and feathery and lack the knobs.

Watch for large, yellow western swallowtails among the meadow wildflowers. A less showy species and one of the earliest butterflies to be on the lookout for is the spring azure, just a floating blue petal of a butterfly. If you temporarily catch one of them, you may notice that your fingers become dusted from handling the wings. This fine dust is a collection of scales that overlap like shingles on the butterfly's wings and provide both strength and color. Try looking at them under a hand lens while a partner gently spreads the wing for you.

a reddish glow to meadows; look for thin clusters of red flowers above arrowhead-shaped leaves. Stonecrop often clings to the rocks of the south-facing meadows, its thick, succulent leaves topped with yellow star-shaped blooms. Cut into those thick leaves for a quick sip if water is scarce. The plant stores water in its leaves to survive drought-like conditions.

It should go without saying that your visits to the meadow should not bring destruction to fragile communities. Wildflower bouquets are a pretty thought, but let them be just that. Take only memories home.

Now let's look at the animals that make the meadow their hunting or nesting ground. One lucky day you may spot a lizard warming itself in a sunny meadow. The alligator lizard is about eighteen inches long, and it is the only lizard we have here in the islands. An interesting bit of information about this fairly nondescript, gray-brown animal is the claim, which I can by no means verify, that you can look through its ear openings right through its head. Next time you have one in hand (watch out—they bite), coax it to calm down long enough that you can take a squint through its head. Let me know the results.

To us, meadows are open spaces inviting our spirits to roam afar, but to others, a meadow is a dense, dark thicket. Meadow mice, more properly called *voles* (they have shorter ears and tails than mice), scurry about in the matted undergrowth of grasses. You won't often see one; if these plump little creatures try hard not to attract the attention of the sharp-eyed owls and hawks that prey on them, how much less apt will we be to notice them. However, you may find their runways in the meadows below the dead grass mat, some of them tunneling through the grass to a burrow opening. Voles are vegetarians, so if you find their tunnels, look for small litter heaps or caches of gnawed plant stems, roots, and bulbs. They're prolific breeders; litters usually number about ten, and females may give birth to up to a hundred young between spring and fall.

There's an even tinier creature scampering through the grasses: the smallest of all mammals, the *shrew*. Its tiny size (it weighs in at only about one-fifth of an ounce) and tapering nose easily distinguish it from mice and voles. It, too, tunnels year-round through the meadow grasses on a frantically focused search for food. Eating to stay alive seems to be the only object in this tiny life; a shrew needs to swallow its own weight in food every twenty-four hours and thus wolfs down insects, berries, plants, worms, and more, as if constantly stoking a fire with nothing but kindling.

Shrews have a musk gland on their velvety fur that secretes such a foul liquid that few animals will eat them. Cats will catch a shrew and torment it but rarely eat it. I've often found whole dead shrews on woodland paths, dropped there perhaps by a small hawk or other bird who had second thoughts about its intended meal. Owls, who apparently can't detect foul odors, are one of the few creatures who'll attack a skunk or feed on shrews; look for shrew bones in disgorged owl pellets.

In the meadows of San Juan Island at Cattle Point lives a large population of *European rabbits*. (Look for them also on the grassy areas of Lopez's Spencer Spit.) Released by breeders in the late 1800s (some accounts say the rabbits escaped), the rabbits have dug extensive warrens in the Cattle Point area. The population swells and shrinks; a virus killed off a large number in the late 1970s, but the rabbits are steadily recovering from their losses. Foxes were brought in many years back to control the garden gluttons but had to be killed after chicken topped their menu instead. (Foxes can still be seen on San Juan.) Devouring any and all vegetation except for a few lucky plants such as daffodils and peonies, the rabbits are in turn a good food source for eagles, owls, and hawks.

Although a few rabbits may be seen during the day, your best chance to view this largely nocturnal creature is at dawn and dusk, when it nibbles on various grasses and herbs. The long, sensitive ears are an indication of its attitude, so watch closely as it feeds. If the ears are flat back, the animal is fairly restful; if straight up, tensely attentive. One ear cocked forward and the other back usually indicates the puzzled searching out of a sound.

Watch, too, the rabbit's cleaning routine. It scrubs its face with the two front paws and pushes its ears forward with the hind legs to be licked. Those hind legs are powerful; a rabbit can vault over its shorter front legs and leap up to eight feet. To wash its hind paws, rabbits first vigorously shake the dirt off and then lick them clean. Note also the nose and whiskers to see how a rabbit uses them to gather information.

A shadow overhead will send a rabbit running for cover, but you can comfortably train your binos on bald and golden eagles hunting over the Cattle Point meadows. Goldens are spotted more often in the islands than in any other part of western Washington and may easily be confused with immature bald eagles. However, goldens are feathered to the toes, whereas balds have a bare tarsus; goldens also have a three-toned bill, black, blue, and yellow, and subadults have white patches in the wings, which you can see flash in the sun from well over a mile away. A regal bird, this eagle is also much more fierce than the bald; so much so that the Chinese once used them to hunt wolves.

Another raptor you're likely to see making long, low swoops over grassy fields is the *northen harrier*, also known as the marsh hawk. Slim, with long wings and tail, the harrier is one of our most social hawks (they roost communally in fields) and one of the easiest to observe thanks to repetitive flights over the same patch of open ground as it scans for food.

The harrier can easily be identified by the bold white rump patch present on both sexes. Always looking down as it quarters the fields, carefully covering every square foot below, the harrier brakes suddenly when it spots its prey, jerking backwards as if it had slammed into something. It then stabs feet first into the grass, scoring a hit perhaps one in ten times. If you're lucky and the harrier isn't, you may also see eagles or red-tails move in on the smaller hawk and rob it of its prey, forcing the harrier to once again resume its undulating flights over the field.

Raptor biologist Bud Anderson gives an account of watching a harrier in a most uncommon hunt. These hawks usually feed on mice and voles, but one with "delusions of grandeur" apparently thought it could catch a wigeon, which is a fairly large duck. "We watched it come in really straight and fast, and these wigeons went *'What?!'* You could actually see them look at this harrier coming in. The ducks flushed in front of it at the last second, and the harrier came up on the rear end of a wigeon and grabbed hold of its rump. The wigeon turned on the speed and the harrier just went *'Whoa!'* It went through the air for about 50 feet and then let go."

Raptors aren't the only birds to watch for in meadows. Small sparrows such as the savannah and vesper sing and nest in the grasses. Ground nesters are common in the meadow, and though it may seem that peeping chicks confined to a ground nest would be easy pickings for predators, most are precocial. Like ducklings, the chicks are covered with down and are able to follow their parents from the nest soon after hatching. Their plumages blend in with the background, and when the birds become alarmed, they freeze and melt into the vegetation.

*Western meadowlark*

Because the meadow lacks an abundance of natural perches, singing is often done on the wing, and the songs, such as those of the meadowlark and skylark, carry exuberantly across open spaces. The vesper has a sweet, finch-type song, but despite its name, the bird doesn't sing more often in the evening than any other sparrow.

Bright yellow with black berets and wings, American goldfinches feed off the summer seeds of thistles, dandelions, and Queen Anne's lace. The western meadowlark, another golden-colored bird, with a black neck collar, boldly trills its cheery, flutelike phrases from open meadow perches. Once an abundant breeding species in the islands, this bird has suffered a decline, and it is not likely you'll find its nest among the grasses. However, the western meadowlark is still a winter visitor, and hope remains that it may one day return to our summer meadows.

## SITE GUIDE

It must be stressed that wildflower meadows are fragile areas and should not be trampled on or picked over. The following areas all have trails from which much can be seen; look, listen, and leave the meadow as you found it. If you spend some time just sitting and soaking up space and insect hum, you'll come away changed without needing to change the meadow.

### San Juan Island

**American Camp:** Large boulders punctuate the meadows here; look for raptors such as bald and golden eagles, red-tails, and rough-legs perched on the rocks or soaring overhead, harriers quartering the fields, and falcons hunting. Sit for a while and soak up nothing but grass, sea, and sky. You may see western long-spurred violets, pellets, rabbit trails, vole tunnels, owls at dusk, pipits during their fall migration, skylarks singing and courting, rabbits feeding, perhaps even a fox.

ACCESS: Follow Spring Street out of Friday Harbor to the San Juan Valley Road and Douglas Road intersection. Turn left on Douglas and travel 1 1/2 miles to the intersection with Little Road. Turn left on Little and proceed about 1/2 mile to the intersection with Cattle Point Road. Follow Cattle Point Road to American Camp and don't turn off but continue on to Pickett's Lane. Turn right, travel about 1/2 mile to the parking lot, and hike out to the meadows.

**Mount Young:** What a treasure this place is on an early spring morning. Look for turkey vultures, golds, balds, and other raptors soaring overhead. Red fescue gives the meadow a burnished look, and camas and blue-eyed Mary grow among the grasses and lichen-covered rocks. When you stumble upon a rather startling plant that looks like a huge, wandering squash vine, you've found the Oregon manroot, a member of the cucumber family. Also check out the wonderful grayed grandpa of a Garry oak. The meadow looks out to Garrison and Mitchell bays and Haro Strait beyond; the honking you hear comes from the Canada geese below at British Camp.

ACCESS: See directions to British Camp in "Forest."

## Orcas Island

**Mount Constitution:** This 2,409-foot mountain is the highest point in the San Juans. Look for wildflowers such as Menzies' larkspur, farewell-to-spring, blue-eyed grass, chickweed, Indian dream, woolly sunflower, and harvest brodiaea. You may see black-tailed deer browsing the slopes and turkey vultures, eagles, ravens, or black swifts overhead. For the wildflower shows, visit the meadows mid-May to early June; by June's end, all will be brown.

ACCESS: From the ferry, follow the Horseshoe Highway approximately 12 1/2 miles to Moran State Park. Go about 1 1/2 miles further to Mount Constitution Road and follow this road 2 1/4 miles to a lookout on the left side of the road. Parking is available for about five cars. This spot overlooks what has been described to me as the "best wildflower meadow on the mountain." Be careful to stay on the trail so as not to damage the fragile habitat. Another spot to try is Little Summit. Travel 3 miles up Mount Constitution Road to the Little Summit parking lot on the right (elevation 2,200 feet). A short trail (about 500 feet) leads in to meadow slopes.

## Fidalgo Island

**Cranberry Lake Meadows:** High above the lake with good views down to the bog islands and beaver habitat, three small meadows gift the hiker with flaming colonies of paintbrush, spring gold, purple camas, chocolate lilies, wild rose, chickweed, vetch, and kinnickinnick.

ACCESS: Follow the directions in "Wetlands" to the Beaver Ponds as far as crossing the first bridge. Instead of taking trail No. 108-B to the pond, follow No. 108 to No. 107 (don't take the right-branching fork of No. 107). When you come to the main intersection above the lake, head uphill to your right on trail No. 104 to No. 103, which will lead you to the meadows.

**Rosario Head:** In late spring, these rocky, salt-washed slopes sparkle with wild-flowers like sea thrift, spring gold, camas, blue-eyed Mary, prairie stars, saxifrage, chickweed, lupine, larkspur, onions, and stonecrop. The bright yellow bushes are nonnative Scotch broom.

ACCESS: Take Highway 20 south to the intersection with Rosario Road, just after Pass Lake. Turn right and proceed north to the intersection with Rosario Beach Road, which signs to the Walla Walla College Marine Station. The road leads down to the parking lot. From there, follow the trail out to the meadows on Rosario Head.

**Sugarloaf Mountain:** Look for western buttercup, spring gold, yellow violet, prairie star, blue-eyed Mary, camas, chickweed, paintbrush, sorrel, Menzies's lark-spur, and in the uppermost, south-facing meadows, kinnickinnick and fawn lilies decorating the moss carpets.

ACCESS: Coming into Anacortes from Highway 20, turn right onto Commercial Avenue. Proceed to 32d Street and turn left. Continue up 32d to H Avenue, which becomes Heart Lake Road. Turn left and travel 2 miles to Mount Erie Park on your left. Two options: park in the bottom lot and hike the steep trail up to the meadows, or drive 1/2 mile up Mount Erie Road to the ACFL Sugarloaf trailhead and head in from there.

**Washington Park:** Follow the park's loop road around to south- and west-facing slopes where spring puts on a real show. Look for the showy white heads of death camas, the somewhat scarcer purple camas, sea thrift, field chickweed, blue-eyed Mary, and purple carpets of sea blush. You may even spot a chocolate lily. Hooker's onion blooms later in the season, and monkeyflower, which we usually associate with wetlands, is also present in a smaller form. Stay on the sun-baked red clay trails to avoid damaging flowers and grasses. Watch for bald eagles, and note the gnarled junipers and madrones.

ACCESS: See directions to Washington Park in "Forest."

# MARK LEWIS

### His Work is For the Birds

Over the south side of San Juan Island sweep open grasslands born centuries ago of a retreating glacier. Windswept and sun-blazed, the rolling meadows are home to a sizable population of European rabbits, which have found the soft glacial till perfect for burrow building and which have grazed the grasses and herbs down to a putting green or, in many places, bare earth. The population of these nonnative animals fluctuates, however, and one year when it was at its lowest, local ornithologist Mark Lewis noticed a huge upsurge in the native voles.

"They were just scampering everywhere, like lemmings in the Arctic," he says, "and that brought in all sorts of smaller raptors that were migrating through—they stumbled on this bountiful prey source and decided to stay." Only the larger birds, such as eagles, red-tails, and great horned owls, are able to take advantage of the rabbits as a prey source, but voles feed all raptors from the tiniest kestrel on up. Commonly called meadow mice, voles create interlocking tunnels under the grass mats: "They need overhead cover to conceal themselves; they don't have the eyesight or speed of a rabbit to elude predators," says Mark. When the rabbits no longer chewed the grasses to stubs, the vole population prospered. Consequently, so did the raptors.

According to Mark, short-eared owls, which usually don't nest in the islands but migrate through and winter over, found the grasslands a convenient grocery that year and stayed to reproduce. He adds that the rabbit population is once again on the upswing and that the short-eared owls are gone.

The short-eareds may be gone, but larger raptors, especially, continue to scan the grasslands for grub, mostly the long-eared, twitchy-nosed type. Boulders left by the glacier are scattered over the ground, and Mark points out that many are favorite perches for birds of prey, whose guano deposits nourish the lichen and create large green, orange, and yellow patches.

Author of the popular field guide *Birding in the San Juan Islands*, Mark has a few concerns about the local raptor population, including a suspicion that the red-tails and great horned owls are suffering a rollback in their numbers, possibly as a result of escalating development. "Open space is diminishing here in the islands," he says, noting that eagles, especially, are "on the top of everybody's mind. The shoreline's being sliced up into so many tiny lots and being so intensively developed that eagles get pushed out of nest sites and favorite roosting and hunting perches."

The eagles, however, seem to have some aptitude for adapting to human activity. Once the bustle has burnt itself out, Mark says, the balds often return to former nest sites that now overlook buildings instead of brush. Whether or not that will be a consistent or successful pattern, he feels, is still open to question.

Likewise, he has noticed a similar adaptation in that Cyrano of our rocky shores, the black oystercatcher. Both the bald eagle and the oystercatcher, he notes, are long-lived, territorial birds that were once extremely wary of people. "It seems they're coming back to areas now that they originally had been spooked away from," Mark says. He recalls observing a flock of oystercatchers seemingly unruffled by the launching of thirty or more kayaks as they single-mindedly pursued their territorial disputes in Smallpox Bay.

One unique seabird that *has* likely suffered from human impact (in the form of commercial fishing) is the puffin. "We don't have any scientific data to back this up," Mark cautions, "but there used to be an awful lot of puffins nesting in San Juan

County, and I think, with the advent of monofilament gill nets and drift nets, that the puffins just weren't able to deal with it." He explains that puffins have to be quite old before they're capable of reproducing and are able to rear only a single chick annually. If that effort fails, they don't get another chance that year.

In the summertime, islanders can spot the thick-billed "sea parrot" in his gaudy breeding colors, a long plume swept stylishly back from his eye. The birds are very tame, swimming unconcernedly up to boats if their foraging takes them in that direction, Mark says, adding that "puffins are relatively shallow divers, and they do operate around the depths where the gill nets work." To further back up his suspicions, he mentions a report from the Fish and Wildlife Service in Alaska which indicated that during the past winters, up to a quarter of the puffin population were being destroyed annually by the drift-net industry off the Alaska coast. Fortunately, Mark adds, there are far fewer drift nets in operation among the international fishing fleet, but much long-term damage has already been done.

Common murres, too, fall victim to the nets. While sailing during the summer's end, I've come upon what looked like dozens of buoys floating in the water but which were really the upturned white bellies of drowned murres. The experience is unfortunately not uncommon. "I've gone out in a single day and found sixty of them," Mark says. "Right after a gill-net opening. You'll see them pulling birds out of nets occasionally and just tossing them overboard."

In 1993, the National Marine Fisheries Service put observers on commercial fishing boats to see what the birds' mortality rate was, an action inspired by the need to develop a fishery management plan for the endangered marbled murrelet. "It'll be interesting to see what was learned from that because up until now, all you could do was go out and watch the boats in action or talk to fishermen and try to get candid remarks on what the by-catch was on bird species," says Mark, adding, "It's unlikely that we'd have enough mortality of murres and auklets to really affect the populations around here, but the San Juan Islands' puffin population was never particularly large—perhaps around a hundred pairs—and they seem to be more susceptible with their foraging habits and dive profiles and such. They got nailed." He notes that a dozen or two tufted puffins may be found along the south side of Lopez during the summer months; occasional loners seen anywhere in the archipelago are almost certainly breeders commuting from Smith and Protection islands.

Returning now from the open water to the open meadow, Mark notes that here, too, problems exist. "A lot of the ground-dwelling, open-country birds have disappeared from the San Juan Islands." The western meadowlark, one of the few birds that sings lustily from a perch in the open, was once one of the most common nesting species of the county grasslands, at least up until 1960. It can still be sighted here, especially in the American Camp area during winter or migration, but it is no longer found in the islands as a breeder.

Native horned larks were also once common nesters of the grasslands, and though they still move through the area, they too no longer make the island meadows their breeding ground. The nonnative Eurasian skylark, first introduced by the English on Vancouver Island, remains a permanent resident and in fact is not known to nest anywhere in the U.S. other than at American Camp. However, according to Mark, it too has suffered a major rollback in its population, although its incredible song still haunts the area, especially during courtship time. "It goes on forever, all these complex notes coming down out of the sky."

Mark's love for birds began when he was a youngster in the suburbs of Detroit. Suburban wildlife was mostly to be found by railroad track easements, where a small greenbelt of trees yielded such wonders as cardinals and blue jays. "For some reason," he says, "I got very excited about seeing those things." Encouraged in his interest by a mother who showered him with natural history books, he was an avid birder by the time he reached junior high: "When my friends were going out to football practice and such, I was going to the woods tracking foxes in snow or identifying birds." He grins. "I took a lot of heat for it; it wasn't a cool thing to do."

After veering off on a premed track for a while, Mark rekindled his interest in field ornithology by traveling to different natural areas, sometimes by kayak. Eventually he reenrolled in college and completed his book on San Juan birds while a student at Evergreen State, earning thirty-two credits for the project.

After the book was published, he became county coordinator for the Washington Breeding Bird Atlas project, an ambitious attempt to record every breeding species of bird in the county. He also works on the photo-ID database for the local minke whale population and oversees Sea Quest Expeditions, which runs kayak trips in the San Juans, the Sea of Cortez, and Alaska: "Back in '89, a friend and I decided we wanted to start our own little program of natural history education," he says. "Sea kayaks were a great way to introduce people to the marine environment." Earnings from the trips help fund research projects, which normally receive little monetary support unless they focus on a commercially valuable species. "Basically," explains Mark, "we all feel that there's no funding available from any kind of government organization anymore and that we have to find ourselves a little niche, an occupation, that keeps us in enough funding that we can do our own projects on the side."

One of those projects included a novel attempt to reintroduce the western bluebird to the islands. This beautiful bird with the blue back and chestnut breast is another species that has almost completely disappeared from the islands because of competition from the European starling. According to Mark, the last breeding pair was reported on Lopez in 1964; now the bird is seen only rarely on its migratory route.

Trails of bluebird nesting boxes have been established elsewhere to help faltering populations, but in the islands, the problem had a hopeless twist to it. "In San Juan County, the bluebirds were already wiped out," says Mark. "They couldn't breed successfully as nest sites were completely co-opted by starlings, and the resident population just vanished. So we had no base to work from. There was just this tiny relict population on a couple of the Gulf Islands." Whether or not the Gulf Island birds would ever reach the San Juans was open to question; however, there was no question that it would be many years before the Canadian numbers were built up sufficiently again, even with help from British Columbian birders.

Unwilling to wait for time and chance to blow the bluebirds back this way, Mark and fellow San Juan Islander Ken McCann (see "Ken McCann: Walking in the Garden of Whales") hatched an innovative plan to help. Having no core group of bluebirds to encourage with nesting boxes, they instead placed bluebird eggs into the nests of surrogate parents such as English sparrows (poetic justice indeed). Mark points out that it's not unusual to transplant the eggs of one species to another's nest, but although it had been tried with birds such as whooping cranes, to his knowledge it had never been tried with bluebirds.

In 1989, twenty eggs were taken from a bluebird colony down at Fort Lewis and put into the surrogate nests of English sparrows, swallows, and a house wren on San Juan Island. Eight eventually hatched, with the most success coming from the nests of violet-green swallows and the sparrows. The wren rejected the eggs, and the barn swallows deserted the infiltrated nests to start over with new ones.

Mark was disappointed with the results, but he still feels that the project has merit and that it's just a matter of finding the time and funds to try it again. "It took so much more observer effort to watch the sites than we had available to us. Without rallying a lot of people to participate in the project, you can't really do it properly."

In the meantime, a lot of nesting boxes are out and waiting. Mark and others concerned with the survival of island birds will see that the boxes are checked and maintained. The birds are worth the effort, he feels.

"Birds epitomize the exuberance of life on this planet," he says. "I just think they're great."

# Chapter 9

# REFUGE AREAS

IN THE SAN JUAN ISLANDS, a number of areas have been given special status to protect their habitats and wildlife. The U.S. Fish and Wildlife Service has jurisdiction over the San Juan National Wildlife Refuge and Wilderness Area, and the Nature Conservancy oversees several islands within its San Juan Preserve. Let's take a look at these two systems and at some of the wildlife they're designed to protect.

Eighty-four islands, rocks, and reefs make up the San Juan National Wildlife Refuge and Wilderness Area. All are closed to the public except for Matia Island, north of Orcas, and Turn Island, near Friday Harbor. Many of the refuge areas support breeding colonies of birds such as glaucous-winged gulls, pelagic and double-crested cormorants, oystercatchers, rhinoceros auklets, pigeon guillemots, and tufted puffins. For those of you who explore the islands by boat, it's important to observe the restrictions placed on these areas. Stay at least 200 yards off so as not to disturb nesting or resting birds or seals on haulouts. Alarmed birds may abandon nests, leaving the eggs vulnerable to raids by gulls, crows, and ravens, and stampeding seals may trample their young.

Many folks are exploring the San Juans now by sea kayak, and although this can be one of the best ways to see island wildlife, kayakers must remember that seals on haulouts can easily be panicked by boats that to them may resemble orca pods. (For an excellent discussion on this topic, nonbelievers should read Winston Shaw's article "Seals and Sea Kayaks," in the Spring 1991 issue of *Sea Kayaker* magazine.) Kayakers should not consider their sport noninvasive and themselves consequently exempt from restrictions but should keep far away from haulouts.

Some of our most flamboyant-looking birds frequent the refuge areas. *Black oystercatchers* nest on the offshore islets in the spring, although beach walkers may also see them poking among rocks closer in during the nonbreeding season. This inhabitant of the rocky shore is easily identified by a strong bright-red bill (twice the length of its head) used to break open the shells of mollusks and pry limpets off rocks.

Rhinoceros auklets and tufted puffins also breed on refuge islets and are always a special treat to see when you're out boating in the summer. The first has white, feathery head plumes and a small, upright "rhino" horn at the base of its bill in the breeding season. It uses this unique bill, as well as its feet, to scrape out a nesting burrow sometimes as long as 20 feet into the sides of sandy cliffs.

Puffins, too, dig burrows for nesting on rocky offshore refuges, and their plumage is even more fantastic than the rhino's. These seabirds have yellow plumes that sweep out from the eyes and around the back of the head, as well as a bizarre, parrotlike bill with yellow and orange plates that eventually are shed, along with the plumes, after the breeding season. Here in the islands, we see the puffins only in their summer breeding plumage, for the birds head out to sea in the winter.

An alcid less flashily attired but much more commonly seen is the *pigeon guille-mot*, which nests in the crevices and burrows of offshore rocks and refuges. If the tufted puffin is also known as the "sea parrot" for its thick bill, the pigeon guillemot is commonly called the "sea pigeon" because of its somewhat similar shape. Look for a black bird with red legs and feet and white wing patches. These birds use their short wings to "fly" underwater and capture food. Listen for a low whistling sound or sometimes a warning hiss if you approach too closely during the breeding season.

The Nature Conservancy is a private land conservation group that oversees Yellow, Sentinel, Goose, and Deadman islands (as well as 400 acres on Waldron Island) in its San Juan preserve system. Only Yellow Island is open to the public for nature viewing. The other areas are closed off completely for the sake of nesting eagles, peregrines, and seabirds as well as for their fragile ecology.

Yellow Island, however, is a gem well worth seeing if you have the opportunity. This 11-acre island was purchased by the Conservancy in 1980 and serves as home base for the management of other Conservancy sanctuaries in the San Juans.

*Black oystercatcher*

133

Treat yourself to a spring visit to view the magnificent wildflower displays. Yellow Island supports over eighty-five species of flowering plants, including white fawn lilies, shooting stars, Indian paintbrush, and blue camas. Although these species grow throughout the San Juans, their presence on Yellow Island is particularly dense, in part because of the absence of plant-munching animals and the fresh water necessary to their survival. Even cactus has bloomed in these meadows, impressing those visitors lucky enough to see them with large yellow blossoms that lasted only a day.

Yellow Island is only a twenty-minute boat ride from Friday Harbor. People are allowed to visit the island in small numbers if they obey the posted rules, and the Nature Conservancy also offers guided field trips to members during the spring bloom. Visitors are asked to remain on designated trails, refrain from collecting plants or animals, including clams, and visit only during the daylight hours.

Flowers may be the island's most famous wildlife attraction, but they are not the only one. Watch for bald eagles in the island's tall snags, harlequin ducks along its rocky shoreline, rufous hummingbirds, minks, and river otters. Harbor seals haul out on the island's two spits, and orca and minke whales, as well as porpoises, can often be observed offshore.

All San Juan shores, from the refuge islands to the ferry-served, are designated a state marine biological preserve, and state law prohibits taking or destroying any living specimens except for food use. Marine mammals are further protected under the federal Marine Mammal Protection Act of 1972, which makes it illegal to intentionally harass or disturb these animals. Harassment includes approaching hauled-out seals closely enough to spook them into the water and pursuing whales with boats.

Federal whale-watch guidelines prohibit vessels from approaching marine mammals more closely than 100 yards. Aircraft should not fly lower than 1000 feet above marine mammals, and operators of either boats or planes should not perform any action that substantially disrupts the normal behavior of these animals. Do not separate whales from their offspring with your boat, and approach whales slowly from the side, traveling parallel to the pod and no faster than its slowest swimmers. Should the whales approach your boat and you're either not moving or on a course parallel to the pod, you are not in violation as long as your boat stays still or else moves back outside the 100-yard limit.

You may possibly see vessels following the whales more closely than these guidelines permit. Whale scientists have permits from the National Marine Fisheries Service that allow them to get closer in; their boats are marked as research vessels with a yellow flag displaying their permit number. Should you observe an unmarked boat pursuing whales or otherwise disturbing marine mammals, record the vessel's name and identification number and report it to the enforcement division of the National Marine Fisheries Service at (206) 526-6133, or call the Whale Hotline, 1-800-562-8832.

# MARY HANSEN
## In the Steps of the Great Spirit

*It was long ago . . . so long ago. In this time, everyone was the same. The animals and the humans were equal. Children could see the faces in the flowers. The people's imagination could penetrate the plants. Our people understood the animals to be their brothers and sisters. And the animals and people could talk to one another."*

—from "The Night People," a traditional Samish teaching story

In the old times, tribes of the Pacific Northwest believed that long before the first humans appeared, the earth was home to a race of animal people who could shed their skins or furs at will. Today, the raven, salmon, eagle, beaver, and other animals figure in Indian tales such as the Samish story "The Night People," which not only tells how beavers came to Fidalgo Island's Pass Lake but also illustrates several lessons, among them the need to live in harmony and cooperation, as the beavers do.

The tribes found much to emulate in the lives of animals; their young men went on quests to discover the animal spirits that would guide them. Mary Hansen, an elder of the Samish tribe, remembers listening to a friend tell in detail about his own quest, from which he returned with a frog spirit. "Henry used to hop around sometimes," she laughs. "But when it came to the winter dance, that was his spirit. There are some dancers who have a bear spirit. There's one man in particular, a Swinomish Indian, a heavy-set man. When he lets out his cry to start singing and he starts lumbering along, he does look like a bear. One friend from Canada has the loon spirit, and her song is just piercing. I've never known of a dancer who didn't have his or her spirit related to an animal."

Animal spirits were found in sacred places such as Mount Erie on Fidalgo Island. "I've never been up to Mount Erie becase it's so spiritual," says Mary, adding that her son, however, came back from the mountain one time and told her that while up there, he had heard the song of a friend who had died.

"Mount Erie was a sacred place," Mary says softly. "Just to look up there now and see all that electronic hardware and stuff . . ." It's difficult for her, she acknowledges, and then she shrugs. "Sometimes it's better to say nothing at all about how special something is to you, because it gets overrun."

The Samish, who today number about six hundred and maintain a tribal office in Anacortes, claim the San Juan Islands as their traditional and spiritual home.

135

They are now a landless tribe fighting in the courts for federal recognition and an "affirmation of our status as human beings and Indians and not the bastards the federal government has called us," says Mary.

There is no anger in her voice, only a little weariness. The tribe struggles to keep its traditions and sensibilities alive in its young and hopes one day to have a cultural center at their old Ship Harbor site on Fidalgo Island. (The Port of Anacortes, which owns the land, wanted to put the center by the city's steam train attraction instead, but as Mary drily notes, "We're not a theme park. We're not going to go out and attack the railroad.")

Great-granddaughter of a tribal medicine woman, she has seen a lot in her seventy years, "some of it good, some of it very distressing." She speaks mostly of the sadness, of a skull dug up on Guemes, of Anacortes's incinerator rising out of an old tribal site, of development along a Samish trail from Mount Erie to Shannon Point and the great unrest, or the "physical sense things are not right," connected with it.

She does not claim a power of vision others have claimed, but she is nonetheless sensitive to spiritual disturbances. For instance, she keeps an old cooking basket covered with a red cloth, because of her feeling that it wants to return home, wherever that may be, possibly somewhere up the Skagit River. "And my other baskets— I can't say they talk to me, but sometimes I can smell smoke from one of my great-grandmother's cooking baskets, just this little aura of wood smoke." The unrest over the development project was "almost like a rush of dizziness coming through here," she says. "I had a prickly-skin feeling and knew that the spirits were disturbed."

Her unease and that of other tribal members was the moving force behind a position paper put out by the Samish on the detrimental effects of a glut of hydropower permits proposed for the Skagit and Sauk rivers. Under the Native American Religious Freedom Act, government and other agencies must consult with tribes on projects in "sensitive" areas, but the Samish refused their approval of the hydro projects until a study showing their *cumulative effect* was made available. They were told there was no money for such a study.

The Samish tribe's concern for the effects of various forms of development on the total picture extends to the San Juan archipelago, all of which the tribe lays claim to and holds dear. "If we had had the money and the staff, we probably would have objected to every development that's gone in on Fidalgo," she says. "I don't know how Lopez is faring these days. San Juan's an obscenity."

Samish tribal villages once existed on Guemes, Samish, and Fidalgo islands. Families made seasonal food migrations through the San Juans, carrying shelters made of cattails, gathering camas roots, wild carrots, and onions, and fishing off places like Cattle Point and Iceberg Point.

Native plants were heavily used by the tribe for everything from tonics to smokes to baskets. Camas bulbs were an important food staple dug up after the plants had finished blooming in the late spring and then usually steamed in pits and stored in cattail bags. Because of their sweet taste, the bulbs were often combined with other foods, such as soapberries, which were whipped to a froth and then sweetened with the camas for an ice-cream-like treat. The Samish also roasted bracken rhizomes and pounded them into flour for bread. Salal berries were mashed together and dried in small cakes, as were thimbleberries and blackberries.

Of greatest importance to the Samish and other Northwest tribes was the cedar. Almost no part of this beneficent tree was wasted. Baskets were made from its roots, and from the trunks came canoes, house posts, roof planks, and more. The bark was finely shredded for clothing, towels, cradle bedding, and sanitary pads, and the tree's long, thin branches were twisted into rope.

The Samish have a special use for a cedar tree that shows signs of having "power." A strongly spiritual people, the tribe makes rectangular boards with four handholds on them; the boards are believed to have special powers in the hands of certain people. These powers include the ability to find lost objects or people, although they apparently aren't limited to crisis situations. ("One thing I was taught early on is that a man takes his hat off," says Mary, "and I've seen hats literally lifted off with the boards 15 feet away.")

If the cedar was for the tribe their most valued plant, its animal equivalent was the salmon. In the old times, Northwest natives believed salmon were eternal beings who lived in a house in the sea. Each year, the salmon people put on fish skins and offered themselves as food to the tribes, who welcomed them back with a special ceremony in the spring. Later, the tribes returned the fish skeletons to the sea so that the underwater spirits could once again claim their old bodies.

The dwindling salmon runs are of special concern today. "In our area, we had a late run of kings," says Mary, "but down at Willapa Harbor, they're having five-year chinooks come back, and that's a four-year cycle. They didn't come in last June, and they're coming in this year late. Now that has to be caused by the fact that the waters are not hospitable." She pauses and considers. "Indian life was very much measured by time and seasons. When to go out to Lopez, when to fish off Guemes, or when to go to Orcas. The seasons are changing; I hear this from fishermen. They're very much aware something is wrong."

She and other tribal members suggest a moratorium on development to allow time to investigate its effect on the whole. "It's like everybody's life cycle is out of whack," she says. "The fish come back at a little different time, and the run is split. Ordinarily, when the Fraser River sockeye came around from the Hein Bank, it was in a steady stream. I think this year there were about three days and then nothing. Then some more came through, but they weren't Fraser River. So the question is, What happened to the Fraser River sockeye that should have been coming through our waters?"

For the Samish, their relation to the water is the vital one. They depended heavily not only on salmon but also on shellfish, gathering clams, mussels, and oysters in woven cedar-strip baskets. The tribe was careful not to overclam, and they also took care not to defile the water with their body wastes; to do so was a serious offense that resulted in banishment from the tribe. "Without water, there is no being," says Mary. "Our trees breathe so long as the water flows." The Samish always expected the water to be eternal, but now she says she is not so certain.

Furthermore, she is afraid the Samish, the original caretakers of this area, will one day be held responsible for its ruin.

The Samish creation story takes place at Deception Pass on Fidalgo Island and identifies the tribe as the first people, from whom all other Northwest tribes are descended. Samish belief holds that the tribe was placed in this area with a mandate by the Creator to care for its natural resources.

One of Mary's great-aunts tells of a time when the Creator walked the earth and left a footprint on one of the islands. Indeed, a people so bountifully blessed for thousands of years here must feel singled out. But along with the blessing comes a grave charge to care for the land and waters as the Samish themselves have been cared for.

Mary is only too well aware of the responsibility. "I think," she says quietly but firmly, "it's time to show respect."

# PART 3

# Furthering the Relationship

## Resources for Wildlife Study

*"The conservation of waters, forest,
mountains and wildlife are far more
than saving terrain. It is the conservation
of the human spirit which is the goal."*

*—Sigurd Olson*

# Chapter 10

# PADILLA BAY RESERVE

OH, WHAT MIGHT HAVE BEEN.

Picture, if you will, a power plant on the tip of Samish Island. A magnesium smelter by the bay. Or perhaps no bay at all. Put the dikes out another couple of miles west of the existing ones, from Samish and Hat islands to the Highway 20 bridge, and see the bay disappear into 12,000 acres of farmland, with a railroad spur joining a deepwater port on Hat. Still not right? Try yet another option: dredge channels through the bay and create sites for hundreds of homes with private docks in a development described as the "Venice of the Northwest."

Over the years, there have been nearly as many visions of Padilla Bay as fish in her waters. Some were shouted down; others were tried but failed. In the early 1920s, the major diking project out to Hat Island was begun but was finally abandoned when the dike wouldn't hold and finances were exhausted. Today, hanging on the theatre wall of the reserve's interpretive center, a huge canvas of what might have been is all that remains of an ambitious dream.

A project that flourished for a while was oyster production. Over 900 1-acre parcels in Padilla Bay were subdivided and managed by a company that seeded the plots with oyster spat (larvae) and sold them to investors who would share in the rewards of harvest. But by the early 1940s, that dream too had disappeared, defeated by heavy sediments and the predacious oyster drill.

About twenty years after the oyster project dissolved, a Seattle company bought up over 8,000 acres of tidelands, the majority of which they hoped to develop into the dredge-and-fill housing community mentioned above. However, with the passage of the Washington State Shoreline Management Act in 1971, coastal areas became protected or otherwise managed by local and state governments, and in August 1980, portions of Padilla Bay were named a national reserve, effectively limiting development plans. The corporation engaged in a twelve-year lawsuit over the value and taking of its holdings, and the case was finally settled in 1993 after two reviews by the state supreme court and a lengthy jury trial. The $3.6 million settlement added 8,004 acres of tidelands to the reserve, nearly tripling its size.

About 900 acres of tidelands within the reserve's original proposed boundary still remain in private ownership, and negotiations continue with willing sellers for the purchase of those lands. Although it may seem surprising to us now, tidelands were sold and leased by the state up until 1970; at one time, a survey of the bay showed 1,746 individual parcels. Selling off tidelands to individuals or for port and commercial activities was a common practice because "historically, we didn't realize the biological value of some of these areas and what they mean to commercial species like crab or salmon," points out reserve director Terry Stevens, "and to others that are critical as linkages to those species, or just to creatures we appreciate simply because they're here."

Today, the visions of farmlands, industrial plants, marinas, and private homes dissolve into the shining waters of Washington's only estuarine reserve.

Just what *is* an estuary? Simply, it is a place where fresh water meets and mixes with salt water. Long ago, Padilla was a deepwater bay, but sediments from the Skagit River slowly filled it in to create the shallow estuary there today. The bay receives its fresh water no longer from the river, which now empties into Skagit Bay, but from several agricultural drainage sloughs that follow old river channels.

The most unusual feature of the Padilla Bay estuary, the main reason it was selected to be a national reserve, is its huge eelgrass meadow. Nearly 8,000 acres of the 10,700-acre reserve are covered with the plant, which looks like a seaweed but is not. Seaweeds reproduce by spores, but eelgrass flowers, spreading its seeds in an underwater world that is one of the most biologically rich on earth.

Two species of eelgrass grow in Padilla Bay. *Zostera marina*, the native plant, has broad leaves that grow to six feet long. *Zostera japonica* is an introduced species that came in from Japan with the oyster-farming project in the 1930s. It can be distinguished from the native species by its short, narrow leaves and its preferred growth area higher up on the beach. Research so far indicates that the two species can coexist quite well, as they favor different habitats.

After the passage of the Shoreline Management Act, the state began looking at estuaries and evaluating them. Out of a dozen sites, Padilla Bay was nominated as a reserve because it was unpolluted, almost totally undeveloped, and had the state's largest bed of eelgrass. Eelgrass meadows elsewhere are generally much smaller, mainly because the optimum conditions for their growth simply don't exist as they do at Padilla. In most bays around Puget Sound, the beach slopes out into the water, and at low tide, grasses on the sloping part of the beach die as the area dries up. Likewise, they can't grow farther out in the bay, because the water is too deep to allow enough light in to stimulate growth. Hence, in most areas, eelgrass is limited to a narrow subtidal zone where it can have both the water and the light it needs.

Padilla, on the other hand, is a large, shallow bay where enough light penetrates the water even at high tide to encourage eelgrass to grow. Some bays such as the Skagit are also shallow but don't produce huge eelgrass beds because sediments from the river cloud the water and restrict the light.

At low tide, when Padilla's water sometimes recedes all the way to Hat Island and the view looks to be nothing but mud, the grasses are still there, flat but full of water. "It's pretty amazing to be out there at low tide and have all this water draining out of the mudflats, and yet you walk into an area where there's a seagrass bed, and you're in water up to your thighs," says Sharon Riggs, program coordinator for the reserve. The lush plant life that sponges up the water also has an extensive root system that anchors it to the muddy substrates and helps to stabilize the soils in the bay. Without these rhizome mats, ocean currents would scour the bottom of the bay by regularly carrying off mud and sand.

All well and good, but is that the only reason this weedy-looking plant rates having a reserve around it? Not exactly. Far more important is that the annual growth and decay of the eelgrass makes a hearty, life-giving soup for bay animals from crab to waterfowl, which feed not only on the living plant but also on detritus, a combination of the dead grass and bacteria.

The estuary meadow is also home, nursery, and hotel to a host of animals. When the tide is in, gases in the seagrass blades raise them to the bay's surface, slowing the water action and creating a calm habitat for the sea slugs, anemones, isopods, and amphipods that live on the blades and for the clams, crab, shrimp, sole, and salmon that live among them for protection.

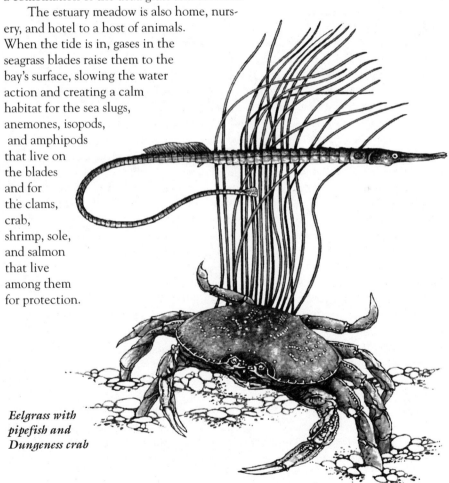

*Eelgrass with pipefish and Dungeness crab*

Juvenile Dungeness crabs come here to molt (shed their shells), and salmon use the estuary as a "halfway house" between fresh and salt water, fattening up on plankton before their ocean plunge.

People, too, have long benefited from eelgrass. The Kwakiutls prepared the plant as a feast food, dipping the roots and bases of the leaves in fish oil and then eating them raw. Other tribes used the rhizomes in their steaming pits to flavor meat or pounded them into cakes, which were dried and stored for the winter.

Eelgrass has also been used for weaving, doll stuffing, wall insulation, fuel, and even in cigars. Sharon notes that in the Netherlands six hundred years ago, people used it to make dikes, "piling up huge heaps to hold the water back."

As with so many other things, eelgrass became more widely valued once it was lost. In 1930, 90 percent of the eelgrass along the North Atlantic coast was wiped out by a disease that may have been caused by a rise in water temperatures. Largely because of the loss of the grass, bird populations along the Atlantic Flyway dropped, banks started eroding faster, and turbid waters suffocated many fish and shellfish.

To form a firsthand acquaintance with some of the fish and crustaceans that depend on the estuary, I headed down to the beach with Alex, the reserve's education coordinator, who leads beach seines twice monthly during the summer. He and a helper waded into the water carrying two wooden poles attached to a net weighted along the bottom and strung with floats across the top. The two dragged the net while walking sideways to the shore and then turned and pulled it up to the beach. Quickly, our group dropped to hands and knees and plunked the slippery catch into waiting water-filled buckets. "A lot easier said than done!" yelped one man trying to capture a wriggling pipefish.

Many of the catch were juveniles, tiny creatures that use the estuary as a nursery. "Look at that itsy-bitsy shrimp," shrieked a small girl. Shrimp, hermit crabs, baby flounders, sticklebacks, sculpins, and small transparent fish with shining eyes swam in the buckets. Threadlike wisps of baby pipefish wove in and out among the others; someday their slender green bodies would look like free-floating eelgrass topped with tiny heads.

It is not only fish and crabs that forage in these watery meadows but a wide variety of birds as well. Snow geese, brant, and dabbling ducks (mallards, wigeons, teals) feed directly on the grasses, whereas the diving ducks (loons, grebes, goldeneyes) prefer the detritus.

The brant's breeding grounds are in Alaska, and just before migrating south to Baja in the fall, the geese gather to fatten up on the 22,000 acres of eelgrass at Izembek Lagoon in the Aleutian Islands. Alex's voice grows reverent as he notes that Izembek has almost three times the amount of eelgrass in Padilla Bay. "I would just love to see what that place looks like."

The brant arrive in Padilla Bay usually in late October, depending on the weather up north. (If northern temperatures are mild, they may come in later.) Some winter over at the bay; others rest and feed and then continue south. In

March or April, the number of brant at the bay may increase into the tens of thousands as flocks head north again to their breeding grounds.

"We've got approximately one-half the flyway population using Padilla Bay as a fueling station on their way to California and Mexico and on their return to Alaska," says Terry. He notes that the hunting season on brant was closed in the early 1980s when the locally wintering brant population dropped drastically to only 1,000 birds. Shooting was banned and the brant's gravel spots were declared off-limits by the Department of Wildlife to help the population recover (brant need gravel in their diets to help them digest the eelgrass). Today their numbers are once again healthy, with the annual average of wintering brant now between 12,000 and 15,000 birds.

Wildlife preservation and hunting may seem a strange partnership, but the reserve is not a "hands-off" sanctuary. "When the whole national program was set up, it was called the Estuarine Sanctuary Program," says Terry. "It was very confusing, because the intent of the program was research and education. The word *sanctuary* implies, 'Stay away, don't do anything.'" So Congress changed the name in 1984 from the National Estuarine Sanctuary program to the National Estuarine Research Reserve Program."

Although certain areas are closed to preserve critical waterfowl habitat, the rest of the publicly owned property in the reserve is open to hunting, fishing, hiking, and boating. Foremost, however, it remains a natural field laboratory to enhance our understanding of estuaries and improve their management. Research focuses on figuring out just how an estuary works. For instance, how do these shallow intertidal areas serve the rest of Puget Sound, and what values do they have that are not yet apparent?

One research project involved scientists from the UW School of Fisheries who studied the connection between eelgrass and the population of Dungeness crab in the bay. What they found is that the estuary nourishes and shelters juvenile crabs for their first year of life. After a three- to four-month planktonic stage, pea-sized infant crabs settle to the bottom of the eelgrass (which may shelter up to a million crab in only 2$^{1}/_{2}$ acres). Predation by birds and fish normally takes about 95 to 99 percent of the population during the next year. Survivors winter over in the eelgrass beds and then move out to the deeper waters of the bay, where males generally reach legal harvest size in three or four years.

Areas around Puget Sound have lost as much as 95 percent of their eelgrass habitat due to dredging and industrial or residential filling. Data such as the reserve's crab study will be used to forestall or mitigate any further loss. With the value of estuaries generally recognized today, outright destruction of tidelands by dredging or filling is no longer a major threat, but other, less obvious threats still exist.

Since Padilla Bay is bordered by oil refineries to the west and farmlands to the east, potential pollution from both of these sources is a concern. The reserve receives a modest amount of federal funds for monitoring the health of the waters.

145

Working with local farmers, scientists did a two-year pesticide study on seventeen chemicals used in the fields, drawing samples from the water and bottom sediments. "We couldn't find but one or two of them, and we found those at levels that weren't as damaging as herbicides," says Terry.

Oil spills are another threat, prompting the reserve to regularly document the hydrocarbon content in the bay sediments. "We've done many sample stations looking at sediments for hydrocarbons, and we haven't found any comprehensive problems in Padilla Bay." But Terry goes on to note that these studies monitor the "chronic effect. The acute effect would be a major spill from a regional shipment of oil." Tankers coming into the refineries often draw too much water to immediately dock at the wharves and must discharge the oil onto barges farther out.

"Usually when you're having a problem with losing oil or a petroleum product, it's when you're transferring it," says Terry. "Seagrass habitats are very sensitive to oil. Rocky surfaces can be cleaned up pretty easily. Sand and gravel can be excavated off the face of a beach. But when you get into seagrass beds, you can't steam-clean them. You can't wipe them off, and you can't walk on them. All you do is push the material down farther into the sediments and delay its decomposition." The view now on how to deal with a spill in such a delicate habitat is simply not to deal with it. "Let it be, let it decompose," says Terry, at the same time recognizing that because of the visibility of the damage, that can be a hard course to defend.

The refineries have put together contingency plans for a spill, in conjunction with various agencies and reserve personnel who provided a detailed habitat map covering sensitive areas such as seagrass beds and harbor seal haulouts. For instance, says Terry, if a spill occurs in November, by using this map, "they know what to expect at that time of year, what key species are there, what

*Brant*

146

spawning areas and nesting areas." Two of the reserve's recent monitoring projects focused on what the tides and currents do at particular times of the day and year. "If you've got a tanker spill here, and it happens on a low tide just before a high tide sequence, is that going to push into the bay, and if so, where's it going to be carried before the tide changes?"

There is yet another threat to the bay that relates to human intervention: the infestation of a nonnative grass, Spartina. "Here at Padilla Bay, I believe it was brought in by hunters," says Terry. "They brought it in back in the thirties and planted it as an attraction and cover for waterfowl." Should Spartina eventually supplant the eelgrass, at least one species of waterfowl, the brant, would probably disappear from the bay.

Padilla Bay now has about twelve acres of Spartina, which, like eelgrass, spreads by rhizomes (underground stems), and it is difficult, if not impossible, to eradicate. "Manage is a much better word," says Terry, who goes on to describe possible management methods, such as biological controls or spraying: "We didn't kill any Spartina during recent trials with spraying, possibly because tidal action may have washed the spray off before it could take effect. We also tried it on some small plots of seagrass to see if spraying Spartina would also impact the seagrass, but it wasn't damaged, mainly because the seagrass in Padilla Bay is hardly ever totally dehydrated. Even at lowest low tide, it's so thick and dense it holds water like a sponge." Digging up the Spartina is as ineffective as trying to kill a sea star by chopping it up; the digging simply spreads it farther if pieces of the rhizome float free and root elsewhere.

Terry attended an international conference in Seattle on Spartina, where, almost to a person, the consensus was to redouble efforts to contain the plaguelike growth. Yet there was also a solitary suggestion that the Spartina might have some value. "The question is, Can this function with our other species and serve a purpose in Pacific Northwest habitats?" asks Terry. Noting that the final jury is still out, he remains cautiously open to the possibility of as yet unknown benefits while sharply aware of the present danger and the need to control it, especially if the plant begins producing seed, as it has down in Willapa Bay.

In Willapa, Spartina spread by rhizomes for thirty to forty years; then suddenly it began to produce viable seed. "In Willapa, it's growing out over the mudflats. It's running into the oyster grounds. The shorebirds are losing habitat," says Terry. "It grows in such density it traps sediments and builds landward, creating marshland." He points out that the typical gradient on the East Coast, where Spartina has long flourished, is first shoreline, then huge expanses of Spartina marsh plunging into deep channels. "They don't get wide-open barren mudflats like this. We don't have that complex of Spartina here. We're about to get it."

Spartina is not yet producing viable seed in Padilla Bay. Before it does, if it does, management methods may prove successful in at least slowing the spread. If not, in another twenty years or so, it may be necessary to visit the reserve's interpretive center to see the life that now flourishes in and around the bay.

The Breazeale–Padilla Bay interpretive center opened in 1982, two years after the establishment of the reserve, on the site of the Breazeale family's farm. Edna Breazeale and her brothers, Fred and Marcellus, decided to give the land to the state, and after her brothers died, Ms. Breazeale followed through on the family decision. A schoolteacher for over forty years, she desired that somehow the property be used for conservation education for children. The reserve's proximity to her land and its educational mandate suited perfectly, although "she admitted that watching the field get bulldozed for construction of the center was hard," says Terry. Two years later, though, "when the landscape had healed, school buses were rolling in and kids were using the building, the beach, and the fields—she just loved that."

A paper mural hangs in the center's fish room, one of many testimonies from schoolchildren who have enjoyed their visit to the estuary. The mural goes beyond simple thanks, however; the students have drawn their idea of the "perfect" estuary and provided an explicit set of laws to keep it that way: no gas motors, no net fishing, no hunting, no cutting down of trees. Shellfish limits. A filter to keep the water from the river pure.

Children easily fall in love with a place where they can thumb their noses at Mom and luxuriate in mud. The interpretive center stokes that excitement with close-up views of living estuary creatures in large aquariums, nonliving but lifelike displays of the area's mammals and raptors, and a hands-on room where children can mix up estuary "soup" and explore in a tidier but no less fun fashion. "The hands-on room was patterned after the discovery room at the Smithsonian, a huge room with artifacts in it, costumes, everything else." Terry laughs. "We didn't have quite their budget."

Terry worked on a committee to help design the building, "way before I ever thought I'd be working here." Hindsight would have provided a larger multipurpose room, with countertops and sinks all around the edges and microscope stations.

School groups are the biggest users of the center, but space limits the number who can visit at one time. The center is usually booked solid for the children's education programs: "Four years ago, we had 3,500 kids coming through our K–8 program. We were turning away more than that; we could not accommodate them." (The center also provides a high-school outreach program, which won a national award for excellence. "It's an interdisciplinary program. We can take it to English classes for writing, or we can take it to chemistry classes, biology classes, et cetera.") Students tend to fill up the weekdays, and on weekends, "it's parents and grandparents being led by students into this building," says Terry, who has heard more than one adult admit to being dragged to the center by his children.

Once they arrive, however, adults find plenty to hold their interest. The lecture hall features regular films about the estuary and related topics, and guest speakers talk about seagrasses, local birding, and nature drawing. The library is an excellent resource open to the public, although materials cannot be checked out, and the classroom holds an herbarium of native plants.

To see the plants' living counterparts, walk outside and take the upland trail.

But first borrow a guide from the front desk to fully appreciate the ³/4-mile hike through fields, shrubs, and woods, part of the 64-acre Breazeale bequest.

Walk quietly and slowly up the winding paved path into a dense setting of cedars and firs. Listen for the chitter of a Douglas squirrel, the *scree* of a soaring red-tail. Look back toward the center past green and gold fields to the sparkling blue bay and the distant hump of Mount Erie. The serene picture has a jarring note, for sticking up across the bay are the stacks of the Texaco and Shell refineries, where crude petroleum is processed into fuels. Reserve and refineries share the same waters, working together to ensure that the ticklish pairing remains a peaceful one.

Two other trails focus on the bay itself. One leads west from the center and under the road to an observation deck overlooking the bay, with a steep circular staircase from the deck to the beach. The other is the Padilla Bay dike-top trail, which opened early in 1990. Hard-packed gravel covers the popular 2¹/4-mile trail winding along the estuary and marked with interpretive signs and an occasional bench. The trail was a cooperative effort between Skagit County Parks and Recreation, Dike District 8, and the Padilla Bay Reserve and was built by the county with grants from sources including the Department of Natural Resources and the Department of Ecology.

Snaking its way through Indian Slough and up along the bay to the outskirts of the town of Bayview, the trail meanders through marshes, mudflats, fields, and sloughs (transitional areas where brackish water mixes with water from the open bay). Broken pilings jut up from the mud, and it's not uncommon to see great blue herons standing motionless in the shallows as if they too were forever anchored.

When the tide is in, watch for the smooth heads of harbor seals, as well as puddle ducks, brant, trumpeter swans, Canada geese, kingfishers, scoters, and goldeneyes. When the tide is out, you can find clams, mud shrimp, and other invertebrates buried in the huge mudflat. Keep an eye out for shorebirds such as sandpipers, dowitchers, and yellowlegs, and don't forget to scan for raptors (look for bald eagles soaring or perched in the tops of trees along the shore, northern harriers swooping over the fields for voles, and falcons stooping shorebirds).

As you walk the trails and feast on the life teeming in and around the estuary, close your eyes for a moment and picture what might have been: houses, a smelter, marinas, and more. Then open your eyes and drink in the water, the birds, the grasses waving in the currents like floating forests, and take just one more moment to give thanks.

---

The Padilla Bay National Estuarine Research Reserve can be reached by taking the Bayview-Edison Road north off Highway 20. The Breazeale Interpretive Center is at 1043 Bayview-Edison Road, (360) 428-1558. Hours are 10 A.M. to 5 P.M., Wednesday to Sunday. A quarterly newsletter describing programs and events is available for free on request.

# GLEN ALEXANDER
## *Hunting Miracles in Mud*

Clouds hid the Cascades when Glen Alexander headed north out of Seattle for the first time. He was alarmed: "I was going across all this flat land and I was thinking, Oh my God, I thought there were mountains around here." Today as he drives to work at the Padilla Bay interpretive center, enjoying the bald eagles and red-tails that punctuate his route, he savors the shape of the land. "I find there's a real beauty to the flats that is unique. Maybe it's more subtle, I'm not exactly sure." Although appreciative of mountain vistas, he reserves his strongest sympathies for a landscape that soothes rather than startles. "The flats touch my heart more."

He wonders if his fancy for flatland might stem from having grown up in the Midwest. No matter how his penchant developed, Alex, as he's more often known, seems happily at home in hip boots on the mudflats of the Padilla Bay estuary. During the summer, he takes advantage of the extreme low tides during the new and full moons each month to encourage folks to share his fervor and indulge that most primal of urges: to slop about ankle-deep in mud. Not only is it fun for the feet, but it's a chance to meet oodles of ooze dwellers and beat the lurking "mud monster" at his game.

Mud monster? Alex shows a group of would-be explorers a child's shoe that was found on the flats. "It was stuck in the mud and there was nobody in it!" he says, eyes wide. "This child felt the mud monster sucking on his boot, then pulled his foot up like this . . ." His voice scales upward in shuddering emphasis: "Don't *do* that." He shows how to break the suction—"toe down, heel up"—and then passes along a "magic bag" that holds not only the shoe but also a shovel, a barnacle-covered rock, a plastic six-pack ring, and a limpet shell. All spark discussions on proper behavior in the mudflat environment, which, Alex points out, is home to many shy creatures who have not invited us to visit. "It's kind of like if a bunch of people came over to your house and didn't knock or anything," he says, stomping across the room and feigning gross unconcern as he flings wide an imaginary door, "but just came in, opened the refrigerator, ate a bunch of food, and made a mess in the kitchen."

So that we won't be guilty of such rude behavior, we learn how to fill in all the holes, turn the rocks back over again, pick up any trash, and leave limpets attached to the rocks. Most of the group are already familiar with the rules, except perhaps regarding the limpets. Alex explains that when the tide comes in, a limpet leaves its rock to graze, but when the tide recedes, it hurries back to its special spot, a scar on the rock into which its shell fits perfectly, forming a tight seal at low tide. "It's a problem for an underwater animal to have the water go away two times every day," he says. "But this one has solved the problem—it sticks on the rock and keeps a little water inside." What happens if you were to pull the limpet off the rock, obviously, is that it loses the water. You can't stick the limpet back onto the rock, and even if you place it close to its special spot, it may not be able to find its way back again. So limpets are off bounds.

But we hardly notice the prohibition, because the seemingly lifeless expanse of mud is full of sparks of life in the shapes of snails, hermit crabs, clams, worms, sponges, and tiny, shrimplike amphipods (small crustaceans such as beach fleas). Alex passes out an identification sheet and shows the group how to collect the minuscule mud aliens in a tray or an aquarium jar. There are seven of us on this warm, cloudy day, tightly tied into our yuckiest tennies and concentrating on our mantra, "Toe down, heel up." Alex, rumpled but professionally rigged out in wide-brimmed hat and waders, likes to keep the groups small, although he has taken out as many as thirty gung-ho mud muckers at a time.

Sometimes the enthusiasm is slow in coming, especially for the younger set, who start off with wrinkled-nosed cries of "Gross!" and "Yuck!"

"But generally they leave that behind," says Alex, whose favorite age groups are kindergarten and first grade. "I don't give them any feedback for that."

Alex's feedback focuses on the positive. Though he has walked this way countless times before, his voice never once betrays an overfamiliarity. Instead, our safari is punctuated with exclamations of "Oh, good find!" and "Hey, that's really neat!" as he zeroes in on the tiny miracles at our feet. He praises a young girl who comes up with yet another of several finds, this time a sponge. "It's always neat to get kids like that, and I always like to tell them, 'You're really good at this.' I want to encourage them to pursue that kind of activity."

As education coordinator for the center, Alex, along with his staff, also teaches the mini-explorer group, three- to five-year-olds who come for one hour once a month to learn about the mudflat. The lessons are mostly active: some playacting, storytelling, lots of hands-on chances to interact with the animals. Tots end up familiar with terms like *detritus, plankton,* and *amphipods* and use them appropriately. "They know this stuff, because it's all intertwined. When we're talking about eelgrass, we see amphipods, and we catch and feed them to the salmon in the fish tanks. They learn what those things are, that they're all interconnected," he says, adding, "We just try to keep looking at the concept of the mudflat from different angles."

Education efforts extend up through high school and beyond. Alex and others worked together to come up with a high school curriculum, which has received national acclaim, and have developed an outreach program that includes a computer network for people studying estuarine water quality.

Human impact on the water quality of the estuary was stressed to the group in an educational video that Alex helped to create (and that is for sale at the center). Bilge water pumped from a boat, used motor oil poured down a gutter, toxics put into a sink drain—all can end up in the estuary and poison the plants and animals.

Armed not with guns but with shovels, papers, trays, and jars, our safari begins at the eelgrass wrack, where dead plants and animals are deposited by the high tide every day. We look for eggs clinging to the blades of the two types of eelgrass: first the long-leaved, native *Zostera marina* and then the shorter species introduced from Japan, *Zostera japonica*. Another Japanese import is the mud snail, which covers the flats with twisted cone shells. "When you introduce a species, they can go crazy; you can get too many," Alex says. "Whatever predator eats these snails in their natural habitat doesn't exist here."

He explains that eelgrass is not a seaweed but, as its name says, a grass. In pockets of the blades, we find tiny yellow lumps, which we're told are eelgrass seeds. Just beyond our muddy territory grows a strangely wonderful meadow whose liquid sky is filled with wingless swimmers, a meadow more productive than a hayfield twice as big or a forest three times its size. The bare mud, too, is "covered by billions of little producers, and even on a cloudy day, they're producing sugars, oils, things like that. They're producing so fast they can't even hold it; it just leaks out. When the tide comes in today," Alex predicts, "it's going to be loaded with that brown foam." The foam is sometimes mistaken for pollution, but he explains that it's similar to beer foam. Just as the yeast in beer creates a foamy head by consuming sugar, bacteria in the water produce foam as they swallow up the bay sugars.

Our small-game safari goes on to find shrimp tunnels in the mud (shrimps can burrow down to 2 feet, making them difficult to catch), five different types of crab, worms that tunnel into the mud much like garden worms and feast on the detritus (dead plants and animals), sponges, and sea lettuce ("Looks like it stayed too long on the bottom of the refrigerator, right?").

As our expedition comes to a close, the animals are carefully returned to their proper niches, and we prepare to return to ours. Cleaned-up hermit crabs again become slicked with mud while mud-globbed shoes are hosed clean. Worlds that were traded for a brief time are traded back. It has been the most superficial of exchanges and understanding, and yet the group will never look at the mudflat in quite the same way again.

Alex hoses off his hip boots and looks back to where we've just been. "The place looks uninviting, you don't want to walk out there, it's really yucky, and you can't see anything that's happening," he says, knowing full well that mudflats don't hold the drama and lure of, well, mountains. But today, for seven open-minded seekers, he has evened the score somewhat by pulling back a deceptively drab cover to reveal a world of bizarre beauty. "When you start looking more closely, you see that it's full of valuable things and that this is a really productive place right here."

He pauses and then adds simply, "That's why I wanted you to come out and see it."

# Chapter 11

# WOLF HOLLOW

SUPPOSE, JUST FOR AN INSTANT, that while hiking over an island trail one day, your boot comes down on the back of a sunning garter snake. Assuming a certain soft-heartedness and lack of squeamishness in your character, you'd like to aid your victim, but where do you take a stepped-on snake? In the San Juan Islands, it's simple. You call or head for the Wolf Hollow Wildlife Rehabilitation Center, where squashed snakes find help, and you'll find out what in the world *happens* to a snake that meets the underside of a shoe. Does it permanently and fatally flatten out? According to Shona Aitken, education director for Wolf Hollow, it depends on which part has been stepped on.

Along with garter snakes, the clinic has treated an occasional alligator lizard and even a bullfrog, but reptiles and amphibians make up a small percentage of the incoming tide of wounded and orphaned that regularly washes into Wolf Hollow, approximately 400 animals a year, in varying stages of distress. The condition of a stepped-on snake is less serious than that of reptiles who've been run over by cars or caught in mowers; feet do far less damage than machines. One shoe-squashed victim with a split skin was held by Friday Harbor Middle School personnel, who were only too glad to hand it over to Wolf Hollow. After a little cleaning up at the wildlife clinic, the snake slithered free again.

Wolf Hollow is located on 40 acres about 5 miles west of Friday Harbor, and from a walk through the buildings and grounds, it's evident where the priorities are. A large yellow metal building houses a food preparation area, a treatment room, and a tiny office space with fridge, desk, and walls covered with papers. The phone shrills a constant summons while steam billows from a stove where treatment tubes boil away like someone's lunch noodles, completing the picture of a place far less concerned with its effect on human visitors than with its mission of mercy to orphaned, injured, and sick animals.

The first contact for most animals that come to the center is with the treatment room, where they receive a thorough exam and assessment. An animal that requires a good deal of care will remain in this area until it is well enough to be moved to outdoor enclosures away from human contact, which not only is stressful but also encourages a closeness with humans that wild animals can ill afford.

Wolf Hollow originated in a private veterinary clinic in Friday Harbor run by Dr. Jessica Lainson and Judy Carter. The pair's first wild patient was a great horned owl with a fractured wing, and from there, according to Judy, "it sort of snowballed. People started calling about wild animals and bringing them in. We started building cages and finally said, 'Well, we'd better call the state and find out what we need to do. It appears we're going to be treating wild animals.'"

For the next few years, the pair treated both domestic and wild animals, but by the end of 1986, they realized they couldn't keep up both jobs. Since nobody else was treating wildlife and "that's where our hearts were," they decided to focus their treatment on wild animals. But the decision created a problem. Because it's not possible to send a wild creature home to recuperate as one would do with a pet, additional space was needed for long-term care. In the fall of 1986, the clinic moved to its present 40-acre home and became a full-fledged wildlife rehab center. "The building was there," says Judy, who worked at the center for ten years, "but it had a dirt floor and big doors at the end, and that was it. No windows, no floors, no nothing. It was a real labor of the heart."

A wide range of wounded and orphaned has passed through the doors of Wolf Hollow since that time. Most of the animals come from the islands, but others are brought from Anacortes and eastern Skagit County. The clinic's species list numbers more than 140 different types of animals, from bats and rats to teals and seals. Because the islands have no possums, skunks, or coyotes, the center sees very few or none of these unless they come in from the mainland. Birds make up the bulk of the center's clientele.

Wolf Hollow also cares for stranded harbor seal pups and the occasional elephant seal that needs care. Normally, when an elephant seal is brought in, it's a yearling, a 250-pound youngster that has come up on shore to molt. Although the animal may not look healthy, the molt is a natural process that occurs annually. What is not healthy or natural is the increasing number of severe skin lesions, which has been noted all down the coast and which may possibly be related to pollutants in the water.

Most of the animals are here because of some human-related activity: car hits (the major cause); cat and dog atttacks; run-ins with barbed wire fences, windows, powerlines, fish lines, hooks, or nets; accidental poisoning; deliberate shooting.

Visitors to the center are likely to be greeted by not only Shona but also Sinead, a red-tailed hawk that was hit by a car. Her left wing was so badly injured in the accident that she will never fly again and thus has become one of Wolf Hollow's "unreleasables." In good weather, she sits on a perch outside the office with a long tether attached to her leg, sometimes hopping up onto the picnic table but most of the time content to sit and watch what's going on. *Content* may or may not be the right word, but Shona feels that at least Sinead is not stressed by her captivity. "You see other birds of prey, they're flying against the wall the minute you go into their cage. They're pulling at their feathers because they're stressed. Of course, I can't read her mind," she admits, "but in comparison to similar animals, she seems very calm." So calm is Sinead that she's used as an educational bird on the site and is occasionally taken into schools.

Some visitors to the center are saddened by the sight of a hawk in captivity and feel death would be far better for such a creature. As already mentioned, however, Sinead does not demonstrate a high level of anxiety, although, never having imprinted on people as a nestling, she is not fully comfortable around them. The staff tries not to inflict on her more than she can apparently handle, and so school-children are asked not to touch but to observe quietly from a respectful distance.

Sinead's impact on the children is a beneficial one: "A lot of children unfortu-nately think of birds of prey as being nasty things with big sharp claws that come down and grab little floppy bunnies," says Shona. "It's nice for them to see that a hawk is in itself a beautiful creature." And it's not only children who are impressed. People who have seen red-tails for years flying overhead or perched on power poles tend to shrug them off with a 'Yeah, yeah, they're ten a penny.' Then they actually see them up close, see the face, the talons, the red tail, and it's just 'Oooohhhh'— they're quite awed by the look of her. People think of eagles as being the regal ones. They're quite surprised sometimes when they see a hawk."

The sentiment that an injured animal should be left to die, however, is a strong one, and Wolf Hollow often encounters those who criticize its efforts to intervene with nature. Generally soft-spoken, with a lovely Scottish lilt to her words, Shona stoutly voices her disagreement: "A lot of people say, 'That animal was supposed to die, so leave it to die.' I can see their point there, but many animals come to us and we don't know why they were hurt or orphaned. But when we do know the reasons, more than 90 percent are related to human activity. So it's not a simple case of 'nature taking its course.'"

Before coming to Wolf Hollow, Shona worked as a ranger in Scotland, and when people would bring her injured wild animals, she felt at a loss as to what to do. After she moved to San Juan Island and started volunteering at the center, that feel-ing changed as she learned how to help animals that were suffering and how to "push the balance back their way a bit. There's so many obstacles that humans are putting in their path, deliberately or otherwise. You suddenly realize maybe there's something you can do" to even up the score somewhat, and though the difference made may be slight, it is, as she says, *something*.

Nevertheless, she is not sentimental about the center's work and has to explain to those on the other side of the fence, who reject euthanasia in any case, why not every animal can be saved. Although Sinead seems to have adjusted well to her cap-tivity, other animals do not. "When it's an animal that's severely hurt and in pain, and you can't do anything to fix the injury, then it's not so much of a decision," says Shona. "When you have an animal that has an injury it could recover from but that'll never be released, then you have a different sort of decision to make. Is this animal suitable to be kept in captivity? Would it be more like prolonged torture?" Different rehab centers have different philosophies. Some never euthanize an ani-mal that could survive, regardless of whether it's going to be in captivity for the rest of its life, whereas others do triage the moment an animal comes through the door—they judge its chances then and there and euthanize on the spot if they deem such action necessary.

Wolf Hollow falls somewhere in the middle, considering each case individually. "On the practical side, there's no way that we could keep every animal," says Shona. "We couldn't do our job. Our cages would be full of gulls with broken wings. That's a terrible way to have to look at it, but we couldn't care for the ones that can be rehabilitated." While Wolf Hollow keeps a few resident animals that will never be released, it also looks for situations for others that might do well as breeders or educational animals.

The center uses consultant vets in both Friday Harbor and Anacortes and has an on-site rehabilitator. Treating wild animals is often a guessing game; many times it's unclear just what caused an injury, and to further muddle matters, wild animals instinctively conceal their pain. But an advantage exists in treating wild animals instead of beloved pets whose owners are less willing to depart from the tried and true. With the wildlings, more chances can be taken, more hunches followed. Treatments at Wolf Hollow consequently have run the gamut from standard medicine to a deep-tissue massage therapy, which has been used on birds, seal pups, and once even on a paralyzed possum, which eventually walked again. Homeopathic treatments may be given to boost immune systems or treat minor infections without resorting to antibiotics, which might have side effects.

Wolf Hollow is one of the few centers in Washington that cares for orphaned seal pups. When the center hears from someone concerned about a lone pup on the shore, staffpeople first advise the caller not to touch the seal or try in any way to urge it back into the water and also to keep children and especially dogs away from the animal. They then contact the Marine Mammal Stranding Network, which sends someone out to assess the seal's condition.

"The vast majority of the time what they find is a pup who's severely starved, dehydrated, usually uninjured," says Shona. "Just a baby who's been away from his mother for some time." Mom may have been eaten by a transient orca, may have died of disease, or may have disappeared because of human factors—a more likely scenario since the peak of the pupping season in the islands (July) unfortunately coincides with that of the tourist season. If the young seal is indeed in a desperate way, the Marine Mammal Stranding Network obtains permission to pick it up and bring it to Wolf Hollow for rehab.

At the height of pupping season, baby seals crowd the twelve tubs in the nursery area and fill the air with mournful *boo-boo-boos*. The pups are very vocal when young because one way mother seals recognize their pups is by their plaintive calls.

A pup is immediately isolated in a tub that functions as a miniature intensive-care unit. Usually, the animal is too weak to swim and has lost so much of its blubber layer that it's unable to keep itself warm in the larger rehab pools. In a tub, the pup can rest out of the water on a rack (harbor seals normally spend about half their time lying on rocks) and can be warmly wrapped in towels or hosed down for cooling and cleaning. The first 24 to 48 hours of its care are fairly intensive: first the animal is rehydrated; then it is fed every 2 hours around the clock.

Volunteers regularly make runs to a Bellingham cold storage for 500 pounds of fish, which usually lasts about two weeks, depending on the number of seals. "We use a delicious mixture called fish slop," says Shona, wrinkling her nose, "which is what everything and everybody around here smells of." The mixture is basically ground herring with an electrolyte solution, vitamins, and minerals. What the center tries to do is replace the mother's milk, which has a very high fat content, somewhere around 45 percent. When mother seals nurse their young, the pups put on weight fast, so they need something similar to that natural formula. The pups that are premature or that have digestive problems receive a milk formula, but "most of our seals are raised on good old fish slop."

Tube feedings at 2 A.M. and other dreary hours involve putting a large syringe connected to a long tube down the seal's throat. Wolf Hollow teaches handling skills so feeders can get the tubes down quickly and efficiently without stressing the animals overmuch. It's not as difficult a chore as you might think, but it does have its risks. Interns walk around wearing Band-Aids covering nips from hungry seals.

Once a pup has been tubbed and tubed for a minimum of seven days, it's transferred to a small pool first; from there it progresses to larger pools as its condition improves. When I visited, one tub held four lethargic, mottled-looking pups about six weeks old. They'd come in starved and dehydrated and had since been through complications such as infections. One was sucking on another's back; when a pup is starving, it sucks on all sorts of things, including sand, buoys, and its own flippers.

*Harbor seal*

Seals in the first pool were still being tube-fed, although small fish were being gradually introduced into their diet. Once the pups were well into eating the fish and putting on weight, they'd move into the next pool, where the tenants were definitely bigger and fatter. At that stage, the seals were encouraged to dive off their haulout platforms and swim after fish in the water. The center feeds the seals until they're between 55 and 60 pounds, which is their natural weaning weight and the stage at which Mama Seal says sayonara.

When a seal reaches weaning weight, it's given a thorough physical exam, and live fish are released into the pool to make sure the seal has the smarts to chase after them. Human contact is restricted at this point to netting the seals for a blood sample or weighing in. It's a procedure they hate, and that's fine. It would be far worse if they enjoyed the human contact and stimulation, for then Wolf Hollow would have failed in its mission to keep these creatures true to their wild nature.

Volunteers and staff at the center try to avoid having the seals come up to them by taking the animals through stages of less and less contact. At first the pups have to be held to be fed, but as soon as possible, hand feeding is introduced, and then the fish are simply thrown into the water. At that point, workers try to stay away from the pool and instead observe the seals from afar. Painted markers are placed on their smooth pates like jaunty little caps so the seals can be easily distinguished at a distance.

"We don't hug them and cuddle them and pet them; that's not what they're here for," says Shona. "One of our big jobs is to keep them as wild as possible. There's no sense putting in the effort to make them physically ready to go back into the wild if they're coming up to humans." The decrease in contact works well with the seals, but with other animals, the center goes a step further by using sight barriers.

A great blue heron with a wing injury was in an enclosure boarded up to eye level. Food was slipped in several times a day through a drawer or chute, and the same procedure was used out in the woodlands in the raccoon cages. "Of course, they can smell that we prepared it, but there's a difference from coming up to a two-legged creature and being handed food."

Raccoon kits are often brought in during the busy "baby season" and soon get to know the two resident overlords, Angus and Iggy, adult male raccoons that are unreleasable because they're so comfortable with humans. But even though the raccoons have been domesticized and will never be wild again, they play an important role in helping the young Wolf Hollow kits return to the wild. "They're very limited in what they can teach them," admits Shona. But they do teach the youngsters a certain amount of food handling, and how to behave with adult raccoons. "They've been interacting with their own size of raccoon and don't realize how to change their behavior slightly to deal with an adult male raccoon! Both of these guys are pretty gentle compared to a wild raccoon, but nonetheless it's good for the youngsters to realize that sometimes you have to grovel a little." The adult males easily shovel in more than their fair share of the food, fattening up significantly over the summer baby season.

Another resident "unreleasable" is Beepo the barred owl, although the possibility exists that she may be released after undergoing behavioral rehab elsewhere. She came in as a tiny gray downy owlet who'd been found on the forest floor. Her rescuers couldn't locate a nest, and so they took her to a local vet, who then called Wolf Hollow. "When we opened the box, we expected the threat display, even from a young owl," says Shona. The birds normally fluff up their feathers in a fierce warning and clack when approached. "From this little one, we got an *eek! eek!* which is 'Feed me! Feed me!' And that's very cute, but that to us is a disaster because that means this animal is not scared of humans. In fact, it recognizes us as a source of food."

She explains that birds of prey have a very short imprinting period. The bird basically looks at whoever's feeding it "and more or less says, 'Okay, you're feeding me, so I must be like you.' That's a very difficult thing to reverse. Some people say it's impossible. So we have an owl that's physically perfect but can't be released becaue she's not scared of people. In fact, she's attracted to people. And that could get her into a lot of trouble." Beepo sometimes journeys beyond the center as an educational bird, but she generally spends her days in a large enclosure, which she sometimes has to surrender to other birds recovering from injuries.

A bird is put into a flight cage to verify that it can fly well enough for release. If it's a large raptor such as an eagle, which needs more room and time in which to fly to build up strength in an injured wing, it's usually sent to another rehab center (such as HOWL, Help Our WildLife, in Lynnwood) that has a suitable flight cage. Wolf Hollow has plans to build its own eagle flight cage within the next couple of years.

The islands have one of the largest breeding populations of bald eagles in the contiguous states, and calls to the center about them are not uncommon. One time a call came in from Orcas about a bald eagle sitting hunched up in someone's backyard. Two workers from the center took the next ferry to Orcas. ("Often we just give people advice on how to capture an animal and how to transport it," says Shona, "but obviously with an eagle, we don't do that.") A sheet was thrown over the bird, which was too weak to put up a fight. No injuries could be found, however, and the eagle, which was very uncoordinated and unable to perch properly, was then tested for poisoning. High lead levels explained its weakness, and a substance was injected into the bloodstream that combines with the lead and makes it easier to pass through the body. "So in a few days, this bird went from his nose on the ground, wasn't going to survive the night, to basically flying from top perch to top perch in the flight cage." Shona guesses that the bird had fed on waterfowl that had ingested lead shot or on fish with high lead levels.

When a bird is an endangered species, such as a bald eagle, and is deemed untreatable, as was an eagle that came in with a dislocated shoulder, the final decision is made by the Department of Wildlife whether or not to euthanize the animal.

Bird care probably comprises the bulk of cases at Wolf Hollow and runs the range from hummers to herons. Hummingbirds can be very easy to rehabilitate if they're not injured; a broken wing is a different story. But if the tiny dynamos have simply gotten caught in a house or shed and are only lacking energy, even though it may look as if they're about to expire, the center keeps them warm and fed and 2 hours later can let them go. A cedar waxwing was helped by a dentist, who cemented its beak back together, and a female goldeneye with a split bill was stitched up and glued with the epoxy used for repairing horses' hooves.

It's easier to imagine working with ducks and songbirds than with sharp-taloned raptors or herons, whose daggerlike bills can quickly puncture an eye. Workers wear eye protection and usually throw a towel or sheet over a bird's head to gain control over the feet, beak, or wings and minimize movement that would damage the bird. Once its head is covered, the bird usually lies still and accepts treatment.

Unfortunately, some birds, such as great blue herons, may find human contact so stressful that they simply refuse to eat. Many arrive at the center in very poor condition, often starved, possibly with toxins in their systems. The heron I glimpsed had come in with the front edge of its right wing badly ripped up but was otherwise strong. The bird's overall health was making a difference in its recovery, and volunteers fed it through a chute to help allay the stress of contact. The bandage on the wing had to be changed a couple of times a week, but once the bird was caught, it would usually submit to the process without protest.

The volunteers chasing down the birds, tube-feeding the seals, and mixing the fish slop are the heart of Wolf Hollow, which exists entirely on private donations. Especially during the busy summer season, there may be thirty to fifty animals at the center needing some type of care each day. Most volunteers work on a part-time basis, so the work crews change daily, and the situation is further complicated as animals are often shifted around to different pens, released, or joined by new patients.

Keeping track of what needs to be done in such an ever-changing environment is a challenge met by posting a "day sheet" that lists tasks from 6 A.M. all the way up to midnight (though feedings often continue through till morning). Chores include observing chow time for a variety of animals (throughout the list is the stern injunction "Don't forget the baby birds!" which have to be fed almost constantly), removing leftover fish from the seal pools, putting Sinead out on her day perch, cleaning the treatment room, and cutting browse for the fawns and goats.

Goats are kept at the center to provide milk for the fawns, which cannot tolerate cow's milk. One goat is curiously named Skunk, and Shona laughs at the confusion her name has caused for newcomers reviewing the day sheet. "You'd see 'Milk Skunk,' and of course to everybody who knew her, that was fine, you went and milked Skunk. But then you'd see a new volunteer go, No, no, I'm not going to do this! So now it says, 'Milk goat.'"

Most of the volunteers are folks from the islands who come in once a week for a day or half day. During the busy May-to-October period, the center also takes interns, who stay in trailers on the grounds or in the main building's upstairs apartment and are basically members of the staff for the duration. They range from those with backgrounds in wildlife management or veterinary science to those who simply have a strong interest in learning. "Most of our interns don't want to go on to do rehab as a career but just want to gain practical experience to balance out their theoretical courses," says Shona. "They do their share of the night feedings. Fish slop at midnight, fish slop at two o'clock. . . . Let them learn what the 'glamour' of wildlife rehab is really like!"

Call after the busy summer season, in October or November, for information on internships; applications are taken through February and selections made by early March. "What we're looking for mainly," says Shona, "is people who show a genuine interest in getting hands-on experience in wildlife rehab and who also have the common sense to know what's involved." (Such as fish slop at 2 A.M.) Internships are a minimum of six to eight weeks.

Shona herself began as a volunteer, working a few mornings a week and then some afternoons as well, and now does rehab along with her work as an education coordinator. She feels the educational work is even more important than the rehab, which is necessary but "short-term." Rehab tries to repair some of the damage that has been done, but education can help prevent or lessen that damage.

She has talked to schools, elderhostels, and other groups but hopes to do more, especially with the schools. After writing to all the local schools about how the center's work could be fertile ground for a wide range of projects and discussion groups, she received a less-than-overwhelming response. Elementary schools alone were interested. "It's categorized as cuddly animal stuff," she says. "That to me is really sad, because I deliberately suggested discussion groups for high school kids. I don't care if I go in there and they say, 'I think what you're doing is rubbish.' Good. Why? Tell me about it. Think for yourself, rather than taking someone else's attitude."

Attitudes about Wolf Hollow range from raised eyebrows and razzing to all-out support. Some think that what the center is trying to do amounts to nothing more than a waste of time and money; they find it ridiculous to be rehabilitating "common" animals such as deer, raccoons, crows, and gulls.

A more insidious attitude, however, surfaces with still others: "We're giving a point of view they totally disagree with, that the animals were here, that humans don't always come first," Shona explains, noting that a people-first perception often accompanies the increasing number of calls to the center about "nuisance" animals. "Somebody calls and says that a raccoon is raiding their henhouse, and they want that raccoon out of there, dead, or gone. Someone who tries to express a different opinion and suggest alternative solutions to the problem is lowlife completely." With increasing habitat loss in the islands, animals "just can't take off into deep woodland, because there isn't very much of it left." So Wolf Hollow tries to give advice to prevent or lessen the problem. They have at times relocated animals, "but it's getting to the stage where that's almost impossible."

Many problems won't be solved by trapping and relocating an animal, because often single animals aren't causing the problem. Trapping a raccoon probably won't stop others from coming to feed on a cat's food; feeding the cat inside is the obvious solution. Some people do very well with suggestions, says Shona, whereas others become angry: "Their attitude is, 'I have a problem, solve it.' And you say, 'No, it's not that simple.' Some people don't want to put out any effort whatsoever" and may even resort to what Shona calls "emotional blackmail" by threatening to shoot the animal if it's not removed.

Calls to the center from those concerned about injured or abandoned animals still far outnumber the nuisance calls. Often, however, people are not certain about what they're seeing. One time a very excited woman called in about an injured pileated woodpecker, which was actually a golden bantam chicken. Another time a caller mistook a woodpecker for a "baby eagle." So now the center asks callers to carefully describe the animals they've seen; doing that has certainly saved time but has also turned up a few surprises from those who *do* know their animals.

When the center received a call a few years back about a beaver on the runway of a small airport on Orcas, the patient, somewhat patronizing reply was "No, ma'am, that is not a beaver. There are no beavers in the islands. That is an otter." The woman replied, "Well, this *otter* has a *flat tail*." So Wolf Hollow volunteers rushed out to indeed find a beaver. Another year, the center received a similar call about a beaver on San Juan Island and gave the standard reply: "No, there are no beavers on the island; that is an otter." Sure enough, after the caller's insistence that this "otter" had a flat tail, Wolf Hollow brought in another beaver.

With the increasing number of animals coming in to Wolf Hollow each year, resources are being stretched to their limits, and fund-raising has become more aggressive to supplement private donations. Additional cages are needed, including the planned-for flight cage for large raptors, and so are facilities for waterbirds. (When feathers get dirty, their insulation is ruined, so the birds cannot be held in a pond.) Another priority is a new well to replace the present slow pumper. Two huge blue tanks store fresh water at present for the seal pools; salt water would be ideal, but purchase waterfront property in the islands? Shona laughs and shakes her head.

One of the center's sympathizers, however, lives in a sheltered bay on San Juan where seals can be released "without going from a pool to the open ocean, which is a bit scary." A seal ready for release is netted, placed on a tarp in the back of the center's enclosed pickup, and taken to the bay. A large ramp is then set up from the truck bed to the beach so that the seal can inch its way down and into the water.

It's an emotional moment. Some might think there would be a certain sadness or wistfulness in watching a seal, or any other animal that has received care, charge off without a backward glance. Not so for the workers of Wolf Hollow. "What you feel is success," says Shona. "To me, a great big 55- to 65-pound seal with double chins disappearing off into the ocean is . . . *YES!*"

---

Wolf Hollow is a hospital for animals, and under state law, it is allowed visitors only at the times of educational programs: Tuesdays, Thursdays, and Saturdays, 11 A.M.–2 P.M. Call ahead to schedule a visit, since the facility cannot cope with large numbers of people. All visitors will be shown around by a staffperson. The center publishes a quarterly newsletter called *Wild Times*, and if you would like to be on their mailing list to receive the publication or would like to become a member to support Wolf Hollow, call (360) 378-5000. The center is located at 240 Boyce Road (P.O. Box 391), Friday Harbor, WA 98250.

# ROSE MARIE ORR

## *Send Her Your Feathered, Your Furred*

Rose Orr's dad says he won't take a bath in her tub until someone else goes in first. The last time he looked, there was a seal in it.

For most of us, a pinniped in the powder room is a radical departure in decor, but for a Wolf Hollow volunteer, a tubbed seal is pretty tame stuff. Rose often cares for injured or orphaned seals until they can be transferred to the wildlife rehab center on San Juan Island, holding them in her tub overnight to rehydrate them before the move. "You open the curtains," she says with a laugh, "and you just better be careful."

The seal pups are her favorite, even though they require feedings every 2 hours through the night, much like human babies. But these babies have to be fed by tubes instead of bottles: "You usually have to be over them," says Rose. "I kind of climb on them and lift their heads up so I have a straight line to put the tube down." The pups' teeth aren't as sharp as the older seals, and "if you can grab their gums and wrap them around their teeth, they're not going to bite their gums, so that's a way to avoid getting bit. But it happens." She should know; a seal once bit her on the chin.

At Wolf Hollow, Rose got a chance to practice the finer points of tube feeding on a wide range of birds and mammals, a priceless opportunity for someone who confesses she was always "soft" on animals. Her involvement with the center began one year at the San Juan County Fair, where a display on Wolf Hollow just happened to catch her eye; eventually she called about volunteering. Surprised and grateful to learn she didn't have to have any experience working with wildlife but simply be willing to commit to one day a week, she soon learned to clean cages, weed gardens, and feed the animals.

She rolls her eyes when she remembers the first task she was given: moving a pile of compost as high as herself. "It's a wonder I came back!" she says now. But go back she did, gaining not only experience but also a good deal of respect for the workers of Wolf Hollow. Describing the center's operation as very much hand-to-mouth, Rose did her part by picking through the Friday Harbor dumpsters for food and begging grocers for day-old bread to feed to the animals. And back at the center, "it was funny seeing people swatting flies and then saving them in a jar to be fed to the birds." The staff also encourages locals who have cat-killed rodents to freeze the casualties in a plastic bag and save them for the center's hawks.

Life at Wolf Hollow might have been bare-boned, but it was certainly never dull. One day, Rose arrived to find that the former director's pet python, Arthur, had escaped his cage. "I'm deathly afraid of snakes," she says, "and I still had to mop the floor and work in there." Another time, she was cleaning out the cage of Angus, the resident raccoon, with her then-twelve-year-old son, Mike, whom she left to get a hose. Suddenly, she heard Mike call out to her in a strange voice; hurrying back, she found the ring-tailed rogue perched happily on her son's head, looking for all the world "like a coonskin cap." Angus ambled off in his own good time.

Rose spends less time at Wolf Hollow these days but works as one of the center's volunteers in Anacortes, caring for everything from baby robins and starlings to deer, owls, raccoons, coyotes, hawks, otters, and herons. She often calls the center to consult with them on primary care methods so that she can stabilize an animal before bringing it to the clinic. West Isle Air of Anacortes and even UPS have provided ambulatory services, and Rose herself takes many of the animals over to San Juan Island on the ferry. She tries not to advertise her cargo to avoid causing the animal additional stress from open-mouthed onlookers, but neither does she restrict all access. On one trip on which she carried an eagle in a dog kennel, an artist took advantage of the unique close-up and carefully noted proportions for a future sculpture.

Another ferry trip involved transporting an eagle that Rose had helped capture out by Campbell Lake on Fidalgo Island. The call, one of her first, came in at 10 P.M. from people concerned about a grounded eagle, and shortly thereafter, she and two other volunteers headed out to search the lake road. They spotted the eagle, but their flashlights scared it, and the chase was on until the animal was finally found in a ravine, "hanging upside down" from a limb. One volunteer threw a blanket over the bird, and the next day it was in a large box on its way to San Juan Island.

Ferry passengers looked askance at the bulky box hopping across the table, but the trip was uneventful and the eagle diagnosed by Wolf Hollow as simply "obese." It was put on a diet, and about a month later, Rose took it back on the international ferry for release on Fidalgo Island. Husband Frank met her at the ferry to help remove the box, forgetting to check first with aggrieved customs officers. "We were getting into all kinds of trouble," recalls Rose.

Getting an eagle through customs was only one of several awkward experiences. After working a day at Wolf Hollow, coming home on the ferry "was always interesting," says Rose with a grin. "I never had trouble finding a seat, because nobody would sit next to me." One time she had to walk around with gull beak marks on either side of her nose. "It was hard trying to explain that!" Another time, after she was sprayed by a skunk, she scrubbed up the best she could and went to work, thinking it was just the residue she was smelling. Her co-workers told her otherwise, and she spent the next two days trying to rid herself of the smell.

Most of her experiences have been positive, however, and far beyond her fondest childhood hopes of having a farm. In addition to the donkeys, dogs, and geese that populate her property, all manner of mammals and birds have trooped through her home. When I spoke with her, she was caring for a chipmunk that was found nearly unconscious on the ground on Guemes. As she picked him up out of his cage, he peed on her hands, and she matter-of-factly excused herself to wash up. She'd be releasing him soon, she said, although she was a bit concerned about the timing: the chipmunk hadn't had a chance to build up a food stash to see him through the winter.

Rose's tenderness for these injured creatures and her delight in their presence are almost palpable. One of her favorite feathered houseguests was Beepo, a barred owl that is now one of the "nonreleasables" at Wolf Hollow. Having imprinted on humans as a very young chick, Beepo had no qualms about making herself right at home with Rose. "She'd always head for the dining room, which had green carpet," Rose recalls. "She probably thought it was the grass or woods." The little owl had a peculiar gait as she sauntered across the floor, "like a little old lady or a Weeble doll. The wing went up and the leg went up." Now and then she'll spend some time with the owl when she picks her up from Wolf Hollow to take with her on lectures. She wraps a towel around her arm for protection, but the bird will have nothing to do with the cloth, preferring instead to perch on flesh. "She could dig in with her talons, but she doesn't. She's still such a people person."

It's a special treat to see owls so closely, as I discovered one night while helping Rose tube a barn owl. As she says, "They're gorgeous; the colors are really something." And the young ones that are orphaned but healthy, such as Beepo, can be constantly entertaining. Rose once cared for two baby barn owls found in a cleaned-out silo. "One was dominant, and when he wanted to be boss, the other would lie on his back. They were just hilarious; they'd fight like two little kids." She pauses and then adds, "We're not that much different."

She has boarded bats, weasels, several pileated woodpeckers, and baby possums. "You usually don't get just one possum, you get a group of them, and they have to be fed on demand like any baby." Rose uses an eyedropper for the feedings. "They'll hang on your finger with their tails."

Once she called Wolf Hollow to ask how to pick up a porcupine. With the help of a couple of campers armed with brooms out at Washington Park, she finally persuaded the prickly fellow into a box. Another time, a vet called her about a great blue heron that had been brought in by construction workers.

"Normally when I get a call, the animal is in a box or a kennel or something," says Rose. But when she got to the vet's office and asked where the heron was, the receptionist just pointed across the room. "I looked at her and said, 'Where?' And she said, 'Under the chair.'" Nobody knew how to handle the dagger-beaked bird sitting quietly in a corner, so Rose carefully pulled out the chair and grabbed the bird's beak when it lunged. She enjoys working with herons, at the same time acknowledging how stressful human contact is for them.

"That's against them in the first place," she says. "A lot of the birds are like that. Flickers are real hard to handle, and rabbits. Deer are almost hopeless." Because these are prey species, she explains, they're extremely skittish, especially the mature deer. "We get enough of those and it's really sad. To try to capture an adult deer with a hurt leg would probably hurt him more than it would do him good. Then once you bring him back, he's in a caged situation and hurts himself again."

Fawns are a little easier to help. Rose has pictures of one curled up at her husband's feet and says, "That's where he wanted to be." Other pictures in her album show a little flying squirrel, baby seals ("just their eyes are so beautiful"), a red fox, a grebe that got caught in a fishing line, and a raccoon kit snuggled down on Frank's shoulder as he talks on the phone. Oh, yes, and a coyote that was making a few too many appearances at the Starbird Motel in Mount Vernon.

"Not that he ever hurt anything, but they were worried about the guests getting scared," says Rose. "One day the maid was working in a room with the door open. He walked in, jumped up, and put his feet on her. I think she lost ten years of her life." Rose was called to pick up the animal, which had probably been raised as a pet and later released. "He was tame to a certain point. If you'd get too close, he'd growl and let you know." The coyote was eventually deemed unreleasable and transferred to a rehab center that abutted a large wildlife reserve.

Another houseguest was a baby otter abandoned in a crawlspace in downtown Anacortes. After Rose fattened him up at home, he was brought to Wolf Hollow, where he was raised, and he was eventually released with another otter (Pogo) off Patos Island. Rose enjoys the otters for their antics. "They're characters; they get into everything. You go in to clean their cages and they're up your leg."

She usually doesn't take the animals out of their cages to let them run around inside the house since she doesn't want to make pets of them. Sometimes, though, her best efforts are thwarted. "I had a baby seagull, which you don't see very often," she says. The gull, called Scuttles, was in a cage that supposedly was locked when Rose left the house to pick up a heron. When she returned with the bird, "as I opened the door, I heard *slap, slap, slap* on the linoleum. Scuttles had gotten loose and was all over my kitchen, leaving me all these little presents. Here I was carrying this great blue heron in, and Scuttles was on the loose."

Although escapes will happen and her heart is tender, Rose nevertheless tries to keep the animals confined and minimize human contact for their own good. "I guess the biggest thing I've learned is the importance of wild animals being wild," she says. "I was the kind of person who would have brought home a squirrel and tried to make him a pet, and at times I still have feelings like that." But she knows wild animals don't make good pets: "They were meant to fly or crawl or swim. They weren't meant to be in a cage."

At the other end of the spectrum from those who make pets of wild creatures are those who can't see why they should be helped at all. Rose talks to various groups, sometimes with Beepo in tow, and once ran across the sentiment that it was a waste of money to spend twelve dollars trying to save, of all things, a silly gull. But she feels strongly that "we can't just say, 'Let nature take its course.' We really have messed a lot of things up." Many of the distressed animals she sees come to her with human-caused complaints, which convinces her that education is even more important than rehab, "so that we're not constantly losing species of animals or plants. We've got to do something. We can't just take over everything and think, Well, we can send them someplace else."

She was presently working on a problem involving a beaver that had injured a dog. Neighbors were up in arms, wanting to set a trap and relocate the animal, but Rose felt that sentiment was so strong that they'd probably end up taking the unfortunate creature's life. "Is that right?" she asks. "The dog was off his land. I'm sure the beaver did not initiate this, but they're worried about their kids and their dog, which should probably be tied up, and their kids told not to go down to the pond." She shakes her head. "How do you go in and try to say this animal was here first?"

For her part, Rose will continue trying to right the balance by tending to wild things that need her help. Does her family ever complain about having to share their home with the wild and woolly? "My family has put up with a lot," she admits. "Most of the time there are cages in the kitchen or an animal somewhere. The first time I had a seal in the bathtub, I think Frank figured he'd be showering with friends or something." Her husband and sons pitch in if she needs help holding an animal while tube-feeding and often go out with her on late-night calls. "They're all pretty soft-hearted that way. They've been trained."

She grins. "In fact, my sons bring their friends over to see what Mom has *this* time."

---

Rose stresses that anyone finding abandoned or injured wildlife should not attempt to trap or pick up the animal but instead should "watch, monitor, and then call" either Wolf Hollow day or night at (360) 378-5000 or the local police for assistance. Usually a trained volunteer such as herself will be called to come out and help. In addition, Wolf Hollow asks that you also do not attempt to feed or water any of these animals, since improper feeding could harm or kill them. For further information on helping wildlife in need, see the "Baby Season" guidelines at the back of the book.

## Chapter 12

# THE WHALE MUSEUM

WALK INTO THE OLD BUILDING ON FIRST STREET *in Friday Harbor and, with the closing of the door behind you, enter the ocean depths. The gentle voices of orca whales call and sing as you move up the long, heavy wooden staircase to a new knowledge and understanding. Green sea foam colors the walls and, as you reach the head of the stairs, melts into blue water and sky and painted whales forever playing.*

The Whale Museum was created when Kenneth Balcomb, well known for his work on photo-identifying local orcas, and fellow researcher Mark Anderson got together and decided they should create a place to house their collection of bones, baleen, teeth, and skeletons. "It was a unique concept," says the Museum's executive director, Valerie Bohonus, "because they didn't want to focus on whaling. We've got a very small exhibit that talks about it, but we really wanted the attention to be on the living whale."

*A gallon cider bottle of sperm oil sits in a small corner display, along with samples of the white, waxy spermaceti found in the foreheads of sperm whales. Widely sought after in the nineteenth century for making candles and cosmetics, spermaceti is used to help the whale echolocate and may also help in buoyancy control during dives. The whale's head, which whalers once split open for its wealth of oil, also houses the world's largest brain.*

Over four hundred volunteers contributed their time, talents, and money to transform the upstairs of the old Oddfellows Hall into a museum. "It was all out of a passion and dedication to whales," says Valerie. "These were people from the islands and people who came from off-island that Ken knew, whale biologists. They wanted to help create this because nothing else like it existed." Artists and other volunteers made stained-glass windows, painted murals, carved wooden sculptures, and built partitions and exhibits, and in July 1979, the Museum was officially opened.

The place had an air of funkiness about it from the start. Built in 1893, it was saved from destruction in 1959 by Emilia Bave, who put in a gallery on the top floor and a theatre downstairs, where players reenacted the Pig War story. The Museum rented the upper floor in 1979 and finally purchased the entire building ten years later.

"I think a lot of people in town referred to this place as 'the hippies on the hill,' because in the late seventies, you had a lot of people who had long hair, wore blue jeans and T-shirts, and were interested in whales," Valerie says, smiling. "We've broken out of that somewhat, although there are still some of those perceptions because people haven't been here since it opened." Noting that the Museum is still pretty much what it was in 1979, Valerie says that a few new displays have been added but no "high-tech exhibitry. It's not that we're averse to that, but we don't want to get it to where it's sterile. We want it to be a comfortable place for people, so they enjoy being here. One person I talked to said, 'You know, of all the things in the Whale Museum, the thing I remember most is the smell. You've got all those bones around you.' And it's true, you walk in and there's this smell, not a bad smell, just kind of this old smell. . . ."

*A gray whale vertebra sits on the floor, like a small tree stump with flippers. A minke whale skeleton lies entombed in a display case, and hanging from the ceiling is the skeleton of a gray whale calf that became entangled in a gill net and died of asphyxiation off Neah Bay. In another spot sits a minke scapula, or shoulder blade. It once had muscles attached to it that allowed the flipper to move like a paddle, steering the whale's body through miles of liquid space.*

The board of directors hopes to upgrade the Museum in the near future by putting in access for the disabled, as well as classroom space, and moving the second-floor store downstairs for street-level shopping. The entire top floor will then be devoted to exhibits. "I can't wait for the day when we can really revamp the upstairs and put in some more interactive stuff that involves more of the senses, because I think a lot of it is very static right now," admits Valerie. The board will seek special funds for the renovations beyond the normal financial support that comes mainly through admission fees, store sales, orca "adoptions," and memberships. The membership base is diverse and currently numbers about three thousand, with the majority of those off-island. Sign-ups mount steadily as the Museum feeds the appetite of a public hungry for information on the Goliaths of the deep.

Valerie's own interest in whales began back in high school. It eventually led her to a degree in aquatic biology and then to studies on manatees in West Africa, work with the Seattle Aquarium Society, and, in 1992, management of the Whale Museum. She believes that "whales are one of those animals that people feel very tight with. They attribute mystical powers to them. They're gentle animals, they've been around for a long time, and they're intelligent."

*One display case holds a fin whale's brain; the other, a human brain, several sizes smaller. An accompanying discussion of whale physiology includes the observation that several animals possess a larger, more complex brain than that of humans and that "of this group, all but the elephant are marine mammals and all evolved for a much longer time and under completely different conditions than have we. We are not the only conscious and communicative beings on earth, but it has taken us nearly a million years to discover it."*

For those eager to learn more about whales, the Museum offers a range of programs. The downstairs hall hosts a children's "Pod Nod" every summer; mattresses

*Minke whale and Dall porpoise*

are set up
on the floor, and
kids bring sleeping bags
and spend the night working
on crafts, telling stories, or watch-
ing whale videos. A waitress at one of the local restaurants told me she does twenty-minute sessions "on blubber" for fourth-graders at the Museum. To demonstrate the effectiveness of a whale's insulation, she has her students coat their fingers with shortening and then dip them into ice water.

*My daughter and I open one of the several children's discovery boxes and find inside a dolphin's jawbone, a sperm whale tooth, a piece of baleen, and the vertebra of a whale. A small jar holds whale lice taken from a humpback in 1952; the tiny, loathsome-looking creatures benefit the whale by cleaning it of dead skin.*

According to Valerie, "there's never an end to programs and projects" at the Museum and "never a shortage of great ideas." One of those ideas became the –Museum's *Gentle Giants of the Sea* K–6 curriculum guide. It's one of the only, if not *the* only, guide for educators that deals specifically with whales. Currently, it has sold around ten thousand copies and is being sent throughout the country to teachers, camp counselors, and parents who want to help children to have a better understanding of these ancient creatures.

*Fifty million years ago, according to fossil evidence in an Egyptian seabed, whales left the land to return to the sea. Researchers have discovered small leg and foot bones that eventually disappeared over the millions of years spent in salt water. A wall display links the cetaceans (whales, dolphins, and porpoises) to the creodonts, an early order of land carnivores that were closely related to the ancestors of cows and sheep and that had skeletons similar to those of the first whales, particularly in the shape of the vertebrae and the pattern of the teeth.*

The Museum also offers a summer lecture series that usually averages fifty to sixty people a night and is free to members. Kids' nature workshops focus on activities such as tidepooling, kayaking, Native American culture, and dock explorations, and adults can sign up for a six-week series of marine mammal classes.

*Whales are mammals, not fish. Their tails move up and down, not side to side like fish tails; they are warm-blooded, and they nurse their young. The bumps on the heads of humpbacks are hair follicles; like other mammals, whales have hair, though in very sparse amounts, since blubber is a far more effective means of insulation in water. Dolphins and porpoises are also marine mammals; along with whales, they are the only mammals that spend their lives entirely in the sea. A skeleton of a spotted dolphin hangs from the ceiling, and a wall display describes the differences between dolphins and porpoises: dolphins' teeth are pointed and conical, whereas porpoises' are small and spade-shaped. Dolphins also have longer, narrower snouts, prefer offshore habitats, and have a sickle-shaped dorsal fin, as distinguished from the porpoises' triangular one. The largest dolphin of all is the orca.*

Orca. Traveling on the ferry to San Juan Island in October, I listened to the family seated behind me wonder excitedly when they would see the whales. No matter that both the month and the place were wrong; kids and adults were on a fervently devoted lookout. "I can guarantee that the majority of people coming up here come for the whales," says Valerie. "They're an accent here. They're the spice that really sets this place apart from anyplace else."

The Museum staff encourages people to call the 24-hour whale hotline number, 1-800-562-8832 (Washington) or 1-800-665-5939 (British Columbia), whenever whales are spotted. Simply record the day and time of the sighting, where the observation was made, the number of whales, and their direction of travel. Try also to note behavior. For instance, says Valerie, were the whales all surfacing at the same time, going back down, and then surfacing again (a resting type of behavior)? Or did it look as though they were chasing after salmon? Staffpeople use this data to track the whales' distribution. Puget Sound whales have been monitored since the early 1970s, and it's now known that they reside year-round within a 150- to 200-mile coastal range stretching between Tacoma and lower British Columbia.

Information is especially needed in the winter, when the islands' resident orcas forage in other areas. "That's when it's very important for people down in Tacoma or Seattle, Vashon Island, Port Angeles, if they see orcas, to give us a call and let us know. Because we really don't know where they go," says Valerie. "It's not like we have radio tags on them and just turn the radio on every day to find out where they are."

171

*A huge wall display shows the migration routes and ranges of different whales. The gray whale, which may at times be seen in our inland waters or off the west side of San Juan Island, has the longest migration route of any mammal: 10,000 miles round-trip between Alaska and Baja California. Their migration is also amazingly punctual, with grays arriving at the same location on the same day each year. Preyed on by orcas, these whales will dramatically alter their course when orca sounds are played underwater.*

Three pods of orcas swim the islands: L Pod, with just over fifty members, is seen the least often; J Pod is the smallest, numbering between fifteen and eighteen, and the most frequently observed; and K Pod has about nineteen whales and is sighted somewhere in between the other two in frequency. Sometimes the pods intermingle and form superpods. Although she has yet to see them herself, Valerie describes the special gatherings: "There's all kinds of activity—breaching, spy-hopping, lob-tailing [banging their tails on the water]. It's really quite extraordinary. There are several theories of why this happens. Some people think it may be a way of mating; some think it's just a big greeting like the days when different villages would get in their boats and go over and have a big celebration. It's hard to say."

*A sign describes how orcas often cluster so tightly that all are touching and the pod moves as a unit, lifting each other out of the water, "almost intertwining their bodies together," for reasons unknown. What is known is that this unique behavior points to an intensely social nature. Orcas are rarely seen traveling alone, and the pods, which are centered around a dominant female, are so cohesive that they will break into smaller groups for no more than a short time. Orcas apparently become members of a pod only through birth and leave it only through death.*

The islands' resident pods frequent the areas spring through fall, especially on the east side of Haro Strait, where flood currents bring the migrating Fraser River salmon down along the west side of San Juan Island. One of the most popular Museum displays is its giant hotline map, which records the latest sightings of orcas and other whales and porpoises from calls to the hotline.

Transient pods also pass through but focus their feeding more on seals than on salmon. According to Valerie, other differences in this transient population include a more pointed dorsal fin and saddle patches (gray areas behind the dorsal fins) that are more closed than those of the resident whales: "You can have a saddle patch that's open, where you've got the black that comes into it," she explains. "The transients tend not to have that openness." They're also more quiet, have smaller pods, and often travel alone.

A Canadian researcher named Michael Biggs discovered that orcas could be individually identified by their dorsal fin and saddle patch and began photo-ID-ing the pods up north. Ken Balcomb used the technique to identify the whales of the southern pods in the islands, and today, devoted whale-watchers can take a field guide along (*Marine Mammals of Greater Puget Sound* describes all the known orcas), put a name to that breaching whale, and find out a little about its background and personality. A few of the whales are more obvious than others. Take, for instance,

Taku, an older bull easily recognized by two small notches cut into his fin. The notching was done by scientists before the photo-ID technique was developed, so they'd be able to recognize the whale in the wild.

The Museum encourages a first-name relationship with the whales through its orca adoption certificates. Begun in 1984, the program was the only one in existence to offer orca "adoptions" and was very likely one of the first whale adoption programs. "It's a good outreach tool for us," says Valerie, "because one of the disadvantages we have is being located on the island, somewhat geographically isolated." Skip the ferry ride if you must, but don't pass on getting to know the orcas. For a fee, a parchment adoption certificate is sent with the whale's name and photo-ID picture, along with a short biography; an annual report with the latest updates on orca research is also included.

*A huge model of an orca swims through the Museum sky. Mature males can reach a length of 30 feet, with a dorsal fin up to 6 feet high. Orcas are the top predators of the oceans, capable of capturing almost any animal that swims. But they too know what it is to be hunted and captured. The ceiling model is a 2:3 scale replica of a male that was first photographed in 1970 when orcas were rounded up by Sea World in Penn Cove off Whidbey Island. In all, sixty-four orcas were taken from Puget Sound and Georgia Strait from 1965 until 1976, when public outcry finally banned the capture of orcas in Washington state.*

Although capture is no longer a problem for local orcas, enough other concerns have bubbled to the surface to set the calmed waters churning again. Increasing boat traffic in the islands raises questions about the effects of noise, fuel, and sewage on the whales, as well as of the blatant harassment of following pods too closely. Each summer, the Museum tries to make would-be whale-watchers aware of the federal guidelines that exist to protect the whales (see "Refuge Areas"). "We've got some signs posted," says Valerie, "and this year we made a brochure that we put down at the port and customs offices and out at the county park where people launch their boats."

As part of the Whale Museum's Soundwatcher program, volunteers personally contact recreational boaters on the water, "welcoming them to the islands and letting them know that we hope they have an enjoyable time here, and we just want them to be aware that there are whale-watching guidelines, for their own protection and the protection of the animals. And they don't deal just with whales," she stresses. "Approaching haulout sites where seals are—you don't want to see them scurry and separate mothers from their young. The pups may dehydrate and starve."

The Museum also works closely with the whale-watching industry, sponsoring workshops twice a year, before and after the busy summer season, "really encouraging them to be role models when they're out on the water, and also keeping them informed on what's happening so they're a little more knowledgeable on marine life around here." Some tour operators carry naturalists along, and Valerie feels that most are responsible and concerned about the animals.

*Dial-a-whale? A wooden phone booth allows Museum patrons to call up the eerily beautiful syllables and songs of whales. Orcas, whose hearing is approximately*

*five times as acute as that of humans, make a variety of noises such as clicks and squeals that resemble the sound of air being slowly let out of a balloon. The humpback, which will hopefully return to our waters if the population recovers from years of commercial hunting, is known as the singing whale. Only the males sing, and the repeated songs are believed to identify the singer and/or communicate with others.*

The slowdown of the salmon runs, which the resident orcas follow, is another concern. "If the salmon supply is cut down, what does that do to the orcas?" asks Valerie. "Are they just going to supplement it with another type of fish, or are they going to leave and look for other places?" With concerns of this type—food depletion, harassment, pollution—the Museum's position is not so much one of taking sides as of educating people and enabling them to make wise decisions on their own. "Because we're in more of a neutral position, we're very well postured to sponsor workshops and seminars and other events that deal with particular issues," says Valerie. "We can bring people together who are specialists and can talk about issues and exchange ideas so the public can learn what's going on."

When the Museum originated, it was aggressively involved in research such as identifying the whales, making acoustic recordings, and figuring out social structure and hierarchy, feeding habits and behavior. Now, however, the focus has shifted from active research to providing information.

One of the reasons is that water-based research involves expensive items such as boats, fuel, and equipment built to survive salt water and has simply become too costly to finance along with running the Museum. Staffpeople continue to offer support by providing facilities and equipment for visiting researchers who need an office or boat, but they concentrate their efforts on interpreting for laymen current fieldwork in cetology through newsletters, displays, and seminars.

"It's so hard to study marine animals, because you only see them at the surface, and that's such a small portion of their lives. It's all spent underwater—who knows what they're doing?" Valerie notes that most of the data that *can* be collected on orcas—size, numbers, food preferences, social structure—has pretty much been gathered, "and I think some of the issues we're going to be looking at now really don't have much to do with the orcas. For example, looking at salmon runs as their food source. You don't need to be around orcas to find out about the salmon runs. So I see a lot of research that could happen where you're not even dealing with the orcas."

The Museum provides lab facilities at a lighthouse on the west side of San Juan Island, where shore-based orca research continues. The lighthouse was built in the early 1900s and stands at Lime Kiln, the only whale-watching park in the nation. In the summer months, visitors to the park are often gifted with the sight of orca pods passing through, presumably following the salmon runs. At the lab, a researcher videotapes the orcas each time they pass by, noting how many boats are in the area, how close they're getting to the whales, and what kind of behavior the whales are exhibiting. Survey equipment records precise information about the whales' movements as they pass the lighthouse, and a hydrophone boom, or underwater microphone, records boat noise and whale vocalizations: sonar clicks, whistles, and calls.

For Valerie, it is the sounds that are the most thrilling. "I personally find hearing them to be much more exhilarating than seeing them, especially at night if you're out. You can't see them in the water, but you hear their blows as they come up."

She smiles. "I just love it."

*As you enter the Whale Museum, the first words to catch your eye are this quotation by Heathcote Williams: "From space the planet is blue. From space, the planet is the territory not of humans but of the whale. . . . Blue seas cover seven-tenths of the earth's surface and are the domain of the largest brain ever created, with a fifty-million-year-old smile."*

---

The Whale Museum is located at 62 First Street in Friday Harbor (P.O. Box 945, Friday Harbor, WA 98250), (360) 378-4710. Museum hours are 10 A.M.–5 P.M. from Memorial Day to October 1. Hours shift to 11 A.M.–4 P.M. from October 1 to Memorial Day. Open seven days a week. The Museum publishes a quarterly newsletter, *The Spirit of the Sound*; an activity book, *Whale Mail for Kids*, will be sent free of charge to children. A K–6 curriculum guide, *Gentle Giants of the Sea*, is also available for purchase through the Museum, as are frameable orca adoption certificates.

# KEN MCCANN
## *Walking in the Garden of Whales*

Ken McCann likes to say he holds the record for throwing up over the side of a boat while studying whales. A former director of the Whale Museum and a native New Zealander, dubbed "eccentric" and "radical" by the press and "weird" by students, who nonetheless (or perhaps therefore) love him, Ken studied sperm whales off the rugged New Zealand coast, where seasickness was a regular occurrence for rewards too brief: "You make a sighting that may last for half a day if you're lucky, and everyone gets ecstatic and jumps up and down." Coming to the Pacific Northwest, where he could observe whales all day long in protected waters, he found it "beautiful, a new world."

One of his first jobs working with whales in the Northwest involved a fairly unconventional aspect of research: playing music to orcas. As skipper of the research vessel for Interspecies Communications of San Juan Island, Ken transported groups of whale-lovers out to Robson Bight, where notables such as the Dalai Lama would paddle out to observe and commune with orcas. "The Lama wanted to hold hands with everybody in a big circle around on the rocks every morning and do telepathy. I'm a pretty open-minded person, but I thought this was kind of bizarre."

175

Yet he adds, "At one point when he was doing his thing in the morning, the whales were lob-tailing, and he said later on, 'Yes, that's just what we asked them to do.' He figured, and there's this school of thought that suggests this, that they do pick up images."

A wide variety of instruments was played every night at about eight o'clock, projected down into the depths through an underwater speaker while the boat remained at anchor. "What we said in essence was, well, if you whales like it, you can stay, and if you don't, you can buzz off. We wanted to get away from the harassment," Ken says. Orcas are very sensitive acoustically, and he decries the practice of chasing them in powerboats. "Imagine your head underwater in a tub next to a whirring Mixmaster™, and you have some idea of what an orca is hearing."

The serenaded whales showed a preference for Beethoven, baroque, and bamboo flute. They also enjoyed the violin (although not country-western fiddling) but turned tail on the deep-pitched tones of the double bass and also rock and roll. The group judged the duration of the whales' stays and their vocalization responses to be evidence of their preferences. "While no concrete conclusions were drawn, the whales seemed to prefer instruments with higher tones," says Ken. "They also responded to percussion, which is interesting because of their tremendous ability to echolocate."

Sounds are used by orcas in a variety of ways: to navigate, obtain food, communicate, even comfort. Sound may also be used to deadly effect, as when orcas "burst pulse" on a salmon, hitting or stunning it with machine-gun clicks until it floats unconscious to the surface.

Accents in vocalizations differ among orca pods, and each whale has a unique signature sound. "When playing, there'll be some vocalization," says Ken, "but if they're dispersed, that signature sound appears to be made most often, which may indicate an attempt to let the group know who and where they are."

Communication can also include water slapping, such as lob-tailing. Some suggest that the smack on the water that reverberates into the depths may be another way the whales have of letting each other know where they are. Ken disagrees. Admitting he doesn't know for sure (no one does), he feels that in many cases, the slapping is prompted by agitation: "I think they're letting people in boats know, 'Back off, you're too close!' I've also seen a semicircle of orcas lob-tailing while approaching a small bay and then feeding in the bay. This may be evidence of orcas driving the salmon into a smaller area, like dogs herding sheep, in order to feed more efficiently."

One of the most wondrous applications of whale sound is the clicking used to echolocate, an ability found only in toothed whales. When Ken explains this technique to schoolchildren, he dramatizes the lesson by blindfolding them in front of pieces of wood, carpet, and glass. Then he gives them a Ping-Pong ball. "When they throw the Ping-Pong ball at the carpet," he says, "it makes a noise, a *thunk*. If it hits the glass, it goes *pink*. If it hits the wood, *bop*. So they pretty much know what surface they're hitting even though they can't see. And they also know how far away they are from the object by the amount of time it takes for the ball to return."

The demonstration over, Ken takes on the character of Moby Slick, a ravenous sperm whale hurtling into the depths for breakfast. It's dark down there, and he asks the kids how the whale manages to find its way: "What do I do? Reach out my flipper and hit the headlights? No. I've got to switch on my sonar." He describes how the whale sends out a pulse on a wide beam from the melon (forehead) and catches it back again in the bottom jaw, which is filled with viscous oil. The whale sends out a click, "and that click travels until it hits something; then it bounces back. The whale says, 'Okay, let's see. I sent down a click and got back a click; that must be sand.' He points in a different direction, *click-clack*. Whale says, 'Hmmm, sent down a click, got back a clack; that must be rocks. Can't eat sand, can't eat rocks. I'll go over here. *Click-snap, crackle, pop*. Aha, breakfast!'

"Then the whale changes from wide to narrow beam and bursts pulse. When the sounds hit the object, they bounce back and give the whale a perfect picture, just like an X ray. The whale can see that the squid is this big, going this way, and moving this fast. Then it becomes a simple matter for it to plot its own intercept point."

Besides finding food by using sonar, regulating its body temperature, and collapsing its lungs to withstand the pressures of the deep, the whale must slow down its metabolism to about a tenth of what it is at the surface. "The whale not only has the ability to do all of that, which in itself is very marvelous," he says, "but it's also sending out, on a different frequency, constant signals in this area, which are reminding it, as it were, of the proximity of the sand, of the rocks, of the submarine, or of some twit in a boat fishing up here, while at the same time, on another frequency, it's making a call home to its mother. So they can do all of that at the same time."

The wonder and excitement in his voice show his deep love for the whale. He grows impatient with those who would downplay the capabilities of these creatures, especially to children: "I think it's extremely presumptuous for humans to decide what constitutes intelligence and set the criteria for it. There's just too many variables that humans can't take into account," he stresses. "We use what *we* know, and it doesn't work that way."

In answer to children's questions about whales' intelligence, he'll often use a delightful anecdote that came from a news clipping sent to him by a teacher. Noting that he can't vouch for the authenticity of the story and further noting that dolphins are a type of whale, he explains how a nursing dolphin simply swims up to its mother and touches her side, "and that causes her breast muscle to go into automatic eject mode. She blasts out a big mouthful of milk, which is almost ten times as rich as human milk." He goes on to describe from the article how a baby dolphin in an aquarium came face to face with an old man smoking a cigar. The man blew out a big puff of smoke a few times, and finally the baby dolphin "bopped around the tank quick as he could go, found his mother, hit her in the side. She squirted him a big mouthful of milk, he came back to where the man was, and. . . ."

Ken blows out an imaginary stream of milk. "We know that probably the dolphin had never seen smoke in air before and yet was able to say to itself, 'Well, I can do that. That's not hard.' Somehow it knew that milk in water, visually speaking, is about the same as smoke in air. So I say to the kids, 'How many humans do you know who could do that?'"

Ken got into teaching about whales by accident, he says, although one has to question whether fate doesn't play a large part in urging someone toward what is so obviously his calling. "I *love* what I do," he says. "I firmly believe that our children and our environment are our two most precious resources, and for me to be able to work with both of them is an honor and a privilege."

Currently the director for Island Institute, which specializes in week-long summer camps on Spieden Island in the San Juans, Ken also does programs for the Pacific Science Center and, in the off-season, slide-lecture presentations from elementary up to college levels.

When he teaches children, he exhaustively seeks out that which will hold a youngster's interest. "Most young children would prefer to be entertained rather than educated, so the trick is to find ways of combining both." For instance, if he's trying to convey some idea of size of the largest creature that ever lived, the blue whale, he'll describe how he discovered, over months of unceasing research, that a blue whale weighs exactly as much as four zillion, two trillion, and something M & Ms. "The kids go, Wow, that's a pretty major dude! They can relate to that." In the manner of all gifted teachers, he emphasizes that "all you need to do is somehow inspire them so that when they're no longer with you, they want to continue studying on their own."

Getting kids to think for themselves is another priority. An intense and irrev-

*Orca*

178

erent freethinker who has been called a "radical environmentalist" more times than he cares to remember (*Alaska* magazine described him as "an eccentric New Zealander who is part P. T. Barnum and part new-age seer"), Ken headed up the 1986 field effort to rescue 200 marine mammals trapped by the encroachment of Hubbard Glacier in Alaska's Russell Fjord.

"If there was something happening I didn't believe in, I went for it, threw everything I had into it," he says. Appalled one time when he discovered that because of budget constraints, tissue samples from stranded marine mammals had not been studied to determine cause of death, and concerned because samples in the 1970s had showed an alarming increase in PCBs metabolized by pinnipeds in lower Puget Sound, he worked for several months with the EPA, which consequently volunteered its expertise to analyze tissue samples for a data base in Puget Sound.

He doesn't feel, however, that it's his job to push his opinions on his students. "When people ask me how I feel about whales in captivity, it would be so easy to go about the business of creating what I call 'false disciples' simply because I dislike the practice so intensely. I could easily say I hate it, it's bad for the whale and here's why. But I don't do that. I say to the kids, 'Okay, I want you six to come up with ten good reasons why the whales should be in captivity'—education, making worldwide advocates of people who'll never get to see whales in their natural environment— 'and you six are going to come up with ten good reasons why not.' We do it around the campfire at night, and I sit back and watch them reach their own invariably correct conclusions."

There's much we still don't know about whales, and Ken encourages his students to play with the possibilities. "I try to instill in them that science is nothing more than a bunch of simpletons sitting around the same table doing the same jigsaw puzzle. And everyone who finds a part that fits is crucial to the completion of that puzzle."

One of the puzzles that has long intrigued Ken and other observers is the periodic mass strandings of whales. Basing his own beliefs on the work of Frank Robson, who wrote a book on this phenomenon, Ken suggests that *love* may provide a partial answer. To support his point, he describes how gray whales ferociously protect their young, a trait early harpooners used to their advantage. Hunters would wound a baby gray and drag it up on the beach, and its distress calls ensured that other whales wouldn't leave the area. Orcas stay with their mother's family for their entire lives, he adds, and "we know of at least two instances of dolphins supporting another at the surface in an attempt to save its life. I think we can assume from these and other documented cases that familial bonding is not something reserved exclusively for the human race."

Ken further notes that whales, unlike humans, "literally have to remind themselves to take each and every breath," and when sick, they may possibly fear drowning. "Let's hypothesize for a moment that one such sick whale decides to beach itself in an attempt to avoid the rigors of staying afloat. Now pretend that the tide goes out, leaving the animal without the buoyancy necessary to support its great

weight, which begins slowly and agonizingly to cause suffocation. Add to this the sun's powerful rays beating down on extremely sensitive skin tissue." Trumpeting its distress calls seaward, the whale may innocently lure would-be rescuers to the same fate. If results of a tissue analysis on the stranded whales show that only one suffered from a life-threatening illness and the rest were comparatively healthy, could not one reasonably speculate that something more than pure accident was involved?

Ken isn't reluctant to attribute loyalty and love to whales. "I believe also that instinct comes into play here. Whales may be unable to resist one of their own's cries for help. If one of my sons were in distress, would I consciously think about things before rushing to his assistance? Would any parent? Of any species? Isn't it a most arrogant assumption for humans to believe they're the only ones capable of such great love?" he asks, adding, "I realize, of course, there are many variables, and one explanation doesn't provide an answer for all circumstances."

He remembers a time off San Juan Island when gill nets were spread thick in the water for a one-day opening. The whales were negotiating the nets, and Ruffles, a male, swam under one and off for about a quarter of a mile. A female and her calf that were following swam "this way and came back down this way and then sort of stopped, stayed right in that area. Ruffles came back, went under the net, and swam around the outside and off they went. So there's that kind of thing going on. Somebody else will probably say, 'Well, that wasn't why the male came back. The male came back because, you know, he forgot his lunch,' or something like that. He didn't come back to rescue. But to *me* and to everybody on the boat that day, it was obvious that that was what was going on."

Ken acknowledges that it's easy to jump to conclusions about the reasons behind a whale's behavior, but he maintains that, "at the very least, opinions and theories, no matter how radical, are necessary to learn as much as we can as quickly as we can. More and more today, there are animals and ecological systems that simply cannot afford the luxury of waiting until we prove everything."

For most of us, now and through the centuries, theories and explanations are secondary to the sight of a whale surfacing. Even the simple knowledge that these Gargantuas still roam the seas is enough.

These days, when Ken takes whale-lovers out to see the grays off Westport or the orcas in the San Juans, he gives them ginger to settle their stomachs and sights and stories to inspire them. Chided at times for taking out folks by those who feel that whale-watch boats harass the animals and that only scientists with permits should have the privilege of close-up encounters, he responds with customary bluntness, "How do you figure that? Don't you think, with two thousand oil tankers coming through the Haro Strait every year, that if we have some kind of major disaster, the people willing to help are going to be there as a result of their experiences with the whales? The whales are there to be enjoyed, cared for, and cherished by all who share this planet."

When the whales need help, expect to find Ken McCann leading the way.

*Chapter 13*

# WILDLIFE GROUPS

TALKING TO AND SHARING FIELD EXPERIENCES WITH those who have an intimate knowledge of local wildlife is an excellent way to get to know our area's flora and fauna. The following list describes several wildlife and environmental groups you may wish to contact for further information.

**Friends of the ACFL:** Guardians of the 2,200 acres of Anacortes Community Forest Lands (ACFL), this active group sponsors forest and wetland education in the local elementary schools, a special "watershed" program for middle-schoolers, summer "forest discovery" outings for kids aged seven to twelve, and family and adult nature hikes. Members also assist with trail maintenance and with special projects such as reclamation of an old dump area with native seedlings. Organized in 1987, the group is dedicated to the care, protection, and enjoyment of the community forestlands in their natural state. The group is also politically active; members helped achieve a permanent logging moratorium in the ACFL. Meetings are scheduled for the second Thursday of the month; meeting place varies. Annual dues include a quarterly newsletter. Mailing address: 619 Commercial Avenue, #32, Anacortes, WA 98221.

**Friends of the San Juans:** Since 1979, the goal of this group has been to monitor land-use development in the islands to protect the scenic, natural, and socioeconomic resources of the area. Activities include offering public education workshops in support of long-range environmental planning, performing reviews of forest permits, sponsoring public forums, and generally keeping tabs on the county government. Monthly board meetings. Annual dues include a quarterly newsletter. Contact Nancy DeVaux, executive director, at (360) 378-2319 for further information.

**Guemes Island Environmental Trust:** The purpose of the GIET is "to promote a healthy, diverse natural environment through voluntary research, education, and political action where necessary. To this end, the Trust functions as an advocate for wildlife; monitors air, water, and noise pollution; and supports efforts to conserve land for the use of wildlife and the enjoyment of future generations. A commitment to these goals is the only condition of membership in the Trust." Originally formed in 1988 to fight jet noise over Guemes, the group also has taken on nori farming, logging, wetland destruction, land conservation, roadside spraying, groundwater concerns, and more. Meetings are held the second Saturday of odd-numbered months at the Guemes Island Community Hall. No annual dues. A quarterly newsletter is sent free of charge upon request. Mailing address: P.O. Box 643, Anacortes, WA 98221.

**Island Institute:** This Seattle-based, for-profit organization has a marine field station located on Spieden Island (north of San Juan Island). One-day, overnight, and seven-day marine science camps are offered June through August for all ages and custom-designed programs for groups throughout the year. A 1:5 ratio of staff to campers is maintained, and study topics include Native American traditions, marine mammals and invertebrates, native plant study, orca whale communication, and more. The Institute was founded in 1988 by Jane Howard, a science and environmental educator who has devised field-study programs for the Pacific Science Center and a number of U.S. schools. For rates and further information, call (206) 938-0345. The Institute is located at 4004 58th Place SW, Seattle, WA 98116.

**North Cascades Institute:** Developed in 1986 as a nonprofit school dedicated to studies of the Pacific Northwest's natural wonders, NCI's programs range from field seminars and elderhostels to outreach projects in the public schools. Many seminars focus on the San Juan Islands, including their geology, natural history, birds, and wildflowers. For a catalog of course offerings, write NCI at 2105 Highway 20, Sedro Woolley, WA 98284, or call (360) 856-5700, ext. 209.

**Olympic Park Institute:** OPI is another nonprofit school whose mission "is to inspire environmental stewardship through educational adventures in Nature's classroom." For over ten years, the Institute has emphasized hands-on learning experiences in the Olympic National Park, but the focus is not limited to the park. Field seminars include marine mammals, Northwest amphibians, seabirds, intertidal exploration, and ethnobotany. For the Institute's catalog, write OPI, 111 Barnes Point Road, Port Angeles, WA 98362, or call (360) 928-3720.

**San Juan Audubon Society:** This island arm of the Audubon Society began in 1980 with a group in Friday Harbor and, according to a past president, is probably "one of the most unconventional chapters in the country" because of its lack of regular meetings and committees. Nonetheless, the chapter has a faithful core

*Bufflehead*

group dedicated to both enjoying and protecting nature in the San Juans. Activities include monthly field trips, usually on the third Saturday, and a Christmas bird count. Field trips are open to the public. The chapter has also sponsored the *Audubon Adventures* program for local fourth- and fifth-graders and public education on wetlands. Membership benefits include a subscription to their newsletter, *The Trumpeter*, published five times a year. Mailing address: P.O. Box 85, Deer Harbor, WA 98243.

**San Juan Preservation Trust:** Organized in 1979 to protect farmlands, shorelines, and wildlife habitats in the San Juan Islands, this group now has nearly 6,000 acres under its protection. Members are linked by a desire to preserve the natural beauty of the islands for future generations by setting aside land on which development is either restricted or prevented. Property owners retain ownership but grant deeds of conservation easement to the Trust, which then becomes a steward of the land and safeguards it for posterity. Not opposed to development per se, the Trust supports careful, or limited, development. Membership is over 900, with an annual membership meeting held every April. The group publishes a quarterly newsletter, which can be received for a minimum donation. Mailing address: P.O. Box 327, Lopez Island, WA 98261-0327. Phone: (360) 468-3202.

**Skagit Audubon Society:** This active group offers regular programs, open to the public, on natural history, birds and other wildlife, and environmental concerns. They also sponsor regular half-day and full-day birding field trips in and out of the local area, as well as several hikes each month in the Cascade Mountains. Additional field trips focus on identification of wildflowers and mushrooms. The Skagit chapter sponsors the *Audubon Adventures* magazine, sent to more than seventy-five Skagit County classrooms, and is active in a wide variety of conservation projects in both the county and the state. A Christmas bird count is held annually, as well as a Bird-a-thon fund-raiser in May. The group meets the second Tuesday of each month, September through June, at 7:30 P.M. in the Bayview Civic Center, C Street, in Bayview. Mailing address: P.O. Box 1101, Mount Vernon, WA 98273. A membership fee covers membership in both the national and the Skagit Audubon groups and includes six issues of *Audubon Magazine* and ten of the chapter's newsletter, *The Flyer*.

**Skagit Land Trust:** The new kid on the block, the SLT was organized in 1992 to assist landowners to preserve wetlands, agricultural and forest lands, scenic open space, and shorelines throughout Skagit County. The group works with landowners to develop conservation easements on their property and subsequently monitors those easements. It's also involved in educating the public on the need for local land conservation. Board meetings are held monthly with an annual membership meeting in March. The group publishes a quarterly newsletter, the *Skagit Update*, which is sent to all members. Mailing address: P.O. Box 1017, Mount Vernon, WA 98273.

**Washington Department of Fish and Wildlife:** This state agency manages recreational use of wildlife and freshwater sport fish and marine and commercial food fish and shellfish populations. They also sponsor the Backyard Wildlife

Sanctuary Program (see below). Mailing address: 16018 Mill Creek Boulevard, Mill Creek, WA 98012. Phone: (206) 775-1311.

**Washington Native Plant Society, Salal Chapter:** This local arm of the state chapter was organized in 1990, and members focus on the conservation, appreciation, and study of our native plants and their habitats. The group includes a range of botanical devotees, from curious beginners to experienced botanists. Field trips are open to the public and are offered regularly through the year to areas of unusual or interesting plant communities, often in the archipelago. Meetings are usually held in Mount Vernon on the first Saturday of every month except July and January (during these two months, meetings are held on the second Saturday). Membership dues vary; membership includes a quarterly statewide publication, *Douglasia*, which features in-depth studies of native flora, and the local chapter's newsletter, *The Potent Teller*. Mailing address: WNPS, P.O. Box 576, Woodinville, WA 98072-0576. (They can provide current local contact names.)

---

## BACKYARD WILDLIFE SANCTUARY PROGRAM

"Do birds have any value other than aesthetic?" It was an odd question, coming as it did from a group gathered to learn how to attract wildlife to their yards. The speaker admitted we could probably survive the extinction of much of our wildlife. But he added firmly, "It's a larger question of value and quality of life. Wildlife can be the barometer of our living space, like the canary in the mine shaft."

Wild creatures are also just plain fascinating to have around, although some might not be around much longer without a little help. The speaker, an urban biologist with the Washington Department of Fish and Wildlife (WDFW), went on to ask the group, "What happens when you build a city in the middle of a bird's home?" Although the archipelago isn't Seattle, the same development pressures exist here, and residents who want to help would do well to start by turning their backyards into wildlife "safe homes."

The WDFW began the Backyard Wildlife Sanctuary program in 1985. Partially funded by the sale of personalized license plates, the program now has well over a thousand participants, from those with pocket-sized lawns to those with plantation-sized spreads (including the governor's estate).

If you are interested in encouraging backyard wildlife, write the WDFW at 16018 Mill Creek Boulevard, Mill Creek, WA 98012, and request their backyard sanctuary information. For a fee, the WDFW will send a packet with various tip sheets: how to build nest boxes, how to attract hummingbirds, what to plant for wildlife in western Washington, how to set up water sources for birds, and more. An application for sanctuary status, which simply asks potential members to inventory sources of food, water, and shelter already in their yards, is also included.

Once the inventory is submitted, the property may be designated an "official" wildlife sanctuary. (Such a designation, by the way, places no legal obligation on the owner.) Membership in the program includes an all-weather sanctuary sign, as well as, each spring and fall, a WDFW newsletter, *Crossing Paths*, which provides updates on the program and regular tips for welcoming wildlife.

Let's take a look at some of these tips as a sample of what the WDFW has to offer. First of all, the number and types of plants in your yard are most important in attracting wildlife. Feeders are supplementary to a good variety of trees and shrubs; the more vegetation, the more insects, and thus the more insect-eating birds. Good tree and shrub choices include vine maple, paper birch, hawthorn, red-flowering currant, elderberry, and serviceberry.

Multiple layers of vegetation attract best. Don't "park out" your woodlands, says the WDFW. Instead, leave a natural understory of bushes and deadfalls to provide animals such as raccoons with slugs, snails, berries, insects, and shelter. Leave logs, rocks, and brush piles as homes for small mammals. Include a fencerow of native shrubs for a long, continuous shelter (quail love it), and don't prune the lower branches.

If cavity nesters could talk, they might echo a common complaint heard throughout the islands these days: Where can one find a cozy, modest home to raise a family? Though they aren't being priced out of the area, they're being pushed out nonetheless as more and more trees disappear. So leave those snags for about forty-three different kinds of birds in western Washington, including chickadees, nuthatches, flickers, swallows, and wrens.

How to help out nesters come early spring? Save odds and ends of yarn, thread, string, dryer lint, fur, and hair, and hang them from a limb in a loose mesh bag. Keep cats inside. Allow approximately a quarter acre between nesting boxes, since most species are territorial. Cover openings under eaves where house sparrows or starlings nest, because these nonnative species compete with native ones for nesting sites. Crows should also be discouraged, as they'll kill other birds' offspring.

Finally, some tips on food and water. The WDFW advises against the use of seed mixes; instead try the larger sunflower seeds and cracked corn, with suet in the winter. (Skagit Wild Bird Supply at 1518 Memorial Highway, (360) 424-5575, sells a wide range of seed for avian appetites.) Keep feeder food dry and relatively fresh or it will spoil and may harm the birds (as this is being written, salmonella spread by bird droppings mixed with food is killing local birds). Don't prune all the deadwood out of your yard, because it draws the insects woodpeckers feed on, and plant flowers for butterflies and hummingbirds (good choices include lavender, butterfly bush, coral bells, French marigolds, and foxglove).

*Salmonberry*

Still waters may run deep, but they don't attract half the wildlife moving water does. Try running a hose along a branch over a birdbath and letting it drip. Or punch a hole in an old pail, hang it over a shallow dish or overturned trash can lid (birds aren't fussy), and fill the pail daily with water. Sink an old tub into the ground to attract amphibians, and seed it with a bucket or two of "soup water" from a nearby pond.

Sound intriguing? Why not tap into the WDFW program for guidance and start planning your own wildlife haven now? Begin with a logbook, or nature diary, to help take stock of your property and wildlife: divide a looseleaf notebook into thirds, and use one section to record what animals you've seen doing what and where, and include time of day and weather. Use the next section to inventory your land as it is now by listing all plants (types, sizes, locations) and any large rocks, dead trees, brush piles, or grassy areas.

Then do a scaled diagram of your property's dimensions on graph paper, including buildings and paths, where the windows are (for viewing wildlife), and where the sun falls (for plantings), but not current vegetation. Make a few copies of this skeleton draft and fill one with the items listed in your inventory. This "before" record will help you later decide where to move existing plants and so forth to maximize benefits for wildlife. In the last section, turn one of those drafts into a "dream" plan to guide your sanctuary efforts over the days, weeks, or years to come. The reading list below should help with your planning.

### Suggested Reading

*Attracting Backyard Wildlife*, by Bill Merilees. Stillwater, Minn.: Voyageur Press, 1989.

*Backyard Bird Habitat*, by Will and Jane Curtis. Woodstock, Vt.: Countryman Press, 1980.

*The Backyard Bird Watcher*, by George Harrison. New York: Simon & Schuster, 1979.

*The Backyard Naturalist*, by Craig Tufts. Washington, D.C.: National Wildlife Federation, 1988.

*The Birdhouse Book*, by D. McNeil. Seattle: Pacific Search Press, 1979.

*A Complete Guide to Bird Feeding*, by John Dennis. New York: Alfred A. Knopf, 1982.

*The Naturalist's Garden*, by Ruth Shaw Ernst. Emmaus, Pa.: Rodale Press, 1987.

*Suburban Wildlife*, by Richard Headstrom. Englewood Cliffs, N.J.: Prentice-Hall, 1984.

*Wildlife in Your Garden*, by Gene Logsdon. Emmaus, Pa.: Rodale Press, 1983.

# CHARLIE NASH
## The Islands' Eagle Eye

During the twenty years Charlie Nash spent as Friday Harbor's postmaster, he found a use for the post office building that went a bit beyond business. The postal landing was conveniently high enough that he could step out with a direction finder and track a radio-tagged bald eagle that hung out around Cape San Juan. "He never did leave, hardly," says Charlie, whose placid tone belies a passion for eagles. "It was always the same bearing."

The former postmaster became interested in bald eagles back in the early 1960s when he read an article in *Audubon Magazine* that announced that there were only three active eagle nests in the state. "Well, I knew there were more than that because I'd seen them," says Charlie. "So I thought, Well, I'll see how many I can find to repudiate that." Flying over the islands, he found ten or twelve nests in the San Juans alone. He continued watching for nests from his fishing boat, and pilot friends began telling him when they spotted nests from the air. "It just grew and grew," he says.

Eventually, a formal nesting survey for San Juan County was born. Island eagles mate in mid-February, and in March they lay one to three eggs. The eagle pair trades off covering the nest during the thirty-five-day incubation period, although the female assumes the greater responsibility, and both feed and care for the young, which hatch out in April. For the survey, Charlie would check the nests in early April for any signs of activity and again in June to count the chicks.

Years of close observation have made Charlie into a local expert on the bald eagle. At his home in Friday Harbor, he leans over a chart of the islands heavily measeled with black spots and points to one on Orcas. "That's a very popular nest there. It's been there for ages, probably centuries." One of the first and largest nests he found was on Turn Island, near Friday Harbor, an impressive dwelling estimated at 11 feet deep and 5 feet wide. Bald eagles build the largest nests of all birds in North America, with some weighing in at more than a ton. The nest on Turn finally fell off when the tree rotted out, but Charlie notes that the couple may have rebuilt in another spot, because an eagle pair still frequents the area.

Eagles usually build alternate nests, possibly as backups in case the main one is lost, which happened on Turn, or because, as Charlie believes, the main nest "gets so vermin-infested from food that starts to rot. Then they'll move over to their alternate nest, until the other one leaches out. It might be one year, two years, whatever." Sometimes, he says, you'll find old and brittle trees with hardly a limb left, because eagles have broken off every branch that's small enough for nest building.

The San Juan Audubon Society reports a couple of interesting observations made by a state park ranger who saw immature balds "practicing" nest building on Sucia Island in the alternate nest sites of their parents. The "play-work" of eagle youngsters apparently isn't restricted to familiar nest sites, because immatures were also observed working sticks into an abandoned osprey nest in Moran State Park on Orcas.

According to Charlie, nests are usually built along a shore facing north or northwest, so that the sun is at the birds' backs when they feed in the early morning. There's little glare on the water then as the eagles are hunting for fish or seabirds, their mainstay in the winter. "They like fish," he says, "but there are a lot more seabirds available, like gulls. I'll bet at least half their food is birds, either cormorants or gulls."

Most of the island eagles satisfy their longings for fish by heading north and east to mainland rivers at the end of August to feed on the spawning salmon, with a wave of adults returning to the islands again in October. (A second, larger group of both immature and adult eagles returns in January.) Their diet also includes small mammals and carrion.

Wanting to demonstrate for professors from Switzerland how eagles catch their prey, Charlie once took a 3-pound salmon he had caught, injected it with air so it would float, and threw it out over the water. An eagle picked it up, but "it was pretty heavy for him. He just got off the water and flew real low to the shoreline, stopped on a rock just above the water and rested a little bit, then flew to a limb, and eventually zigzagged his way up to the nest." Eagles may weigh up to 14 pounds and can carry aloft up to half their body weight. I've heard of a cat on Orcas that came home with talon marks on it, but stories of eagles carrying off live lambs or pet poodles are questionable at best.

When an osprey hunts for fish, it may completely submerge itself in its quest. The bird's wing joint is made so that the wide surface of the wing doesn't hit the water. Bald eagles lack that adaptation; when they hit the water, their wings stick to it, giving rise to the many tales of eagles swimming 2 to 3 miles back to shore. Charlie adds that when a fish is too heavy for an eagle to carry aloft, the bird will swim with its wings to shore, clutching the fish in its talons.

Bald eagles apparently mate for life (Charlie equivocates on this) and will defend their nests, which can be found every 2 to 10 miles along the shore, according to *Birding in the San Juan Islands*. "They like the locations they pick, and they'll stay there the rest of their lives if they can. They'll defend it against other eagles." He tells the story of two enemies locking talons and hitting the water. The birds eventually became disconnected and one flew off to its nest, but the other, the interloper, was far too waterlogged to fly. So Charlie and a friend popped him into a sack and took him over to a vacant house where he'd have some cover to cool down and dry off.

When asked if he has ever seen a pair lock talons in a courtship flight, his tone becomes reverent. "Oh, it's spectacular." A commercial fisherman, he spends a lot of time in Alaska and saw the most impressive display when he was anchored in a bay up there. "This pair was flying around like they were getting ready to do their thing, and they grasped talons. One of them was really active," he remembers. "I guess the wind had them all stirred up. Anyway, they grabbed talons and went down, just whirling to the beach." One of life's givens is that courtship carries with it a certain amount of risk, however, and with eagles it's apparently no different. Charlie recalls a story of a couple of fellows out at Mitchell Bay who found two eagles that had locked talons and couldn't *unlock*, perhaps because the talons of one had jammed into the other's toe joints. They were caught over the limb of a tree, one hanging on each side, still alive. The birds' rescuers took a tall pole and "kept working with it till they finally got 'em free."

We're able in the islands to see eagles on a regular basis, thanks to good habitat and food supply. Scan the shorelines for the tallest trees and that telltale spot of white that shows an eagle at rest, perching or preening after having fed. (If the birds are hunting, Charlie says, they'll be down lower, closer to the water.) If you're out in a boat, look for places where the tide changes, and look closely at points of land. He recommends American Camp along South Beach as probably the best place to regularly observe eagles, thanks to the rampant rabbit population. "You get out there the first crack of dawn and you'll see plenty of eagles. They come out and get their breakfast before most people show up."

It's easy to confuse a bald eagle on the wing with another large raptor, the golden eagle. Should you spot the two silhouetted against the sun and thus stripped of distinguishing colors, note the length of the head on each. The bald's head is quite long, more than half the length of its tail, whereas the gold's head profile is shorter than half its tail length. Golden eagles are rarely seen in other parts of western Washington, but the San Juans are blessed with a few resident breeding pairs.

There are approximately ninety-four nesting pairs of bald eagles in the islands, a healthy population. (In 1990, about 315 balds were counted in the midwinter bald eagle survey for the WDFW. The winter population usually swells by about 5 percent with Alaskan migrants.) But development is taking more and more of the prime nesting spots along the shoreline. To help the eagles, San Juan County was one of the first to approve the 330/660 rule, which says a property owner may not cut timber within 330 feet of a nest, and which limits cutting in the next 330 feet. Fines have been levied in the islands for improper cutting, and Charlie recalls a fellow who disregarded the rule and cut down a tree with an active nest in it. A young woman from the county came out, and "this little lady was about that tall and skinny as a rail, I don't think she weighed eighty pounds. She forced that guy right back to California."

There's a certain triumph in his laughter, not surprising from a man who has devoted so much time to and received so much pleasure from watching eagles. "They're just interesting birds," he says with a shrug, "and I like to go on my boat and see if they're still at it."

All of us who hold them dear hope that the island eagles will remain "at it" for a long, long time.

# PART 4

# Wildlife Reference Section

*"The animal shall not be measured by the man.
In a world older and more complete than ours,
they move finished and complete,
gifted with extensions of the senses we have lost
or never attained, living by voices
we shall never hear."*

*—Henry Beston*

(The following is an alphabetized list of the islands' most common species of flora and fauna, discussed and italicized in the previous sections. A review of a few local field guides is also provided for those wishing to further their knowledge in a specific wildlife area.)

# REFERENCE LIST

**Alder, Red** (*Alnus rubra*). Once used by Native Americans to make cradles, dishes, and the long slow fires that cooked the salmon, red alder is the Northwest's fastest-growing tree. It is not, however, long-lived, with a maximum age of only about one hundred years. Leaves are roundish with toothed edges, and the smooth light-gray bark may look as white as birch if heavily colonized by lichens. Male and female flowers are on the same tree; the long male catkins appear in early spring before the leaves and soon disintegrate after pollinating the female cones. The alder is the only broadleaf tree to bear its fruit in a cone; clusters of tiny cones that hold the seeds of future trees mature in late summer and hang until the following spring. Alders like moist soils; nodules on the tree's roots convert the air's nitrogen into chemicals that enhance the soil and inhibit a fungus that causes heart rot in Douglas-firs. Alder leaves also have a high nitrogen content, which further improves the soil as the leaves rot, making the ubiquitous alder a tree vital to the health of our forests.

**Barnacle, Acorn** (*Balanus glandula*). Our most commonly observed barnacle is actually not, as you might suspect, a mollusk like the clam or oyster but a crustacean, related to the shrimp and crab. When we see it, the barnacle is shut up within its white conelike shell plastered to a rock, but at an earlier stage of its life, this creature roamed free and shell-less in the water. Eventually (and it's fascinating to wonder why), the barnacle eschews its wandering life and fastens headfirst to a hard surface such as a rock, piling, or boat bottom. It further vies for the claim of most antisocial creature by then building around itself a fortlike structure of calcified outer and inner plates, out of which it will never again emerge or even see. (Eventually, the adult barnacle loses the sight it never uses.) Inside the shell, the barnacle lies on its back, its head cemented for life and legs extending into the water at high tide to sweep plankton and detritus into its mouth. When the tide is out, the inner plates close up, trapping water inside to keep the gills wet until the tide returns. When the barnacle is again covered with water, the plates open and the feathery legs emerge once more. The barnacle is found worldwide but only in salt water and is preyed upon by sea stars and sea snails. Look for other barnacles in our area also, such as the goose barnacle (*Pollicipes polymerus*), with a leathery brown "neck" or stalk, found on exposed shores, and the heavily ridged thatched barnacle (*Semibalanus cariosus*).

**Bat, Little Brown** (*Myotis lucifugus*). Our most common bat has a 5-inch furred body from head to tail with a wingspread about double that length. It is brown above and lighter beneath, with a hairy face and a tiny, mouselike snout. The tail membrane is unfurred on the top side. During the day, the bat roosts head down in hollow trees, caves, or buildings. It mates in the fall but doesn't give birth until the spring, usually to only one offspring, which is able to fly at three weeks. Solely insect eaters, these bats are most active 1 hour after sunset and 1 hour before sunrise in pursuit of their prey. Extremely capable hunters, bats zero in on insects and avoid obstacles by bouncing sounds off objects and receiving those sounds back into their large, funnel-like ears. Supposedly, the amount of time the sound takes to travel from bat to object to bat again allows the creature to judge distances. You won't hear these ultra-high-frequency sounds, although bats may also make squeaks within our hearing range. Our only true flying mammals (flying squirrels glide), bats may make over a thousand dives per hour in their pursuit of insects and may eat up to a quarter of their weight in one evening. Look for them at dusk above lakes, wetlands, and meadows. (If you spot a larger, reddish-colored bat with a wing size of a foot or more, you've likely caught sight of *Eptesicus fuscus*, the big brown bat.) Little brown bats may live over twenty years, are found throughout North America, and migrate out of our area in the autumn.

**Beaver** (*Castor canadensis*). Weighing in at an average of 40 pounds, the familiar "slaptail" is our largest rodent. Rodents are gnawing mammals, and with large yellow-orange incisors that perform as strong chisels, the beaver is a master at gnawing, cutting down willows, alders, and cottonwoods for food (despite their affinity for water, beavers don't eat fish but are strictly vegetarian) and any trees available for its dams and lodges. The beaver is also a skilled engineer, damming streams to form ponds where it can live, building lodges in or on the edges of those ponds (it may also dig burrows into the banks of ponds or lakes), and digging canals to connect ponds or provide watery routes for floating trees to the ponds.

The beaver has nostrils that close down underwater; protective, transparent eyelids; and flaps of skin (lips) that close behind the incisors to seal out water. Its forefeet are small and clawed, whereas its hind feet are large and webbed. The paddle tail is covered with overlapping scales and, contrary to popular belief, is not used as a trowel to mud its lodge but rather to control the direction of its swimming, to prop itself up as it fells a tree, and to slap warning signals on the water's surface.

Beavers may live fifteen to twenty years and supposedly mate for life. In May or June, two to six kits are born; a typical lodge family includes the parents plus the litters of two successive years. Look for trunks and branches with chiseled tooth marks, wood chips, twigs peeled of bark, and scent mounds—piles of mud, or mud mixed with grass and sticks, on which the beaver has left its scent, castoreum oil. This oil is also combed through the beaver's thick fur to waterproof its coat. Droppings are usually deposited underwater, and tracks are often obscured by the dragging tail, although you may occasionally spot a webbed hind track about 6 inches long.

**Blackberry, Trailing** *(Rubus ursinus)*. Our native blackberry is also known as the dewberry or the wild or Pacific blackberry. A ground creeper with small, tasty fruit enjoyed by birds, deer, and hikers, this prickly vine is often seen twining along forest paths and across tree stumps or, most heavily, over cleared land. Alternate leaves are dull green and usually have three leaflets. Five-petaled white flowers appear in May on male and female plants; male flowers are longer, about 1¹/₂ inches across compared to the female's ³/₄ inch. Berries ripen from red to black in August. We also have two other blackberries in our area, both introduced species: the large Himalayan, which has tall, stiff canes and brutal thorns, and the evergreen, which can be told by its sharply divided, toothed leaves.

**Blackbird, Red-Winged** *(Agelaius phoeniceus)*. The breeding (polygamous) male red-wing is easily identified by scarlet shoulder patches edged with yellow and a ringing *conkaree* song in early spring. (The call is a low *chek*.) The female is a comparatively nondescript brown, with a heavily streaked brown-and-white breast. She weaves a basket nest usually among marsh plants; look for it, once the nesting season is over, hanging on a cattail stem or willow branch. A clutch is usually three to five pale blue, darkly streaked eggs. Found throughout North America, the bird is a year-round resident here and the hothead of the marsh in springtime, when the male aggressively defends territory from other males and even raptors and humans. After the breeding season, the birds may be seen foraging in large flocks for weed seeds in the autumn fields, pastures, and marshlands.

**Bracken** *(Pteridium aquilinum)*. Our tallest-growing fern, the bracken may reach a height of 3 feet. The scientific name is derived from the Greek *pteris*, which means "wing," not a clumsy comparison for these triangular fronds, which resemble pairs of wings decreasing in size the higher they sprout on the stem. The fern grows from a pencil-thin rootstock that spreads quickly in woods or waste areas. Its fiddlehead has a silvery hair covering and is sometimes said to resemble an eagle's claw. This perennial is one of the only ferns to be killed by frost; it dies back each year, becoming tan and brittle. Bracken is found worldwide and has proven both useful as roof thatching and food and inspirational as the crux of countless superstitions. For instance, cutting the stem supposedly reveals the letter C in the cross-section, which has been taken as a symbol of both Christ and the devil's cloven hoof.

**Brant** *(Branta bernicla)*. The brant nests in the arctic and travels through our area on its winter migration to Baja California, with the largest concentrations of birds wintering over on Padilla and Samish bays, usually beginning in late October. (Most of the flocks, which can exceed 200,000 birds, continue south, but several thousand geese remain on the bays throughout the winter; listen for their call, a low, harsh *karr-onk*.) In the islands, look for them taking a break from their spring migration at Spencer Spit, which has a good supply of eelgrass—a mainstay of this bird's diet—and a sandy beach where the brant can access the grit they need to digest the grass. A small black-and-brown goose with white belly and rump, the brant can also be identified by a white half-ring around the neck (immature birds lack this feature); in flight, the leading edges of the wings slope back sharply.

Although a goose, the brant doesn't fly in a V-shaped Canada goose formation but in long, undulating lines that may ball up and then spread out again. Strong, fast flyers, brant make migratory flights of several thousand miles as many as eight times during their lives. Like gulls, they're able to drink sea water on the way because of glands that excrete the salt. Brant are game birds, but the WDFW drastically curtailed hunting here in the early 1980s until faltering populations recovered, and the agency still keeps a close watch on the birds, which don't reproduce as rapidly as other waterfowl.

**Bufflehead** (*Bucephala albeola*). From October until the middle of May, buffies are a common and cheerful sight on our freshwater ponds and saltwater bays. This small, mostly white diving duck breeds in Alaska and western Canada in trees near mountain lakes, laying up to a dozen buff-colored eggs at a time; some nonbreeders remain in our area through the summer. The adult male is easily recognized by its white head patch, although this field mark may lead beginning birders to confuse the bird with a male hooded merganser. The buffy's flanks, however, are white, not brown like the merganser's, and its bill is stubbier. Female buffies have a more subdued appearance; their flanks are duskier, their heads are grayish brown instead of black, and instead of a large white head patch, they have a smaller white cheek patch. Some birds pair up here in the spring before leaving for northern breeding grounds; watch for courtship displays then and some aggressive head bobbing among drakes.

Buffleheads dive to feed on fish and crustaceans and are able to burst out of the water directly into flight. Watch as a group dives for food; supposedly, one buffy will often remain at the surface on sentry duty. Settlers called this bird the "buffalo-head" because, in their view, the large-headed bird resembled the equally large-headed buffalo. (The buffy's genus name, *Bucephala*, actually comes from the Latin for "ox-head.") It has also been called the "butterball" by those who admire its chunky, rounded shape.

**Cattail** (*Typha latifolia*). A plant of the marshes that roots in mud or shallow water, cattails can grow to more than 6 feet high. Stalks end in two flowering spikes; the uppermost becomes golden by early summer with yellowish male flowers, which pollinate the female flowers on the stalk below and then are shed, leaving behind a withered upper spike. The lower, spongy spike is actually a tight mass of female flowers, which become brown when the plant's fruits mature after pollination and then burst into fluff in the autumn. One ripened spike may release as many as two million tiny nutlike fruits borne on downy hairs and set free by the wind all through the winter.

Cattails provide shelter for waterfowl and house construction materials not only for the muskrat's domelike domicile but also for early Northwest natives, who wove the straplike leaves into temporary summer mat shelters. The leaves, which are light green in summer and eventually become tan and brittle, have large air cells that store oxygen, scarce in wet soils, and that make the leaves feel spongy when squeezed. Red-winged blackbirds, marsh wrens, and yellowthroats all nest among cattails.

**Chiton, Black** (*Katharina tunicata*). The second-largest chiton on our coastline, the familiar black chiton grows up to about 4 inches long. Fairly abundant on rocky shores at low tide, this mollusk grazes slowly over the rocks, scraping off algae and diatoms with its rasplike radula, before heading back again to its home spot. Chitons attach to the sides or crevices of rocks by means of a strong muscular foot, which is also used for crawling. This yellowish foot, with lines of fringed gills on either side, clamps so firmly to a rock that to break the suction it's usually necessary to slip a knife (or the bill of an oystercatcher) between it and the rock. Eight overlapping shell plates along its leathery back, or mantle, give it the defensive ability to curve its shell when detached from a rock.

Chitons reproduce by releasing long threads of eggs in the water to be fertilized by the male's sperm. They don't have eyes, but minute bumps scattered over their bodies are sensitive to light and touch. Should you spot a similar-sized, greenish gray chiton with its eight plates covering more of the mantle and edged with bristly hairs, you've come across a mossy chiton or perhaps a hairy chiton, which has softer hairs. These two are not usually found on open rock surfaces, as is the black chiton, but favor tidepools, crevices, and the undersides of rock ledges.

**Cormorant, Double-Crested** (*Phalacrocorax auritus*). Perhaps our most commonly seen cormorant, the double-crested is a year-round resident in the islands, often seen perched on pilings as it spreads wide its wings to dry its soaked plumage. Because the bird lacks complete waterproofing and also possesses a dense skeletal structure, it is able to dive to depths of over 100 feet.

This nearly 3-foot-tall "sea crow" with the long, snaky neck and the bill hooked at its tip is all black except for an orange-yellow coloring around its eyes and throat. The only change in breeding season is a few white plumes on top of the head. (Immatures have more brown in their feathers.) Of the three species seen regularly here in the islands, this is the only one you'll see on lakes as well as on salt water. They're also the only ones that build bulky nests of sticks lined with seaweed, to which they add each year. Double-cresteds nest in colonies on rocky offshore islands, laying three or four pale blue eggs. Though usually voiceless, they will croak hoarsely in the breeding territory or when alarmed.

Two other species are common here in the islands: the Brandt's cormorant and the pelagic cormorant. Brandt's cormorants, which have a buff-colored band across the throat, are also found year-round but breed off the ocean shores; only nonbreeders are seen here during the summer. Pelagic cormorants are resident breeders, slightly smaller and slimmer than the other two and with a red throat patch. To distinguish the three species in flight, look for a kink in the base of the neck of the double-crested; the equally long neck of the Brandt's cormorant lacks the kink. The neck of the pelagic is long, straight, and thin. Its tail is longer and slimmer than the others', and during breeding season white flank patches are visible. In breeding plumage, the pelagic also looks much more "double-crested" with its two distinct head crests than the rather poorly named double-crested cormorant (on whom the narrow crest of feathers above and back of each eye is rarely visible).

**Crab, Hairy Hermit** (*Pagurus hirsutiusculus*). "Harry Hermit" I like to call this comical little animal, as it so definitely seems to have a personality. Far feistier than the barnacle, which retreats from the world within its fortress, the tiny hermit crab is ever ready to seek out new shelter and do battle over empty shells. Only about an inch long at adulthood, as it grows, the hermit faces the continuing challenge of finding an abandoned spiral shell home of a snail or whelk to occupy. When it happens upon a likely prospect, the crab carefully inspects the shell by tapping it with its antennae (its eyes are on stalks between the antennae) and rotating the shell until it determines its suitability. Then, in the fastest home-closing deal in the west, the hermit zips out of its old shell and backs its soft abdomen speedily into the new one, its end pair of limbs clamping the inner shell and its larger front claws blocking the entrance. Speed is of the essence, as the shell-less crab is vulnerable to predators, including other hermits, who have no compunction about nailing a dawdling house hunter.

Hermits are scavengers and eat whatever flesh they can find. Their first pair of legs is used both to gather food and to fight; the second and third pairs are for walking. In June or July, male hermits deposit sperm within the shells of females, whose eggs are later fertilized when laid.

The hairy hermit, with fuzzy legs and antennae, is the most commonly seen crab in tide pools. More often found in pools lower down on the shore is the granular hermit crab, which is comparatively hairless. This species can withdraw completely within its shell, whereas Harry Hermit often settles for a shell that doesn't allow such a full retreat. Pick one of these crabs up and soon it will poke its curious head out; then it will scurry off to safety and perhaps yet another round of house hunting.

**Crow, Common** (*Corvus brachyrhynchos*). In the San Juans, a smaller subspecies of the common crow forages along the shoreline, raids town garbage containers, and steals eggs from the nests of gulls and other seabirds. This is the northwestern crow, which seldom strays far from salt water. It has a more nasal tone than that of the common crow, supposedly sounding more like *car* than *caw*, if you have a fine enough ear to know.

Flocks of crows roost together in the same spot each night and often fly off to the same foraging areas each morning. Nests are bulky masses of twigs and sticks, usually high up in a tree and close to the trunk. Crows lay anywhere from three to nine pale blue-green, blotched eggs and may have more than one brood in a year.

Highly intelligent birds, crows will hide objects, often seeming to prefer shiny ones, and recall their caches without difficulty weeks later. Scientists know of at least twenty-five different sounds made by the crow, which has the ability to imitate other animal sounds and even sings a tuneful song; this may come as a surprise to those who know only the familiar grating squawk. Apparently the crow will indulge in lyricism if it doesn't have an audience, somewhat like a tough guy shedding a tear when no one's looking. Shakespeare noted this in *The Merchant of Venice:* "The crow doth sing as sweetly as the lark / When neither is attended."

**Currant, Red-Flowering** (*Ribes sanguineum*). The blooming of this shrub is one of the very first signs of an island spring. Small clusters of drooping red flowers usually appear in March, although one bush flowered on a south-facing slope at Bowman Bay as early as January 17! The shrub's blooms usually wither in May, after offering up a wellspring of nectar for rufous hummingbirds. Leaves are maplelike, dull green, and roundish, with three to five lobes. Blue-black berries July to September are enjoyed by birds, if not by people. Also known as the winter currant and blood currant, the shrub grows up to 5 feet high in the wild and favors open woods, roadsides, and sunny, dry areas.

**Deer, Columbian Black-tailed** (*Odocoileus hemionus columbianus*). Also called by some the mule deer, of which it's a subspecies, the black-tail's large, sensitive ears earn it the comparison; its other distinguishing field mark is a bushy tail, black on top and white underneath. A fairly small deer, the black-tail stands only about 2$\frac{1}{2}$ to 3 feet high at the shoulder and seldom weighs more than 200 pounds. Its coat is reddish in summer and gray in winter; the belly is white. Antlers of adult males are forked, and often the forks branch into four points on each antler. They're shed well after the November breeding season, in late winter, and either decay or are eaten by rodents. New antlers bud out in the spring, tender and covered with soft "velvet," and as they harden, the bucks polish them against tree trunks and soon have a gleaming pair of weapons with which to challenge others during the mating season.

Mating occurs in the fall and early winter; spotted fawns are born spring and early summer, May to June, usually only one per year, although twins also occur. The spotted coats mimic the dappling light of the forest, effectively camouflaging the youngsters while their mother is off feeding. Fawns lose their spots in the fall and are by that time weaned and feeding on shrubs and grass; a heavier winter coat soon comes in.

Look for deer grazing in open glades or fields or along brushy forest margins. Favorite browse includes the shoots and leaves of forest shrubs such as huckleberry, thimbleberry, and salmonberry, as well as clover, skunk cabbage, hedge nettle, mushrooms, low-growing trees, and plants of the summer meadows. Should you startle a deer, notice its stiff, bounding gait, called stotting, during which all four feet bunch together. Excellent swimmers, black-tails may also be seen paddling between islands, although perhaps less now than formerly, with all the boat traffic! They are common in the San Juans, from the shoreline to the slopes of Mount Constitution and too often, tragically, in the road.

Black-tails seldom live more than ten years in the wild. An albino buck seen on Guemes Island in the 1970s lives on in deer bearing the traces of his lineage in their gray-white flanks. Should you happen to see what look like small albino deer while boating by Spieden Island, you've spotted a nonnative species, the European fallow deer, introduced when the island was tricked out in the 1970s to resemble an African game farm.

**Douglas-Fir** (*Pseudotsuga menziesii*). The largest and most abundant tree in Washington and one of the country's most important lumber trees, this species takes its name from the Scottish botanist David Douglas, who sent its seeds back to Europe in 1827. The Doug-fir name is properly hyphenated because the tree is not a true fir, on which cones stand erect, but more closely resembles a hemlock or spruce. (The name *Pseudotsuga* means "false hemlock.") Cones hang downward and have unique three-pronged, "pitchfork" bracts, which alternate with the seed-bearing scales. Male flowers are yellow, conelike stuctures, near the twig ends, that open and shed pollen in the spring. Female buds, at the twig tips, become brushy tufts of scales and bracts; after pollination, they ripen to the familiar cones in autumn.

Inch-long needles surrounding the branches give a bottlebrush effect. In shaded forests, where the tree is usually associated with hemlock and cedar, the lower limbs drop off, leaving a long branchless trunk. Bark on the younger trees is a smooth gray-brown with resin blisters, which have a wonderful fragrance when broken; as the tree ages, its bark becomes more heavily ridged, or "corky," and sometimes more than an inch thick (over a foot thick in giant specimens), providing good insulation from fire.

Doug-fir may grow to over 250 feet high and 6 feet in diameter; some of these giants can still be seen on the Olympic Peninsula. Well loved by children as the common Christmas tree of our area, Doug-fir also rates high with wildlife. Deer eat the new shoots and foliage; squirrels harvest the cones even before they ripen; crossbills, winter wrens, shrews, and mice feed on the seeds; brown creepers search the bark furrows for insects; and mushrooms grow on the dead wood. Commercial products include structural lumber, plywood, and paper. The tree's straight, strong trunks have also been used as masts; the 214-foot flagpole at Kew Gardens, England, is cut from this tree. Northwest tribes used the tree's boughs in sweat lodges and boiled its needles for a tonic.

**Dragonfly.** Fossils suggest that dragonflies once had a 2-foot or larger wingspan some three hundred million years ago. Today, two pairs of 2-inch gauzy wings laced with veins (each wing able to move independently of the other) carry aloft one of the world's most spectacular flyers. Capable of speeds up to 35 miles per hour, dragonflies can also hover or fly backward and catch and consume flying insects on the wing. Mosquitoes, flies, gnats, and bees are captured in a basket formed by the front four of the dragonfly's six legs; the aerial wonders can eat their own weight in insects in half an hour. They have chewing mouth parts (dragonflies are of the order Odonata, which means "toothed jaws"), as well as bulging eyes, which are the largest in the insect world and which can scope out prey up to 40 yards away.

Dragonflies flying in tandem are mating. After fertilization, a female hovers briefly over the water and dips her abdomen in to release her eggs or else deposits the eggs in mud or plant tissue. Eggs hatch into aquatic nymphs with huge lower "lips" that can be extended like frogs' tongues to shovel up food such as insect larvae.

Several thousand species of dragonflies exist around the world. Some common Northwest species include green darners (green thorax, blue abdomen, clear wings), western flying adders (brown thorax with yellow marks, black abdomen with yellow patches), and the swift long-winged skimmers (blue to violet with yellowish, brown-striped sides). Darners fly high, skimmers low. Damselflies are sometimes confused with dragonflies, but they hold their four wings vertically over the back when at rest, not horizontally as dragonflies do. They're also not as large as dragonflies, and they have a more brilliantly colored, slender, "twiglike" abdomen. Damselflies also are shorter-lived, lasting only for about one or two weeks. Adult dragonflies live at most ten weeks, though the majority probably live less than five.

**Eagle, Bald** (*Haliaeetus leucocephalus*). One of the largest and most magnificently visible birds of prey here in the archipelago, the bald eagle has a 7-foot wingspread, dark-brown body and wings, yellow bill, yellow eye, and yellow, unfeathered feet. Immatures have a dark eye and lack the adult's familiar white head and tail until anywhere from three to seven years, during which time they may be easily confused with the golden eagle. (Golds, however, have a three-toned bill and a tail that is white at the base. They are also feathered to the toes.) As with most raptors, females are larger than males.

The long scientific name means "white-headed sea eagle," which should relieve those who consider turkey vultures the only true bald-headed raptor. This eagle's primary food is fish, but it will also eat waterfowl, crabs, small mammals, and carrion, and it won't hesitate to pirate food from other raptors such as ospreys. Look for pellets (about 3-inch-long cylinders or 1-inch-wide balls) of regurgitated feathers, fur, and now and then a bone; most bones are easily digested in the bird's strong stomach acids.

A bald eagle usually nests near water in a bulky stick platform. The nest is placed high up in the tallest conifer, usually just below the top of the tree, and added to yearly. (Golden eagles normally nest on cliffs, but when using trees they will nest *below* the canopy, whereas ospreys build nests on the tops of dead trees.) Many build more than one nest, possibly as backups for the main one in case of blowdown or parasite infestation, or even as additional declarations of territory.

Bald eagles mate for life, and pairs defend the nesting territory. Breeding occurs here in February; one to three eggs are laid in March, and the young hatch out in April, fledging eight to fourteen weeks later. Both parents incubate the eggs, although the female has the bulk of the responsibility. The islands have about ninety-four pairs of nesting eagles.

Outside the nesting season, the bald eagle, unlike the majority of raptors, can be fairly social, flying in to communal night roosts (usually in winter) and often soaring on flattened wings with other eagles. Their presence in the islands wanes with summer as they move to inland rivers for the salmon runs, returning to the San Juans again in October. Washington is second only to Alaska in its number of wintering bald eagles; listen for their distinctive call, a high-pitched, tremulous scream.

**Eelgrass** (*Zostera marina*). Although it resembles a seaweed, our native eelgrass is actually a flowering maritime herb with grasslike leaves up to 6 feet long. (The flowers are minute single stamens or pistils on flattened fleshy spikes.) Eelgrass reproduces by both rhizomes (creeping root stems) and seeds; in the aquatic world, water currents instead of air distribute the fertilizing pollen. The plant dies back in the winter, and seeds germinate in the spring as the water warms up. Eelgrass favors bays and estuaries, where it's largely protected from violent wave action and where

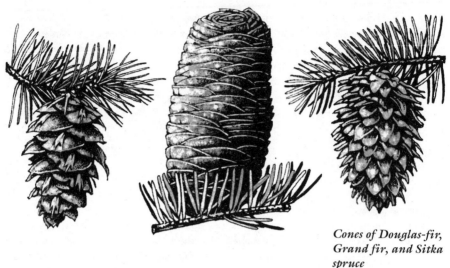

*Cones of Douglas-fir,*
*Grand fir, and Sitka*
*spruce*

it shelters juvenile populations of crab and salmon and is a staple of the brant (almost 90 percent of its diet). Human populations also have made good use of eel-grass, as food, fuel, roof thatching, and dike-construction material; it was also once used to stuff mattresses and pack glass.

**Elderberry, Red** (*Sambucus racemosa*). One of the earliest shrubs to flower in the spring, red elderberry can be easily known by its soft, pithy, bump-covered canes. This native shrub thrives in coastal areas, sometimes growing to 20 feet high in damp, shady conditions. Compound leaves have opposite, elongated leaflets with finely toothed edges, as many as nine leaflets on a shoot. Pyramid clusters of unpleasantly pungent white flowers appear in April; masses of berries ripen to a brilliant red in June and last into fall, unless the birds get them first. Although the berries can be made into wine, most humans find the raw fruit inedible (the berries are supposedly poisonous to people if taken in quantity). Birds such as robins and band-tailed pigeons relish them, however, spreading the one-seeded nutlets across the islands to sprout into the shrubs of early spring.

**Fern, Sword** (*Polystichum munitum*). The most commonly recognized fern in our forests, often seen poking up out of rotting nurse logs, sword fern has dark green fronds up to 5 feet long. Note the diagnostic triangular projection at the base of each sharply pointed leaflet. Sword fern is easily distinguished from another common fern of the moist woodlands, lady fern, which has equally long but light green fronds that are widest just below the center and taper in both directions. Fern fronds are coiled like frog tongues when they come through the ground in the spring; they slowly unroll to lap the air and add lushness to our understory.

**Fir, Grand** (*Abies grandis*). Native to British Columbia and the western United States and common in the San Juans, this fast-growing tree (up to 3 feet a year under some conditions) is one of our tallest true firs. Both the common and scientific names of this tree refer to its size. A few trees in the islands are over 100 feet tall, but grand fir may reach a height of 200 feet (a tree on the Olympic Peninsula grew 231 feet tall, with a circumference of over 20 feet). They rarely form pure stands but usually grow with Doug-fir, western hemlock, and western redcedar in cool, moist areas.

Grand firs are easily known by their long, flat, flexible needles fanning out feather-style, rather than in the bottlebrush fashion of Doug-fir. Dark green above, whitish below, the needles are blunt-tipped and of two different lengths. Cylindrical green or greenish brown cones sit upright on the top branches; seeds of these cones feed forest birds, squirrels, and rodents. The bark of young trunks has blisters that when pinched open give off a fragrant resin, which some folks believe has healing properties. Not an especially long-lived tree (300 years is probably maximum), the grand fir is very susceptible to heart rot fungus. Its soft, light wood is used commercially most often for pulp.

**Flicker, Northern** (*Colaptes auratus*). Our most common woodpecker is also our most unusual. Unlike other woodpecker species, flickers are fairly gregarious birds that hop across the ground to feed. About as big as large jays, these birds are easily distinguished by their handsome plumage: black bib and black-spotted breast, barred cinnamon back, and in the males, a red "mustache." In flight, a white rump patch is visible. Flickers drum and use nest holes, in which six to ten white eggs are deposited between mid-May and mid-June; both sexes incubate the eggs. These birds feed on ants, beetles, grasshoppers, and grubs, as well as berries and rose hips in winter.

**Fox, Red** (*Vulpes fulva*). Small populations of red fox are found on Fidalgo and San Juan islands, where they were once supposedly brought in to control the European rabbit populations. About the size of medium dogs, foxes weigh between 6 and 15 pounds and are approximately 3 feet long from nose to bushy, white-tipped tail (the distinguishing field mark). Tracks are doglike and form a straight line. Red foxes have different color variations, ranging from orangish red to silver to black. Underparts are white, and legs and feet are black. Shy, wary animals, foxes are mostly nocturnal, although they've been spotted during the day here on Fidalgo's Cap Sante and at San Juan's American Camp. Omnivorous feeders, they usually focus on plant life and insects such as grasshoppers during the summer and on small mammals (voles, rabbits, and especially mice) and birds in the winter.

Active year-round, foxes don't usually den up here in the winter but simply snug down to snooze with their tails wrapped tightly around them. In the spring, they use birthing dens in natural cavities such as abandoned burrows or hollow logs. (Dens are often marked with excavated dirt and food and bone scraps.) Foxes mate in January or February, and litters averaging four to eight pups are born from March to May. Pups are weaned after two months but remain with the parents until the family abandons the den by late August.

**Frog, Pacific Chorus** (*Pseudacris regilla*). Also known as the Pacific tree frog (*Hyla regilla*), this frog may be more properly placed in the former genus than the latter. Their resounding *rib-it* chorus, sometimes as early as February, is one of the clarion calls of spring in the islands. These frogs migrate to and breed in shallow, often seasonal ponds and wetlands through late spring.

The chorus frog is fairly tiny (up to 2 inches, but usually smaller) and may be distinguished from other Northwest frogs by the sticky round toe pads that help it climb over slick surfaces, including windows, which they may scale at night in order to feed on insects attracted to light. A heavy, dark eye stripe stretches to the frog's shoulders. The upper skin is smooth; its color may be green or variations of brown, and the skin is commonly marked with irregular bands on the back. Underparts are white and rough. Males, which are smaller than females, can be distinguished by the dark wrinkled skin on the throat. Chorus frogs also have a chameleonic ability to change color according to their surroundings.

Females lay 400 to 750 eggs in irregular, jellylike masses attached to vegetation; each mass contains from 10 to 70 eggs, which are dark on top and white on the bottom. The dark surface of the egg will always present itself topside no matter how the mass is turned. Sources differ on the reason for this; it's suggested that the dark coloring either protects the embryos from UV rays or predators or else absorbs the sunlight to promote development. Embryos hatch in two to three weeks, and tadpoles metamorphose (turn into froglets) usually in June. Chorus tadpoles can be told from red-legged tads by their eyes, which are not as centered but instead are set on the margins of the head. Our most abundant frog species, chorus frogs provide food for numerous predators, such as garter snakes, herons, ducks, otters, and foxes.

**Frog, Northern Red-Legged** (*Rana aurora aurora*). Our second most common frog, the red-legged is larger (up to 4 inches long) than its chorus frog neighbor, but more wary and not anywhere near as vocal. When you're hiking near wetlands, you'll more likely hear the chorus frog croaking than this nearly voiceless species. Red-legs will squeal when alarmed, and their calls at breeding time are several weak notes often made 2 feet under the water. But although this is not the frog you'll usually hear, it's the one you'll probably see, oftentimes alerted by its startled leap into the brush or water.

The bodies of red-legs are generally brown and marked with black flecks to blend in with the leaf litter. The red is predominantly on the undersides of the hind legs. Like the chorus frog, the red-leg usually has a black eye mask; under it, a creamy stripe extends from the jaw to the shoulder. Females are larger than males, and they lay their eggs (750 to 1,300) here during January or February in a large jelly mass attached to pond vegetation. As in chorus frogs, fertilization is external, the male depositing his sperm over the egg mass. Embryos hatch after four weeks, and tadpoles develop over the next four to five months, metamorphosing into froglets just under an inch long.

**Goose, Canada** (*Branta canadensis*). This is our most commonly recognized wild goose, sometimes called the "chinstrap goose" or "cravat goose" for the distinctive broad white band from the chin to behind the eye. Its head, neck, and bill are black, and the rest of its body is brownish gray, except for white on the belly and tail. Also well known for their noisy, V-shaped migration flights and characteristic deep honking, the birds are common migrants here from March to May and again in August to November; a few are resident breeders in the islands.

Canada geese mate for life, although "divorce" sometimes occurs and an individual whose partner dies may mate again. Ground nesters, they breed on the shores of lakes or coastal marshes, and ganders aggressively defend the nest and young. Canada geese feed on submerged grasses and aquatic life in marshes and also on field grains (supposedly with sentries posted).

**Gooseberry, Swamp** (*Ribes lacustre*). A familiar shrub in the islands, the gooseberry, as its common name suggests, likes moist habitats such as swamps, stream banks, and damp woodlands. It belongs to the same genus as the red-flowering currant and is similar except for prickly stems, which have three to seven larger thorns at each leaf node. Gooseberry grows up to 5 feet tall, with dark green, maple-shaped leaves and dark purple berries. The plant flowers in June, and the berries appear in late summer. Too tart for most tastes, they supposedly make good wine and jam.

**Grebe, Western** (*Aechmophorus occidentalis*). This largest of North American grebes, which has also been called the swan grebe, can be easily identified by its long, snakelike neck and black-and-white coloring. This species has a single short black crest on the top of its head (the horned grebe has buff crests on both sides of its head), and its yellow bill is much longer than that of other grebe species (the genus name comes from the Greek for "spear-bearing"). The sexes look alike. Now protected by law, western grebes were once slaughtered for their densely feathered breasts, which were turned into hat adornments.

Awkward on land, where they spend as little time as possible except during nesting season, grebes are exceptional swimmers and are able to dive in a blink. Their feet are different from those of other swimming birds; instead of being webbed between the toes, they have individually webbed toes. Much better swimmers than fliers, grebes must taxi along the water before becoming airborne. A long white wing stripe is visible in flight.

Striking courtship displays involve much vocalization and "dancing" together, in which the birds seem to stand on the surface of the water, and often include hundreds of paired birds. Western grebes nest on floating vegetation mats on lakes in eastern Washington, laying three to ten eggs in May. Chicks swim soon after hatching but will also ride on their parents' backs. The birds feed on fish, small aquatic invertebrates, and water plants. One of six grebe species represented in the San Juans, the western grebe winters on saltwater bays most commonly from October to April, although sometimes nonbreeding individuals will be seen during the summer. Listen for a creaky, whistling call.

**Guillemot, Pigeon** (*Cepphus columba*). This alcid with the strange name is seen regularly throughout our island waters. (*Guillemot* is a French form of "William," though how that applies to this bird is anyone's guess.) Look for a fairly small, pigeon-like bird with bright red feet, long black bill, and black body with white wing patches (in winter, the body is much paler and varied with black; the wings are the same). Listen for its feeble, warbling whistle or a single shrill *zeee*. The "sea pigeon" is a breeding resident here on offshore rocks and islets, laying one or two eggs usually in June, which is the only time the bird comes ashore. Social birds that usually flock, guillemots are also excellent swimmers, using their wings to move swiftly underwater in pursuit of their prey.

**Gull, Glaucous-Winged** (*Larus glaucescens*). This large white bird with the gray mantle is our most commonly seen gull and the only breeding resident of at least six gull species in the islands. Glaucous-wings build grass or seaweed nests on rocky offshore islets and lay two or three light brown or olive, speckled eggs. Mark Lewis, in *Birding in the San Juan Islands*, suggests that the shorebound who wish to view a local breeding colony can focus a spotting scope on Goose Island from the Cattle Point picnic area on San Juan Island. Nest building or repair of old nest sites occurs in early May, and by month's end, the first eggs are laid. Both sexes incubate the eggs and defend the nesting site. First-year gulls have black bills and feet and are grayish brown all over; second-year birds are paler and grayer, and adult plumage comes in the third or fourth year.

*Pigeon guillemot*

For the amount of scavenging this bird does, one might think its head would more closely resemble the naked pate of a turkey vulture rather than the snowy crown of an adult gull. Gulls feed along the shores on carrion and shellfish, as well as on insects, worms, and rodents in fields and garbage dumps, and they catch small fish near the water's surface. Very social birds that often gather in large flocks to feed, gulls are commonly seen in harbors around docks.

**Hardhack** (*Spiraea douglasii*). This locally common shrub of open, moist areas can grow to 6 feet tall, forming dense thickets almost impossible to penetrate. The tough, sinewy, reddish brown stems have 2- to 3-inch toothed, oblong leaves and fluffy plumes of pink flowers in the summer. Also known as steeple bush or Douglas spiraea, hardhack is often found bordering local wetlands.

**Harrier, Northern** (*Circus cyaneus*). One of our most commonly seen raptors, the harrier, or marsh hawk, swoops low over meadows and marshes to capture voles and other small creatures. Flying in a zigzag or undulating pattern and flashing a telltale white rump patch, this slim, medium-sized hawk holds its long wings angled over the horizon as it glides, similar to the turkey vulture's dihedral wing position. A tireless hunter of tall vegetation, often flying back and forth over the same patch of ground, the harrier has a face that is almost owl-like, presumably fitted with similar facial disks to pick up the squeaks of field rodents. When the hawk spots its prey, it suddenly "slams on the brakes," hovers momentarily, and then plunges talons first into the grass.

Males have a silver-gray back; females are brown. (Immature marsh hawks have bright orange breasts.) The birds build nests of grass on the ground and usually lay four to six bluish white eggs. Only a few nest in the area, but harriers winter here September through April in high numbers. After breeding season, these hawks are, like bald eagles, rather social raptors that often roost communally in fields on the ground (balds roost in trees). The harrier's call is a short, nasal whistle and a lower-pitched *choo, choo, choo*. One source notes that the bird is highly curious, and repeated squeaking noises may bring it in closer if the person making the noise remains hidden.

**Hawk, Red-Tailed** (*Buteo jamaicensis*). Next to the bald eagle, this is probably our most well-known raptor. Its large, bulky size, its habit of perching on telephone poles and fence posts, and the red fan tail of the adult are familiar field marks; it also has a dark head, a light bib, a mostly uniform brown back, and a 4-foot wingspread. (When the bird is soaring, the tail looks white from below, although if strongly backlighted, it may show some red. Wait for the hawk to veer off and display the upper side of its tail.)

Red-tails seem to prefer voles as the mainstay of their diet but thrive because they're generalists and will also feed on waterfowl and any ground-dwelling prey—snakes, rabbits, chipmunks, even large insects. These hawks breed here and up to Alaska, building large nests of twigs and sticks (to which they add every year) high up in trees such as cottonwoods or on cliff faces. Most eggs are laid here in April, usually in clutches of two to four eggs. Chicks hatch out in early May and fledge in June. In the winter, northen red-tails migrate into our area and swell the already abundant resident population. Listen for the red-tail's call, a hoarse, descending *kee-er*.

**Hemlock, Western** (*Tsuga heterophylla*). One of the most common trees of our northwest woodlands and the state tree of Washington, western hemlock grows well in the deep shade, often out of "nurse" logs—rotting logs that nourish new growth—and because of this it may eventually come to dominate an undisturbed forest. Nonetheless, the tree has its weaknesses: thin bark makes it vulnerable to fire damage, and shallow roots prove a poor anchor in heavy winds. Hemlock is also fairly slow-growing. It may live five hundred years, reaching a maximum height of about 200 feet.

Younger trees are easily recognized from a distance by their drooping crowns. Closer in, examine the branches for flexible, round-tipped needles in three rather short, intermixed lengths (*heterophylla* means "variable leaves"); these quickly wither and drop when the branches are cut. Clusters of small red male flowers open in spring and scatter pollen to purplish, budlike female flowers at the branch tips; pollinated flowers ripen in the fall to small tan, papery cones. An important timber tree, hemlock is used for pulp, flooring, and siding as well as for making cellophane and plastics. Northwest natives once made a dye from the tree's red inner bark and also boiled the bark into a tonic for sore throats. The low, spreading branches of hemlocks offer shelter to ground-feeding birds such as grouse, and the seeds are eaten by crossbills, pine siskins, and chickadees.

**Heron, Great Blue** (*Ardea herodias*). This 4-foot-tall, bluish gray, spindly-legged heron with the dashing black head plume is a familiar sight in island marshes, along shorelines, and perched on kelp rafts in salt water. In flight, the great blue is easily distinguished from cranes by the S-shaped curve of its neck and by its trailing legs as it flies over with slow, heavy wingbeats. Its voice is equally distinctive, a loud, hoarse, "bad-tempered" squawk when disturbed. Most often a solitary feeder, the great blue heron will at times be seen hunting side by side at choice feeding grounds; I once counted close to a dozen perched in trees overlooking a marsh on Guemes Island. Great blues also roost together and nest in colonies used year after year. Stick platform nests are placed high in the treetops, sometimes several nests to a tree.

Rookeries exist on Samish Island (over three hundred nests) and on Fidalgo Island's March Point (about one hundred nests). Males arrive first at the heronry, choosing a site to build a new nest or picking an old nest to restore. They then engage in courting displays to attract females; new mates are chosen every year. The herons nest here in March and lay three to six bluish eggs in April. Young hatch out in May and fledge by the end of June. Both parents incubate the eggs and feed the chicks, of which usually only two are successfully raised. First-year juveniles are all gray on the tops of their heads.

Herons feed mainly on small fish but also on frogs, snakes, and salamanders in the shallow waters of marshes, bays, and tidal flats and on large insects such as dragonflies; they'll also take small rodents in the fields. The great blue hunts by either quietly stalking its prey through the shallows or standing head hunched to shoulders, perfectly immobile, until it spies its prey and thrusts its long, daggerlike beak in for a lightning-quick kill, capturing the creature between the mandibles, not impaling it as commonly described. Heron bills are finely serrated for holding their slippery catches, and the prey is dropped headfirst into the gullet.

The great blue is the largest of North American herons, common on both fresh and salt water, and has a lifespan as long as seventeen years. Numbers peak in the islands in the fall when breeding adults and young return from the nesting areas. Great blue herons lack oil glands, so instead of preening their feathers with oil, they have another way to keep the feathers clean and water-repellent. Special down feathers form a powdery substance when the heron crumbles them with its bill; it then distributes this powder while preening and finally combs it out with a uniquely made serrated middle claw. Protest over the slaughter of herons and egrets for their "fashionable" feather plumes led to the 1918 Federal Migratory Bird Treaty Act.

**Honeysuckle, Orange** (*Lonicera ciliosa*). This showy vine with inch-long orange trumpet blossoms is pollinated by hummingbirds attracted by sight rather than smell; hence, the flowers have no scent. Roundish leaves are opposite each other on supple vines that may grow to 30 feet and that often entwine around tree trunks and branches, sometimes so tightly that the honeysuckle's stems may embed in the wood and cause the death of the tree. End leaves of the vine form a shallow bowl holding the blossoms. Honeysuckle flowers appear in May, to be replaced in September by reddish berries, which birds appear to enjoy but which are rather bitter to human taste. You may also chance upon another woodland honeysuckle with smaller paired leaves and purple or pink tubular blossoms. This is the hairy honeysuckle, which blooms a little later than its orange cousin but eventually sports similar bitter berries. Enjoy these plants for a beauty that breaks in on the greens of the understory with a startling exoticism.

**Huckleberry, Red** *(Vaccinium parvifolium)*. The lacy, bright-green branches of this deciduous shrub, which belongs to the same family as the madrone, are often seen sprouting out of mossy stumps and logs where birds have dropped the seeds of its berries. Numerous small oval leaves and, in the spring, small pinkish green flowers decorate the huckleberry, which grows to 6 feet high in moist woods. The bright red berries ripen July to August and are rather tart but reputedly make good pies and jams.

**Hummingbird, Rufous** *(Selasphorus rufus)*. The croaking of the chorus frog and the buzz of a rufous hummer are the earliest voices of an island spring. The whirring wings of the adult male, which may beat up to 200 times a second (although usually much less), are what produce that high-energy buzz. The males, known by their flashing red throats and rufous backs and sides, are the first to return in the spring, staking out and aggressively defending food sources with noisy calls and chasing after much larger birds, as well as other hummers. Females have green backs with rufous sides and more colorful tails, which they fan to ward off intruders; males depend on their metallic gorgets (throat patches) to threaten other males.

Rufous hummers breed from southern Oregon to southeast Alaska. After the birds breed, the males leave the territory while the females build the nests and tend to all egg-laying chores. Nests may be reused from one year to the next and added to; the golf-ball-sized cups are made of mosses, lichen, and bits of bark and leaves woven together with spider silk. They are usually not hidden but often placed on the exposed tip of a low conifer branch in April. Watch the female to find the nest, which, even though exposed, may be easily passed over. Usually two tiny white eggs are laid. The young leave the nest after three weeks, and another nest is often constructed in June, higher up in a deciduous tree, for a second brood.

A hummingbird can hover (moving its wings in a horizontal figure-eight pattern), fly backward and forward (up to 50 miles per hour) and up and down, and zip through the air in dazzling courtship display arcs. Its butterfly size (about a nickel's weight) hides a stout heart, for this is a courageous bird that won't hesitate to charge far larger intruders such as jays. The needle-sharp bill is used in combat and is hollow like a butterfly's for ingesting nectar from tubular blossoms such as honeysuckle, flowering currant, columbine, and hedge nettle. (The bills are too long for the birds to properly preen, and so hummers may often be seen cleaning themselves by bathing.) Hummers will also obtain protein from eating insects such as mosquitoes; their high metabolism, on a par with that of the frantic shrew, requires an almost constant focus on food. During cold spells, they may go into a deep torpor, saving vital energy by reducing their metabolism.

Rufous hummers are the most abundant hummingbird in our state and may live up to ten years. The greatest travelers of all migratory hummingbirds in western North America, most are gone by September, on their way to wintering grounds in Mexico, although a few remain into October.

**Indian Pipe** (*Monotropa uniflora*). This ghostly plant of the shadowed, humus-rich forest floor has no need of green tissue or chlorophyll to produce its food; it parasitizes the roots of conifers for its nourishment, and it may also live off decaying woody plants. Several stems arise from spreading masses of roots sheathed with fungus that transfers the nourishment of the tree roots to the plant.

Indian pipe grows to 10 inches tall and flowers from June through August. Its stems are topped by heads that at first look like the drooping bowls of peace pipes but later stand erect when the 1/2-inch brown fruit pod is produced containing masses of tiny seeds. Also known as the "corpse plant," "ice plant," and "ghost flower," this waxy white plant blackens at maturity or when picked. (The Straits Salish believe Indian pipe sprouts wherever a wolf voids; their name for the plant means "wolf's urine.") A somewhat similar plant of the deep woods, spotted coral-root, also functions without chlorophyll, taking its food from either decaying or living plant matter. As is true of the Indian pipe, scales pressed along the stalk are all that remain of this reddish plant's leaves. The exquisite orchidlike blooms (May to June) have white, purple-spotted lower lips; the stalks brown in July but last several months.

**Indian Plum** (*Osmaronia cerasiformis*). Our earliest flowering shrub is also known as osoberry or, less flatteringly, skunk bush, for the rank smell of its blossoms. Like skunk cabbage, Indian plum uses a strong scent to attract early pollinators. The elongated white clusters of blooms appear before the leaves, which are smooth-edged and fairly narrow. Different shrubs produce pollinating and fruit-setting blooms, but they are difficult to distinguish except, of course, when the female plants bear fruit. Bright orange, big-pitted fruits beloved of birds ripen over the summer; people generally find their taste too flat to enjoy. Indian plum may grow to 12 feet in open, moist woodlands and often has several trunks. The shrub is somewhat less common in the San Juans proper than the rest of the archipelago. (*Oso* means "bear" in Spanish; supposedly bears enjoy the berries.)

**Juniper, Rocky Mountain** (*Juniperus scopulorum*). As its common name indicates, this cedarlike tree is usually found in a far different habitat and indeed is narrowly restricted west of the Cascades to the San Juans and western Fidalgo Island. This slow-growing, long-lived tree (one juniper in Utah is three thousand years old) exudes toughness as it bends its twisted, shrublike body to the harsh, windblown habitats of rocky island bluffs. Junipers have thick, bushy foliage and often more than one trunk. The bark is thin and stringy, and the leaves are opposite each other on twigs; on older trees, they're scaly like the western redcedar. Cones, which resemble berries and are eaten by birds when ripe, contain the seeds and take two years to ripen to their blue color. Crush them and the smell will recall a possibly familiar odor; juniper "berries" are used to flavor gin.

Male and female flowers are on separate trees; the yellow male flowers open in spring near the twig tips. Female flowers, which are tiny clusters of scales, receive the pollen and then develop into hard, green berrylike cones. Junipers grow to only about 20 feet, larger in more sheltered situations. Their durable wood has been cut into many a farm fence post beside which other junipers often sprout, having been sown there by birds that perched to feed and expelled the seeds.

**Kelp, Bull** (*Nereocystis luetkeana*). Growing to as much as 100 feet long from a rooted holdfast, bull kelp forms "forests" that provide a sheltering calm for juvenile fish and marine species, such as anemones and sea stars, that lurk in the holdfasts. The holdfasts attach to rocks not much farther out than the lowest tides, so look off rocky shorelines for huge kelp beds. Rising from the holdfast is a long, whiplike stem, or stipe, which ends in a hollow floating bulb. Two groups of 15-foot-long, wavelike blades stream from the stipe's end, indicating the speed and direction of currents and providing resting spots for ducks and tie-ups for small craft. (In Samish myth, the blades are the tresses of the tribal princess Ko-kwal-alwoot, who became a sea spirit to feed her people. See her statue at Rosario Park on Fidalgo Island.) Coastal Indians tied the stipes together for fishing lines and also used the bulbs to carry water.

Bull kelp manufactures its food from sunlight and chemicals in the water; the green chlorophyll is there but masked by a brown pigment. (Rich in minerals such as iron, kelp is harvested for fertilizer and can also be pickled and eaten.) The kelp usually dies off during winter and begins to grow again from microscopic spores in the spring, completing its tremendous growth cycle in just a few short months, during which time it grows as much as several inches a day. In the fall, sacs on the blades release microscopic spores, which develop into tiny plants called gametophytes. These plants winter over, and then, come spring, male and female plants release eggs and sperm, which fuse to form zygotes that become the new kelp sporophytes. Urchins and crustaceans graze on the mature plants; sponges, hydroids, and other invertebrates live on their blades; and fish feed in the sheltered area of the stipes. In the winter, storms wash great tangles of the weed ashore, where it provides habitat for hundreds of sand hoppers; pull up a bunch and watch the action.

**Kingfisher, Belted** (*Ceryle alcyon*). This top-heavy, pugnacious-looking bird with its rattling cry (one source compares it to the clacking of a fish reel) is a familiar sight along lake and saltwater shores. Nearly crow-sized, the kingfisher is slate blue with a white throat and belly, a long fish-catching bill (like a heron's), and a bristling head crest. Both sexes have blue chest belts; females have an additional chestnut band.

Excepting the tern, kingfishers are the only small birds that dive headlong from the air into the water. Look for them patrolling the shallower waters near shores; they often perch on snags projecting out of the water to survey the scene below. If the outlook disappoints, the bird swoops off to another perch, usually punctuating the flight with its dry, characteristic call. Fish are its mainstay, but frogs, mice, insects, berries, and small crabs are also eaten.

Nesting here is in April. The bird burrows with its bill into the banks beside ponds, streams, and salt water; then it scoops out the dirt with its feet, digging a slightly upward-slanting, horizontal tunnel 3 to 7 feet long. In May the female lays five to eight white eggs in the nest chamber at the tunnel's end. (Regurgitated fish bones and scales at the ends of the tunnels form makeshift nests.) Eggs hatch about three weeks later, and both parents feed the young.

The belted is the most common kingfisher in North America and a resident in the islands. (Migrants from the north swell the island population in the winter.) Although often seen, these birds are not terribly easy to study since they're as quick to take alarm as their tall fishing neighbors, the great blue herons.

**Limpet.** Several species exist in our area, inhabiting different tidal zones and shores. Limpets are usually seen tightly attached to rocks, but unlike barnacles, these creatures leave their niches to graze for food when the tide returns, though they usually don't wander more than a yard off. Serrated tongues called radulas are used to scrape algae off the rocks. After feeding, limpets usually "home" to their original spots—where they may have ground an impression into the rock—and form a tight seal to withstand the battering of the waves. (If the rock is harder than the shell, a limpet may grind down the latter to perfectly fit the rock so that water may be retained in the shell at low tide.) The limpet's grip is tight enough that a 70-pound pull is required to loosen it. Its shell is mostly oval and usually ribbed to some degree, depending on the species. These creatures are gastropods, which means "stomach-footed"; they move by the rippling motion of a muscular foot.

**Loon, Common** (*Gavia immer*). The sight of this large, shy bird in its glorious black-and-white breeding plumage is always a special treat no matter how many times one has been favored. Summer plumage includes a white checkerboard back on a black-and-white- speckled background and a zebra-striped necklace. (Winter plumage is comparatively drab, being mostly gray with white underparts.) Like grebes, both sexes have identical plumage.

Goose-sized, with a long, dark, sharp-tipped bill, loons, again like grebes, have legs set well back on the body; hence, the birds are almost helpless on land, but are superlative swimmers. Their bones, unlike those of most birds, are almost solid, making these heavy birds effortless divers. Loons eat crustaceans and water plants, but mostly they dive for small fish, using both their wings and their large webbed feet for propulsion to depths of up to 200 feet. The birds are also strong fliers, though they require a running start of perhaps 100 yards to become airborne.

Loons come on land only to breed; nests are built close to shore so that the birds can simply slide back into the water. They lay two or three brown, spotted eggs, and both parents care for the eggs and young. The loon used to breed in the islands but has forgone our area for less populated ones. It returns here near summer's end (North America's highest numbers of loons—common and yellow-billed—winter here), still in breeding plumage, and this plumage can be seen again in early spring before the birds take their leave in April or May for breeding grounds on northern lakes.

The distinctive call of the loon is given only during the breeding season. Once, out in a kayak on Padilla Bay, I was surrounded by loons calling from different directions in a fog, and it was as if the eerie day had found its voice in the eons-old yodeling. Loons are one of the most primitive of birds, belonging to an ancient family that evolved some fifty million years ago. Three other species occur regularly in the islands: red-throated loons (the smallest, at 17 inches); Pacific loons (breeding plumage has diagnostic vertical white stripes on the side of the throat); and yellow-billed loons (the largest, at 35 inches, with a light bill, as distinct from the common loon's dark one).

**Madrone, Pacific** (*Arbutus menziesii*). Without this snaky red, glossy green tree highlighting the island bluffs, the beauty of the San Juans would pale perceptibly. Native from California to British Columbia (Canadians call it the arbutus), madrone is a member of the heath family (which includes salal, rhododendrons, kinnickinnick, and huckleberry). A slow-growing hardwood, madrone may live up to 250 years. It may also grow to over 100 feet (madrone is North America's tallest broad-leaved evergreen) or else develop a stunted, scraggly form. The tree thrives in rocky, well-drained soils on high bluffs above the salt water, often angling out precariously over the water.

Outer portions of the tree's bark are reddish and paper-thin and annually peel off through the summer to reveal the new green-skinned bark below; the sinuously smooth trunks later change to a glowing reddish orange. Dark green, oblong, leathery leaves, which look like those of a rhododendron, are slowly shed and replaced; second-year leaves drop in summer after new leaves appear and expand in June and July, so the tree remains perpetually green.

Pinkish white, bell-shaped blossoms, like salal blooms or lilies of the valley, scent the air with a honeyed fragrance April through May (hummers and bees enjoy the nectar) and are later replaced by large bunches of red, seedy berries in the fall. Birds such as the robin, quail, varied thrush, waxwing, pileated woodpecker, and band-tailed pigeon (and supposedly raccoons and various smaller mammals) enjoy the berries and help spread their seeds. Deer like to browse on the new leaves and branches.

Because its papery bark offers little protection, madrone is highly susceptible to fire damage, although cut or burnt trees sprout easily from stumps. (The tree is difficult or impossible to transplant successfully.) In Hazel Heckman's *Island Year*, the author tells how one spring many madrones seemed to die as more and more leaves browned with no new crops to replace them. Researchers determined that the trees were "temporarily confused" by an unusually long, cold winter; defoliation set in unseasonably early, and the new growth was late in coming.

**Mallard** (*Anas platyrhynchos*). Who doesn't know this ubiquitous bird of pond, field, and saltwater marsh? Its easily observable presence shouldn't breed a ho-hum attitude, however, for the large, wild mallard is a truly stunning duck. The dapper drake has chocolate breast feathers with a white collar, a bright yellow chocolate-tipped bill, jauntily curled tail feathers, and an iridescent blue-green head. The hen is mottled brown with an orange bill. Both sexes show a purplish speculum (wing patch) in flight.

Mallards mate in February, the drakes bowing to the hens and rearing up to better reveal their showy plumage, and hens lay eight to twelve greenish eggs March to May. Nests are usually made near the water (sometimes in trees) and built of reeds, leaves, and grass lined with down from the hen's breast. The female takes care of the incubation and chick-rearing chores; young are precocial, entering the water within 24 hours after hatching.

In mid- to late summer, drakes gather on sheltered waters to go through a partial molt and acquire a drab eclipse plumage, during which time they cannot fly and are only distinguishable from the females by bill color. Females also lose their flight feathers at this time but remain with the young. Flight feathers are replaced in the fall.

A surface-feeding, or dabbling, duck able to burst from the water immediately into flight, the mallard feeds bottom-up in shallow waters, mostly on aquatic vegetation, along with some crustaceans, small fish, and insects. In fields, the ducks feed on a variety of agricultural crops such as corn. Highly adaptable in terms of both food and environment and easily domesticated, the mallard is the ancestor of most of the world's barnyard ducks. Resident here, this puddle duck is joined during the winter by migrants that swell the local population.

**Maple, Big-Leaf** (*Acer macrophyllum*). True to its common and scientific names, this tree has the largest leaf in the state, sometimes up to 16 inches long (more commonly about 10 inches), and 8 to 12 inches across. The five-lobed leaves turn pale yellow in the autumn, which is perhaps just as well; this tree would overwhelm if it had the blazing red color of our other maples. The leaf stalks bleed a milky sap when broken.

Leaves and flowers appear together in April. A tree that seems to do little by halves, this maple sports streaming clusters of fragrant yellow flowers, which are quite long (4 to 6 inches) and beloved of honeybees. From late summer through fall, look for 2-inch paired maple "wings" or "helicopter" seeds (samaras) fed on by squirrels, mice, and birds such as finches. Black-tailed deer browse on the leaves and twigs of younger trees.

This maple's dense, fine-grained wood is valuable for furniture and was once used by Northwest natives for making tools and canoe paddles. Early coastal peoples also wove the bark into rope and used the huge leaves to cover food in cooking pits. Common in the moist lowland forest, the big-leaf is our only large native maple. It may grow to 100 feet high, often with a forked trunk or several trunks growing together, and live to two hundred years. Two other smaller local maples provide the scarlet show of autumn: the Douglas maple and the vine maple.

**Merganser, Hooded** (*Lophodytes cucullatus*). Also known as the "hairyhead," this beautiful duck with the amazing headgear is a resident breeder in the islands, frequenting freshwater ponds and marshes in the spring and summer and protected bays in the winter. *Merganser* is Latin for "diving goose"; this duck dives easily for small fish and also captures frogs and aquatic insects. It has the typical fish-catching merganser bill: slender, serrated, and hook-tipped.

The smallest of our local mergansers, hooded drakes have black heads and backs with rufous sides and white crests that can be lowered or raised at will.

214

Females are brownish gray with bushy brown crests. Often seen with wood ducks, mergansers may compete with them for nesting cavities; like wood ducks, they'll use nesting boxes put on or by freshwater ponds in wooded areas, where they lay up to a dozen white eggs. Two other merganser species are common in the islands: the red-breasted merganser, seen most frequently on salt water through the winter, and the common merganser, our largest species and other resident breeder.

**Muskrat** (*Ondatra zibethica*). This marsh-dwelling rodent is a common, if not commonly seen, resident of local wetlands. Look for this mostly nocturnal creature in the early morning or evening hours, or check for signs of its presence. You may notice fragments of broken-off plants and shells on shore; 1/2-inch, oblong scats; floating rafts of marsh plants, on which the animal sometimes rests to feed; or small heaps of cut plants mixed with mud, on which the muskrat leaves its scent. Or you may see its thatched, conical shelter of marsh plants piled 2 to 3 feet above the water's surface, although along streams muskrats will burrow into banks. Lodges have underwater entrances and may be worked on for years until attaining a rather massive size.

In the lodge is an above-water chamber with a nest of shredded leaves. Muskrats usually bear up to three litters a year, beginning in March and ending in late summer, with four to nine young per litter, which the female raises alone. The animals eat mostly plants such as cattails and the stems and roots of water lilies and sedges; they also eat shellfish and small aquatic animals such as frogs, salamanders, and turtles. In turn, muskrats may be eaten by hawks, otters, minks, raccoons, or owls. Another enemy is the trapper, who covets the creature's fur; coarse guard hairs conceal a dense, waterproof coat of soft brown hair.

Muskrats are sometimes difficult to distinguish from their wetland neighbors, the beaver and river otter, but the latter two are larger. A muskrat's head and body measure only about 10 to 14 inches. But the major field mark setting it apart from a beaver is an approximately 10-inch tail that is scaly, almost hairless, and vertically flat (instead of horizontally so, as is the beaver's paddle tail) and that often leaves a distinct track. Hind legs, with webbed feet, are longer than the front, and musk glands are present on the lower abdomen.

**Mussel, Blue** (*Mytilus edulus*). Sometimes called the bay mussel, this is the mussel most commonly seen attached to rocks in the intertidal zone. Shells of adults are blue-black (immatures are brown) and about 2 1/2 inches long. Mussels cling to the rocks with strong byssal threads (produced by a gland in the foot), which harden from fluid to tough, brownish fibers almost immediately on contact with the rock. These threads can be broken should the mussel find it necessary to move; new threads are readily formed as the shellfish painstakingly moves along, detaching the old threads and extending the new ones to pull itself onward.

At high tide, mussels open their hinged shells to filter-feed on plankton in the water, and they in turn are preyed upon by sea stars and whelks. You may also notice, on more exposed, wave-swept rocks, the California mussel, which is larger (up to 8 inches), more heavily ribbed, and colored blue, black, and brown.

**Nettle, Stinging** (*Urtica dioica*). In early spring, this unfriendly European transplant pushes up new green shoots along many a trailside, sometimes to an intimidating 6 feet. The perennial plants are covered with tiny, bristling hairs that act as miniature syringes. When these hairs come into contact with the skin of a hapless victim, they break and eject an irritant, which produces a burning sensation (*Urtica* means "to burn") that may last a couple of hours to a couple of days, depending on the individual. Many locals have a favorite antidote to the nettle's sting. You might try rubbing the leaves of broadleaf plantain or thimbleberry on the sting.

Nettle spreads rapidly by rhizomes and is beneficial to the soil in that, like alder, it's a nitrogen-fixing plant. (Soak it in a bucket for a couple of weeks and then pour it over your plants as a fertilizer.) Leaves are opposite and heart-shaped with strongly toothed edges; in spring, strings of tiny greenish wind-pollinated flowers trail from the bases of the leaves (both male and female flowers are on the same plant, the female nearer the top than the male).

Wear gloves to harvest the plants; twenty minutes later, they no longer sting, and the young leaves and shoots can be cooked as a spinach substitute or boiled and enjoyed as tea. Northwest natives used the strong fibers of the plant's stems for making fish and duck nets, hence the common name. One legend tells how a tribe was starving because although there were plenty of salmon, the people had no way of catching them until Spider transformed himself into a man and showed them how to gather nettle and weave it into nets.

**Newt, Rough-Skinned** (*Taricha granulosa*). This approximately 7-inch (nose to tail) newt is often seen crawling along a shady trail, usually not far from water. Large numbers of them may be observed during migrations to and from breeding ponds, especially in the spring and fall. The skin on the upper side is a rough brownish gray, while the underside is a startling orange. (The color supposedly startles predators, warning them of poisonous skin glands. When alarmed, the newt may become rigid and raise its tail and head to expose the underside coloring. At least one predator, however, remains unimpressed and unaffected: the common garter snake.) The newt's rough skin becomes much smoother after it has been in the water for a while during the breeding season.

Newts eat the larvae of amphibians and small aquatic animals, as well as worms, small snails, and slugs. They breed here February to April; females attach single fertilized eggs to submerged plants, and larvae metamorphose into adults in the late summer. We have at least one other salamander often found here under logs or woody debris, the western long-toed salamander, usually dark with white-spotted sides and a green or yellow stripe running down its back.

**Ocean Spray** (*Holodiscus discolor*). Also known as arrowwood (native peoples made arrows from the young, straight limbs), this showy shrub is abundant in island woods. Ocean spray's frothy blooms of small white flowers decorate our woods and hillsides beginning in June and July. In the winter, several sparse trunks with a few dried flower husks still clinging to the twigs make identification easy. The strong, durable wood was known to the English as ironwood, and Northwest tribes used it for roasting food because it wouldn't burn, as well as for clam-digging sticks and other tools and utensils. Ocean spray grows to 15 feet high and has 2- to 3-inch toothed, wedge-shaped leaves.

**Orca** (*Orcinus orca*). If the bald eagle is the spirit of the islands' skies, the orca is the spirit of their waters. Also known as the killer whale for its predatory nature (the orca is the only cetacean that preys on other mammals), this largest member of the dolphin family never fails to thrill as its prominent black dorsal fin slices through the water. The boldly marked orca is black with white undersides and has a white oval behind the eye and a grayish "saddle patch" behind the dorsal fin; this patch, along with the fin itself, is used to photo-ID individual whales. Orca males may grow to 30 feet, and as adults they have a straight, triangular dorsal fin up to 6 feet tall. Females grow to about 24 feet and, as do juveniles, have a more sickle-shaped dorsal fin about half the size of the male's.

Females usually outlive males and may reach a hundred years of age. Orcas most often travel in family groups, or pods, built around a dominant female; the islands have three resident groups of approximately eighty to ninety whales divided up among pods J, K, and L (the largest). Births average one every ten years, and newborns may be 8 feet long. Orcas remain within their birth pod their entire lives.

Most sightings here are in Haro Strait, along the west shore of San Juan Island, and in the Strait of Juan de Fuca. These toothed whales prey mostly on fish here in the islands, coming into the area in June to follow the salmon runs. (They supposedly stay within a 200-mile radius of the islands the rest of the year.) Transient pods also pass through but are more likely to include mammals such as seals in their diet.

Orca pods have their own dialects and communicate with a variety of sounds, including sonar clicks and whistles or siren-type calls; they also use sound pulses to navigate, as well as to locate and even stun prey. Orcas are one of the fastest swimmers in the ocean, able to attain speeds of up to 25 knots, and seem very playful; if you're lucky, you may see them leaping out of the water, spy-hopping, or lob-tailing.

**Oregon Grape, Tall** (*Berberis aquifolium*). No, it's not a grape, and it's not a young holly. This common evergreen shrub is often confused with holly because of the prickly similarity of their leaves (Oregon grape leaflets are arranged opposite on the leaf, however, whereas holly leaflets alternate). Dark green, prickly, glossy leaflets (aquifolium means

*Tall Oregon grape, flowering and fruiting*

217

"water leaf"), usually five to seven per leaf, often turn scarlet in the fall before dropping. Northwest Indians boiled the yellow wood of the plant's twigs and bark to make a yellow dye.

This tall species may grow up to 5 feet high or more, especially in more exposed areas such as hillsides or open woodlands. Fragrant clusters of yellow flowers begin to bloom in March and are replaced in late summer and fall by rather sour, waxy blue berries, which can be made into wine or a tart jelly. Try touching the center of one of the flowers with a straw and watch the stamens spring together; the anthers open and scatter pollen as they normally would onto the body of a foraging honeybee.

The tall Oregon grape is the state flower of Oregon and is a member of the barberry family. Our other familiar species is the low Oregon grape (*Berberis nervosa*), which, as its common name implies, is a squatter version of the first (about 2 feet high) and is usually found in more shaded woodlands. Leaflets of this shrub are dull, not shiny, green; they're also not as strongly prickled. The shrub has longer sprays of leaves and more greenish yellow flowers than its taller cousin.

**Osprey** (*Pandion haliaetus*). One of our most widespread bird species, familiarly known as the "fish hawk" because of its wholly fish diet, the osprey is a summer visitor to the islands. Most frequently seen around freshwater lakes, it may also be spotted along saltwater shores. Lucky people may see it hunt, hovering briefly over the water on beating wings before plunging in for the kill. This hawk will dive feet first into the water, sometimes completely submerging itself (the nostrils close down when they hit the water) and usually exiting with a hapless fish clutched in its talons.

218

The osprey's large body is dark brown above, white below (females usually show a brown "necklace" on the white breast). Its head is white with a dark eye stripe, its tail short, rounded, and strongly barred. The hawk's long and pointed wings are diagnostic in flight. You can easily distinguish an osprey from a soaring eagle by the M crook of its wings and black wrist marks (carpal patches).

In May and June, females lay two to four eggs in nests that are large bulky platforms of sticks, vegetation, and trash usually placed at the top of a tall snag near the water and reused year after year. The osprey flies in to the islands in April, departing again in September or October for South American wintering grounds.

**Otter, River** (*Lutra canadensis*). Despite its name, this is the otter we see not only in freshwater habitats but also along our marine shores. (Sea otters aren't found in the archipelago but along the outer coast.) The sinuous, weasel-like body weighs in at about 30 pounds, and with a nose-to-tail length of 5 feet, the river otter is easy to spot whether scurrying over beach logs or splashing in the water. They generally live from ten to fifteen years and have dense brown fur, external ears, webbed feet, and the diagnostic long, muscular tail thickened at the base and tapered to the tip.

River otters mate here in May or June and give birth the following spring (March or April). Litters of one to five kits are born in dens, which may be either natural or other cavities (otters nesting in island crawlspaces are not uncommon). These mammals eat mainly fish but may also kill waterfowl, frogs, and baby mink and rabbits. Otter droppings are irregularly shaped, slimy when fresh, and often full of shell and fish bone fragments.

**Owl, Great Horned** (*Bubo virginianus*). The classic, deeply solemn *hoo-hoo* heard in island forests comes from the large, dark brown "hoot owl" with the ear-tuft "horns." The hooting calls (typically four to seven at a time and something on the order of *hoo, hoo-hoo, hoo, hoo*) are heard most frequently in late winter, near the nesting season. One of our earliest nesters, this owl may

Far left: *Great horned owl*
Above: *Barn owl and western screech owl*

breed as soon as February and lay two to four white eggs in March, often in an old hawk, heron, or crow nest.

The great horned is a fierce, fearless bird that doesn't hesitate to attack larger animals, including humans who trespass too close to a nest. Its diet includes rodents, birds (even smaller owls), squirrels, and rabbits. It's also one of the few creatures that will attack a skunk, which suggests that the owl's sense of smell is nowhere near as developed as its sight or hearing.

Like the osprey, the great horned has the ability to move one toe from front to back, leaving X tracks when it walks on the ground. But these stealthy nocturnal predators are usually detected by either their haunting calls or their pellets of indigestible fur, feathers, and bones found under roosts. They often roost hidden close in to the trunks of conifers, and may be harassed (mobbed) there by flocks of crows or robins that know this owl for their enemy. A smaller species commonly heard in the islands is the western screech owl, which has similar but shorter ear tufts and a call that sounds like a soft, tremulous series of bouncing whistles. Barn owls, perhaps the most commonly seen owls, have pale, heart-shaped faces and long legs. They feed mostly on rats, whereas screech owls take mice and insects.

**Oystercatcher, Black** (*Haematopus bachmani*). This somewhat comical-looking black, stocky shorebird with a long red bill, yellow eyes, and pink legs is a common resident of our rocky shorelines. The bill, which is laterally flattened and twice as long as the bird's head, is used for prying open the shells of mollusks, digging up crabs, or crowbarring limpets and chitons off the rocks. The sexes look the same, and both care for the young. Oystercatchers nest in hollow, pebble-lined scrapes on offshore rocks and lay two or three buff-colored, spotted eggs. The birds often flock together in the winter; their commonly heard calls are repeated ringing whistles. Oystercatchers may live over thirty years.

**Pine, Shore** (*Pinus contorta contorta*). A close relative of the inland-dwelling lodgepole pine, shore pine has a heavier, more furrowed bark and is most often seen here on windswept bluffs in stunted, twisted forms usually not more than 60 feet high, the height depending on the growing site. (Where sheltered from high winds, shore pine develops a large crown and sometimes forms dense stands.) The only two-needled pine in our state (pines are conifers with evergreen needles that grow in bunches of two, three, or five), this pine has 2-inch-long paired needles, and its cones can easily be identified by a stiff prickle on each scale. Many of the tree's cones remain clustered and closed for several years unless fire opens them up and releases the seeds. Others are unsealed and open normally at maturity to spread their seeds. Northwest tribes chewed the buds of this tree to relieve sore throats, much as they used the buds of the Douglas-fir.

**Pond Lily, Indian** (*Nuphar polysepalum*). The sunny yellow bowls of this aquatic perennial are a familiar sight in island wetlands as they sit among large, leathery, heart-shaped leaves April through September. The knob in the center of the flower cup is formed of petals and other plant organs. Leaves and flowers are attached to long stems anchored in the mud and provide a protective habitat for young fish, as well as convenient places for insects and amphibians to lay their eggs.

(Air pockets in the stems and leaves keep them afloat.) Northwest natives once ground the plant's seeds for flour and roasted them like popcorn; ducks also enjoy the seeds, and beavers and muskrats eat the submerged stems of the plants.

**Porpoise, Dall** *(Phocoenoides dalli)*. Oftentimes mistaken for a "small" orca, the Dall porpoise is somewhat similarly colored. Its body is black with white belly and flank patches. Unlike the orca, however, it has no gray saddle patch behind the dorsal fin and no white oval eye patch. The comparatively small size of the body (to $6^1/2$ feet) and dorsal fin (also marked with white) are other good indicators that the "whale pod" is in fact a group of porpoises. From a distance, watch for the diagnostic "rooster tail" spray of water as these porpoises, our fastest cetaceans, race through the water at speeds of up to 30 knots. You may also see them playing in the bow waves of fast-moving boats or spot them feeding; sonar is used to locate prey, which includes small fish and squid. Named after an American zoologist, William Dall, this porpoise has a distinct hump on the back, just forward of the flukes, that earned it the Northwest Native American name "broken tail." The Dall has a high mortality rate due to entanglement and drowning in gill nets.

Another porpoise fairly common in the archipelago, but less commonly seen because of its reticent nature, is our smallest cetacean, the harbor porpoise. Slightly smaller than the Dall, the harbor porpoise is dark gray or brown above with no white markings, although the flanks shade to a whitish belly. It doesn't play in bow waves, and it usually travels in smaller groups or singly. Harbor porpoises are also more apt to frequent the shallower bays, whereas Dall porpoises are usually seen in deeper waters. To distinguish the two at a distance, note the shape of the dorsal fin. The Dall's fin has a longer following edge, the harbor's longer leading edge.

To further challenge you, the Pacific white-sided dolphin is sometimes seen here in the summer, most often in Haro Strait off San Juan Island. Like the Dall, the white-sided also seems to enjoy playing near boats and has white on its dorsal fin. But the prominent curve of its fin will distinguish it from the porpoise. The dolphin is mentioned here with the porpoise simply because the two are often one and the same to many people; they are from different families, however (dolphins and orcas, *Delphinidae*; porpoises, *Phocoenidae*), and can be distinguished by their teeth (dolphins, conical; porpoises, spade-shaped).

**Quail, California** *(Callipepla california)*. This shy but vocal little bird is a familiar sight in the San Juans, often spotted scurrying across roads and into shrubby thickets followed by a long line of chicks. Quail are monogamous, and families tend to stay in coveys that may number over a hundred birds, though coveys disband for nesting in the spring. The birds nest on the ground in scrapes lined with grass or leaves and lay ten to fifteen buff-colored, spotted eggs usually twice a year, once in May or June and again in July or August. Listen for the quail's distinctive three-note call, with the accent hard on the middle note, sounding much like *ka KA kow*, or *Where ARE you?* (The call is often preceded by two-note "warm-ups.") The birds also use a soft *pit pit pit* when flocking. Cocks are especially handsome, with black faces outlined in white, blue-gray breasts, and jaunty, curved head plumes. Hens also have plumes, although much shorter, and are predominantly brownish gray. Quail are common residents here in open, brushy areas and farmlands, having been introduced to the islands as a game bird in the 1930s.

**Rabbit, European** (*Oryctolagus cuniculi*). This species was introduced on San Juan Island by breeders in the late 1800s. Stories differ as to whether they escaped or were released, but no matter; the rabbits are here. A virus killed off a majority of the flourishing population in the 1970s, but the rabbits rebounded (they average three litters a year), and a large number still exist in the American Camp area, where they've dug extensive warrens, and on Lopez. Reddish brown to dark gray, with ears only about 4 inches long, the rabbits usually feed at night, although they're commonly seen here during the daytime. These voracious vegetarians eat just about any plant life, with the exception of daffodils. Rabbits are preyed on by raptors such as eagles, large hawks, and owls and by foxes, dogs, cats, and humans, and may sometimes give warning signs to each other by thumping their hind feet on the ground. Look for clusters of rabbit droppings shaped like thick disks or small pellets.

**Raccoon** (*Procyon lotor*). It's not unusual to catch sight of this bold, black-masked animal raiding picnic sites, and I well remember one at the James Island pier that turned us back every time we tried to go ashore. Raccoons are curious, social, mostly nocturnal animals that favor wooded areas near the water, so you might try looking for their tiny, five-toed "hand" prints along the muddy shores of ponds and streams. They're good swimmers and climbers and supposedly have a call somewhat similar to that of the screech owl—a long, wavering *who-oo-oo.*

Omnivorous feeders, raccoons enjoy a varied diet, including fish, frogs, berries, nuts, corn, carrion, nestlings, eggs, snails, and reptiles. If they approach for handouts, as they are known to do on Jones and other islands, they should not be fed directly by hand because of the chance of a misplaced bite.

Raccoons don't hibernate here, although they may sleep for several days during very cold spells. They live to about seven years in the wild, breeding at one year of age, usually in February. In April to May, females produce litters of four cubs on average in large leaf nests made in tree holes, hollow logs, rock cavities, or burrows under roots. According to Wolf Hollow, raccoons need 2 square miles of forest and wetland to feed and raise a family, and if crowded out by humans, they are resourceful enough to take advantage of them.

**Raven, Common** (*Corvus corax*). Fabled for cunning and mischief making as well as for supernatural powers, ravens figure in many Northwest native myths. They are extremely intelligent birds, smart enough to post sentries while feeding or to figure out how to pull up food attached to a string. Ravens can be distinguished from crows by their larger size, thicker bill, shaggier throat, and wedge-shaped tail (crows' tails are squared off). They enjoy soaring as hawks do; when they come flapping through the forest, you can often hear the steady *whoosh* of their wingbeats. Listen also for a wonderful variety of croaking calls, from a hollow knocking to a melodious *gu-lulp.*

The monogamous pairs build a large basket nest of sticks 100 feet or higher in trees or on cliff faces and lay six to eight green, spotted eggs in the spring. Nests are often reused, and both parents feed and rear the young. During the nonbreeding season, you may spot ravens flying in long lines back and forth from communal roosts. Their omnivorous diet includes grains and berries, voles, nestlings, eggs, crustaceans, and carrion.

**Redcedar, Western** (*Thuja plicata*). This is perhaps our most easily recognized conifer; its scaly sprays and stringy bark make it unmistakable. The thin bark can be pulled off in long strips and was used by Northwest natives to make such items as blankets, cloaks, and cradle pads. Tribes also hollowed out 60-foot canoes from single trunks of these trees, which can grow up to 200 feet high. Redcedar's fragrant wood is highly resistant to decay because of a natural fungicide in the heartwood, and it is used for siding, shingles, fence posts, and boat building.

The flat, many-branched sprays of the tree's foliage are aromatic, smelling a bit like pineapple. In the spring, small red male flowers give off pollen, which falls on the conelike female flowers growing on tiny stalks on the outer branchlets. The cones ripen to brown in the fall and are small and upright; they eventually open to a spreading form, instead of remaining in tight ovals as do many other cones. Shallow roots make redcedar susceptible to blowdowns, and its thin bark leaves it vulnerable to fire damage. The blending together of the terms *red* and *cedar* is not a misprint; western redcedar is not a true cedar but a member of the cypress family.

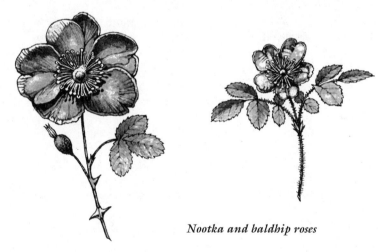

*Nootka and baldhip roses*

**Rose, Nootka** (*Rosa nutkana*). First discovered in Nootka Sound on Vancouver Island, this common bush rose often creates fairly dense thickets along forest edges or other open areas and has large, showy, blush blossoms (up to 3 inches across), which appear May through July. Shrubs grow to 10 feet high, and their stems are double-thorned at the base of each leaf. Hips form in late summer and fall; pick them after a frost and mash them into jam or brew a delicious tea rich in vitamin C. Our other wild rose, smaller cousin to the Nootka, is the baldhip. It can be easily distinguished from the Nootka by stems that are completely prickled and by smaller flowers (less than 1 inch across). Shrubs are generally only to 4 feet high and, unlike the Nootka, may often be found growing alone.

**Salal** (*Gaultheria shallon*). The shiny green, leathery leaves of salal are a staple in the woodland understory. Its fragrant pink bell blooms scent the forest and beckon honeybees from mid-May through July. Dark purple berries usually ripen by late July and are a source of food for wildlife. Salal is the coastal native word for this ubiquitous evergreen shrub; Northwest tribes dried and mashed its berries into cakes.

**Salmon, Chinook** (*Onchorhynchus tshawytscha*). Also known as the king, spring, or tyee, the Chinook is our largest salmon, with an average length of 3 feet and a 10-to-50-pound average weight, although some may exceed 100 pounds. The Chinook has black gums, silver sides, dark spots on its back and both lobes of its tail, and a small fatty fin between the dorsal fin and the tail. Not only a favorite food source for humans, revered by Northwest natives, salmon also draw foraging orca pods into the islands and large numbers of bald eagles to the fish's spawning rivers. They spend their adult lives in salt water, returning to the freshwater streams of their birth to spawn; spring runs return February to April, and fall runs return July to November. Using her tail, the female scoops out a shallow nest in the streambed gravel and lays her eggs (several thousand among several nests), which the male then fertilizes. Soon after spawning is over, both sexes die and become a prime food source for eagles.

Spring-run juveniles stay in streams for one year (fall-run for six months); they then move into estuaries to fatten up for one to three months before the transition to salt water. Adults remain in the sea for three to five years, traveling to British Columbia and Alaska waters before migrating back to their spawning grounds, presumably guided by currents, sun, and even the smell of their home streams. (Dams blocking migration routes in rivers have seriously affected local salmon runs.) The Chinook and the four other species of salmon in the Northwest—coho (silver), sockeye (red), chum (dog), and pink (humpback)—are all alike in that they hatch in fresh water, migrate to the sea as juveniles, return to fresh water when mature to spawn, and then die after spawning.

**Salmonberry** (*Rubus spectabilis*). One of the most common shrubs of island forests, salmonberry gifts us with its rosy blooms when little else except flowering currant brightens the early spring. Its shrubby stems are sparsely prickled (new growth is free of thorns) and in damp areas often form impenetrable thickets to 10 feet high. Leaves have three leaflets with serrated margins; tissue-thin blooms somewhat resembling wild roses are only about 1 inch across and may appear before the leaves, as early as February. Red or yellow-orange raspberrylike berries, which Northwest natives believed resembled salmon eggs, ripen by July and have a sweet flavor. Native peoples also ate the young shoots of the plant raw or roasted as a special spring treat.

**Scoter, Surf** (*Melanitta perspicillata*). Sometimes called the "skunk duck," the scoter is a large, chunky bird with a beak that almost looks deformed because of a large swelling at its base. Males are black with white patches on the crown and nape (breeding plumage only), and their bills have bold markings of orange, black, and white. Females also have swollen beaks, but theirs are black, and their bodies are brown except for light cheek patches. A sea duck able to dive deeply and swim underwater with both feet and wings, the scoter also doesn't hesitate to take on strong surf, plunging through the breakers as the crests come over. Scoters feed on mussels, clams, and crabs and are common in the islands mid-August through early May, breeding in Alaska and northern Canada. Listen for the whistling noise of their wings as they take off or land on the water.

**Sea Anemone, Red and Green** (*Urticina crassicornis*). Somewhat like the Venus flytrap, the sea anemone is designed to trap living prey within its deadly "bloom." What looks like a lovely underwater flower, however, isn't a plant at all but an animal whose numerous snakelike "petals" are really poison-tipped tentacles. This anemone attaches to rocks by a disk and is often found in tidepools, where its contrasting olive green and red colors blend in with the seaweed when the creature closes in on itself. The withdrawal of its tentacles turns the "sea flower" into a drab blob of jelly whenever it senses danger or is in the process of digesting a small shrimp or crab. (That crab's indigestible shell may be stripped clean of meat and ejected within 15 minutes.)

Anemones are eaten by sea slugs apparently immune to their stinging tentacles; should they escape the slugs, they may live up to sixty years or more. They are able to move, if slowly, and they reproduce by ejecting either eggs or sperm through the mouth. Several other anemones are common here, among them the elegant anemone, which is smaller than the red and green and has pink-tipped tentacles.

**Sea Lion, Northern** (*Eumetopius jubatus*). With its thick, yellowish mane and bellowing roar, the lion of the sea is well named. Also known as the Steller sea lion, this marine mammal can be distinguished from the harbor seal by its buff color, small external ears, and large size (males may be over 11 feet long and weigh more than a ton, three times as large as females). Not as highly specialized as the seal for aquatic life, the sea lion has the ability to rotate its hind flippers to propel itself on land, whereas the harbor seal must hunch along on its belly. The head profile of the sea lion is also distinctive with its somewhat long, upturned snout.

Diet includes a variety of fish such as flounder, cod, rockfish, sculpin, herring, squid, and skate; salmon is only occasionally taken. Breeding occurs during June and July, with bulls and harems gathering on rookeries off Alaska and British Columbia down to the California coast (none have been noted off Washington). Females each bear one pup at this time (and breed again two weeks after the birth); the pup is usually weaned within a year. Look for sea lions in island waters fall through spring; Sucia Island is a favored haulout spot.

This sea lion occasionally gives a deep roar, whereas the California sea lion regularly barks. The California—the "circus and zoo seal"—also has a brown coat that looks very dark when wet (the northern's coat turns almost white in the water), and the forehead is pronounced in the males. Some of the males migrate up from California in the fall and may occasionally be seen here through the winter (a friend who lived close to a fish-packing plant on Fidalgo heard persistent barking from these opportunistic feeders.)

**Sea Star, Ochre** (*Pisaster ochraceus*). This is the thick, five-rayed, spiny-skinned star you'll see most often clinging to subtidal rocks and pilings; it's also known as the common or purple star. It may be purple, orange, or brown and grow up to 16 inches across. (It has been suggested that the color variations may depend on location, since the orange color seems more common on the outer coast, while purple predominates in sheltered waters.)

Tiny pincers (pedicellariae) on the back of a sea star provide a hostile environment for freeloaders such as algae and barnacles by nipping whatever comes into contact with them, thus keeping the stars free of the growth usually found on other rocky-shore inhabitants. Sea stars don't have eyes, but a small red spot on the end of each ray is sensitive to light. The thick rays taper from a central disk, under which lies the creature's mouth; a star feeds on barnacles, mussels, limpets, snails, and clams by attaching the suction-tipped tube feet on its rays to a victim's shell and steadily, relentlessly pulling it apart with a pressure of up to $2^{1}/_{2}$ pounds. The star's stomach then pushes through its mouth and into the shell to digest the animal, withdrawing again when its meal is complete (sometimes not for two to three days).

The star has still another amazing ability; should one of its rays be cut off, it can regenerate another, and if the detached ray retains part of the central disk, the missing parts may regenerate into a new star. Stars also reproduce more normally; separate sexes release eggs and sperm into the water.

The ochre sea star is thought to be our longest-lived sea star at twenty years. Gulls are one of its few natural enemies.

**Sea Urchin, Green** (*Strongylocentrotus droebachiensis*). This little porcupine of the tidepool has its mouth on its underside, as does its relative the sea star, but unlike the toothless star, the urchin projects five chisel-like teeth through its mouth to scrape detritus and seaweeds, especially kelp, off the rocks. The spines of the sea star are also much less developed than those of the urchin, which is covered with stout, sharp, inch-long spines that can move on ball-and-socket joints. But again like the sea star, the urchin's shell is covered with tiny pincers, the pedicellariae, to ward off parasites.

Inside this well-armed shell is mostly fluid, as well as a lengthy, coiled digestive tube, the urchin's jaws, and sex glands. Poking out through holes in the shell among the spines are five double rows of tubular feet with suction cups, which are extensible and which help the creature move and fasten to rocks. When urchins die, they lose their spines, and knobby shells called tests can be found on the shore. Shells are most often green, sometimes brown, and have a five-ray pattern, like a sea star that has coiled its arms in on itself.

Several million eggs per female urchin are expelled through pores. The urchin's bright orange gonads are considered a delicacy in many parts of the world, but humans are far from the urchin's only threat. Chief among its enemies, which include gulls and some crab species, is its relative the sea star.

Two other urchins occur on rocky shores here: the purple urchin, which is about the same size as the green, only with longer, blunter spines, and the giant red urchin, which grows to $6^{1}/_{2}$ inches across. Look for urchins in tidepools attached to rock crevices or undersides for protection from the pounding waves.

**Seal, Harbor** (*Phoca vitulina*). It's not uncommon to be walking a beach, riding the ferry, or sitting at anchor in some harbor and to spot the smooth, earless head of this curious seal as it makes its surveillance with large, liquid brown eyes. In another moment or two, all is sadly normal again as the head sinks quietly below the surface. Harbor seals can dive to 300 feet; they usually stay under for no more than 5 minutes, though they're able to remain perhaps another 15 minutes longer.

Adults are gray or tan with dark spots (this seal was once appropriately called the leopard seal), and males, which may grow to 6 feet long, are slightly larger than females. Hind foreflippers cannot be rotated like a sea lion's for walking; thus, the seals are quite clumsy on land, hunching and squirming along and resting near the edges of haulouts where they can quickly belly flop into the water.

Harbor seals are year-round residents in the islands and the only pinnipeds that breed here (as opposed to sea lions and elephant seals). Mostly solitary in water, they'll gather together on rocky haulouts, where they're often seen lying awkwardly on their backs or sides, hind flippers upturned, and where they give birth, nurse the young, or rest for several hours a day. Our least vocal pinniped, a harbor seal will warn other seals off with snorts, grunts, and growls or by waving its foreflippers.

Seals are promiscuous and mate in the water, chasing each other, embracing, and biting (females bite the necks and shoulders of males). The female bears a single pup here in July, and as is true of sea lions, mating takes place again soon after birth. Pups swim at birth and are abandoned by the mother after weaning.

Life expectancy for the harbor seal is about thirty years. Now the Northwest's most abundant sea mammal since it was afforded protection under the 1972 Marine Mammal Protection Act, the seal has the most to fear from the orca. In the archipelago, however, these seals coexist quite peacefully with local orca pods, which feed mainly on the salmon runs; should those runs disappear, perhaps the orca-seal truce will disappear with them. (Transient orca pods will take seals.) Harbor seals feed primarily on fish, squid, and crustaceans.

It really *is* a jungle out there. We have not only leopards and lions in the water but also elephants. The northern elephant seal is our only other true seal, a migrant through this region during spring (from breeding islands off California and Mexico to feeding grounds as far north as Alaska) and autumn (as they pass back through to breeding grounds). Usually only solitary males are seen. They are easily told from harbor seals by their large size (to 20 feet), unspotted skin, and, in males only, thick, trunklike snouts. Some may also be seen through the summer hauled out for several weeks during their annual molt.

**Serviceberry, Western** (*Amelanchier alnifolia*). This island shrub goes by a variety of names, such as Saskatoon berry, Juneberry, and shadbush. Although it may reach 15 feet or higher, it's often stunted to no more than a couple of feet by browsing wildlife. Serviceberry is easy to recognize by the small, round leaves notched along their top margins and fragrant clusters of white blooms appearing in April and May. Birds enjoy the seedy berries, which ripen from red to black in early August.

**Shrew** (*Sorex* spp.). The hummingbird of the mammal world, the tiny, sharp-nosed shrew is sheer frenetic energy, with a heart rate of some eight hundred beats per minute. This pennyweight creature is mostly nocturnal, although it may be seen in the daylight as it scurries through forest leaf mold or meadow grass engaged in a constant quest for food to maintain a high metabolism. Its voice is extremely high-pitched, and there's evidence to suggest that, like bats, it may use that sound to hunt. The shrew's chief food is insects, although an animal with such pressing dietary needs can't afford to be too picky and so will ferociously consume other animal life, even salamanders or mice, and occasionally plant food. Shrews usually require two-thirds or more of their body weight in food every 24 hours, although some species consume much more. Prevented from eating for just 6 hours, they will starve to death.

The smallest of all mammals (and not a rodent but an insectivore), the shrew is short-lived, lasting only up to a year or a year and a half. The female bears five to nine young to a litter and up to three litters a year. A musk gland on the shrew's velvety soft body secretes a smelly fluid that repels most predators, although owls will regularly take shrews.

**Skunk Cabbage** (*Lysichiton americanum*). Another early sign of spring is the yellow tongue of this common wetland plant pushing out of the mud to lick the chilly air. A thick spike of tiny green flowers is surrounded by a waxy yellow spathe open on one side. (Later the spike will fruit into small red berries.) The spathe, a slipperlike hood, can maintain a warm inner temperature even in freezing weather, intensifying the plant's odor. Green leaves that superficially resemble cabbage unroll after the spathes and are huge, their blades sometimes reaching 5 feet long. The name refers to the famous odor, which attracts pollinating flies that feed on carrion.

**Slug, Banana** (*Ariolimax columbianus*). "A slug 'neath your shoe makes a whole lot of goo." Perhaps it's a bit crude to begin with such a line, but let's face it—slugs do not inspire sonnets. If they stir us to any emotion, it is more likely to be lethal than lofty as we hunt them down in our gardens. Let it be known, however, that those garden pests are not our native slugs but European interlopers such as the great gray garden slug, the milky slug, and the black slug. Banana slugs are olive or brownish olive, with or without dark spots, a benevolent woodland species that like the turkey vulture inspires disgust but that performs a similar janitorial role in its ecosystem. Banana slugs basically consume whatever plant or animal substance falls in their way and are themselves eaten by shrews, garter snakes, crows, ducks, geese, and amphibians.

Slugs are snails that in the course of evolution have lost their shells, or else the shells have been internalized into small plates. The slug's body is quite remarkable. Sensory data are received from cells along the foot and around the mouth, as well as from retractile tentacles that can move independently. The longer set of tentacles is tipped with eyes that can only distinguish black and white; the shorter set on either side of the mouth is used to smell and taste.

The slug secretes mucus, which leaves a silvery path and prevents both abrasion and dehydration. Especially thick secretions may occur in the presence of danger, causing a predator to gag on its meal. (Since the slime absorbs water, trying to wash it off your hands only makes matters worse; use a towel instead.) A slug can also hang on a thread of this slime and may even mate in that position. Although they are hermaphroditic, slugs usually cross-fertilize rather than self-fertilize. A slug can lay up to five hundred eggs a year, depositing clusters of about thirty transparent or pearly spheres at a time in moist places under stones or debris. A slug's life expectancy is one to six years, depending on the species.

**Snake, Common Garter** (*Thamnophis sirtalis*). There are at least three species and two subspecies of snakes in the archipelago. The common garter is basically a water snake with two yellowish stripes running the length of its body (the Puget Sound red-spotted garter, a subspecies, has a good deal of red between its stripes). The snake grows to about 3 feet long and is probably one of the most common reptiles in North America, as well as one of the most prolific. It mates here in early spring and bears twelve to seventy earthworm-sized young in late summer. The garter's diet includes frogs, salamanders, worms, slugs, insects, and small fish; it's preyed on by hawks, crows, skunks, and weasels. When captured, this snake will often put forth an offensive secretion from anal musk glands and also strike at its handler. The Northwestern garter is mostly an upland snake found in fields or brushy areas, variously colored and with generally just a distinct dorsal stripe. The wandering garter, a subspecies of the western terrestrial garter (which looks much like the common garter), has light dorsal and lateral stripes and may be found along the shore as well as in the uplands.

**Snowberry** (*Symphoricarpos albus*). This deciduous shrub grows just about anywhere and is easily known by its clusters of white berries, which cling to wispy stems often through the winter. Also aptly known as waxberry, the bushy plant usually reaches about 3 feet in height. Leaves grow opposite each other, as do the thin twigs; pink bell flowers form at the ends of the twigs in June and bloom through the summer. The bitter berries are favored by neither people nor wildlife, although when crushed they provide a good scrub-up lotion for hikers and campers.

**Soopolallie** (*Shepherdia canadensis*). This deciduous shrub with the Chinook name that rolls so trippingly off the tongue is also more prosaically known as soapberry or buffalo berry. Common in the archipelago, soopolallie stands up to 4 feet tall, though it may easily be higher and more sprawling on moist, shady slopes. It's easy to tell this plant by the spotted coppery coloring of its twigs and by the hairy undersides of its opposite leaves (leaves are dark green above). Buff-colored flowers are borne on separate male and female shrubs. Small, bright, reddish orange berries ripen in midsummer and are sometimes called soapberries because coastal natives whipped the bitter fruits into a soapy froth, which they then sweetened and ate as a treat.

**Spruce, Sitka** (*Picea sitchensis*). This tree, the world's largest spruce, is seen fairly commonly in the islands in damp soils near fresh water and sometimes along island shores. Also known as the coast spruce, Sitka seldom grows more than a few dozen miles from salt water. Its natural range is south from Alaska into Oregon along a mild, misty coastal belt. In favorable conditions, Sitka may grow over 200 feet high.

The tree grows vigorously, sometimes as much as 3 feet per year. Bristling, sharp-pointed needles surround the twigs, and the pale papery cones with wavy-edged, "bran flake" scales are distinctive. Coastal natives wove baskets out of the flexible roots, and campers know that the resinous tree limbs are good for long-lasting fires. The Sitka's fine-grained wood was once used to build airplanes; it's now used for purposes such as piano sounding boards and boat building. The main timber tree of Alaska, this spruce takes its name from the Alaskan coastal city.

**Squirrel, Douglas** (*Tamiasciurus douglasi*). This scolding bigmouth of the woods was once referred to by John Muir as "a hot spark of life . . . peppery, full of brag and fight and show." Equally blessed with bravado and curiosity, this squirrel will often hold its own with those it considers intruders, pinning them with its large, blazing black eyes. Its repertoire of sound approaches that of the raven and includes a prolonged *chirr* or trilling, which sounds like some wild, exotic bird.

Brownish gray above and reddish orange below, the Douglas squirrel (whose name honors the same famous botanist for whom the Doug-fir is named), or chickaree, as it was known to early European settlers, measures up to 14 inches long, including its bushy tail. A black line along the side separates the colors and is far more distinct in the summer. Chickarees mate in early spring, and a brood of five to six young are born in May or June. The young are weaned at about two months, when nearly two-thirds their adult size. Look for a large round nest high in a conifer, made of twigs, leaves, mosses, bark, and needles; tree holes are also used if available.

The chickaree is most active in autumn when it's defending a territory about the size of 2 1/2 acres, where it collects and caches cones. Look under trees for piles of scales that mark the squirrel's presence; larger masses of cone remnants, called middens, may be stored aboveground, in hollow logs, or in cavities in tree roots. In addition to cones, the squirrel's diet includes berries, mushrooms, and conifer seeds. Its lifespan averages five years.

**Swan, Trumpeter** (*Cygnus buccinator*). One of only eight swan species in the world and unique to North America, the trumpeter migrates through our area in the spring and fall on its way to and from breeding grounds in Alaska. Some swans stay over in the islands, but most of the population winters in the Skagit Valley and other areas on the west coasts of Washington, Oregon, and northern California. This swan with the 8-foot wingspread is snow white with a heavy black bill marked by a red "grin" line; immatures have black at the base and tip of a pink bill, yellow instead of black legs and feet, and dusky gray-brown bodies.

Flocks fly in V formation or long lines; their buglelike calls can be heard from over a mile away—two deep, sonorous notes followed by three higher-pitched sounds, which some compare to the tones of a French horn. The swans fly in to marshes, lakes, rivers, or even flooded fields with dense vegetation, dipping their heads underwater to feed on freshwater plants and crustaceans and also browsing on shore grasses or field crops such as corn, peas, carrots, and potatoes.

Trumpeters mate for life, although if one dies, its partner will mate again. They nest on Alaskan islands and peninsulas on large, grassy mounds (sometimes even old muskrat lodges) and lay about four to six white eggs. The female incubates the eggs about 95 percent of the time, during which time the male is extremely protective. Parents remain with their young through the first year.

Although trumpeters were on the brink of extinction in the early 1930s because of hunting, loss of habitat, and the ingestion of poisonous lead shot in fields and muddy marsh bottoms, their numbers are rising thanks to increased legal protection. (In 1933, the official count for North America was only 66; by 1989, that number had rocketed to 14,000). They came to the San Juans in 1976 and have since wintered on most of the large island lakes; at least one pair remained here to breed through more than one summer. According to the 1993 Audubon bird census here, twenty-one swans were counted on San Juan, three on Orcas, and three on Lopez. Flocks also return to the Skagit Valley farmlands in late October or early November, and they migrate north again in late February through the middle of March. Trumpeters may live more than thirty years.

**Thimbleberry** (*Rubus parviflorus*). The thimbleberry's large (up to 8 inches wide), softly haired, maple-shaped leaves and raspberrylike fruit make it easy to identify. This common woodland berry grows to 6 feet high in branching, prickle-free canes (younger twigs may be bristled) often infiltrated by insects that lay their eggs within and cause galls to form. Large white five-petaled crepe-paper blooms emerge in May and last until July. Many species of birds, as well as some forest animals, enjoy the seedy red berries that form in midsummer; some people find them as tasteless as they are formless, while others, perhaps picking at an optimum time and place, call them sweet. Thimbleberry is one of three raspberry plants in our area, the other two being the salmonberry and the blackcap.

**Towhee, Rufous-Sided** (*Pipilo erythrophthalmus*). This noisy robinlike bird is probably more often heard than seen, either as it energetically scratches through leaves in the understory for insects and seeds or as it gives its characteristic "rusty-hinge" or meowlike call. A handsome bird, the towhee has reddish sides, red eyes, and a white belly; the male has a black head, chest, and back, whereas the female has brown coloring instead of black. The tail is long and rounded, and the dark back and wings are heavily spotted with white, giving rise to the bird's former name, "spotted towhee." The towhee not only feeds in the shrubbery but builds its nest cup there as well, laying three to five white eggs dotted with brown between April and June. A common breeding resident here, the towhee is a curious bird that may respond to attempts to mimic its call.

**Vole** (*Microtus* spp.). Also known more commonly as the meadow mouse, the vole is a fatter but smaller-eared and shorter-tailed version of the familiar house mouse. Dark brown above and light gray beneath, a vole grows up to 7 inches long, with a fur-covered tail shorter than its body, only about a quarter of the total length. They tunnel out 1- to 2-inch runways, usually through the dead grass mats of fields, but may also inhabit woods and marshy regions (they're good swimmers), depending on the species. Pull apart the dense grass cover to find runways unraveling from the creatures' burrows. Small piles of droppings and cut grass stems along the paths are good signs of voles, which eat mostly stems and other green parts of plants, although in winter they'll also gnaw the bark of shrubs. Some species will even store food for the winter. Voles bear several litters in a year, providing a good supply of food for hawks, owls, and many other flesh eaters. Their average lifespan is about the same as a shrew's.

**Vulture, Turkey** (*Cathartes aura*). With its naked red head looking ridiculously small on a heavy black body, and with its fondness for rotting flesh, the turkey vulture is more apt to inspire revulsion than appreciation. But it's a beautiful creature as it effortlessly soars on air currents over the islands, its mighty 6-foot wingspread showing a two-toned underside. Unlike the flat spread of the eagle, the vulture's wings are held above the horizontal in a distinct dihedral V (V for *vulture*). The broad wings often have distinctly splayed primaries, and the dark gray flight feathers look lighter than the black wing linings.

The vulture is very useful as a scavenger of dead flesh; a highly developed sense of smell helps it zero in on carrion. Unlike the bald eagle, the adult vulture is truly bald, a hygienic adaptation to the bird's diet (immatures have black heads). Turkey vultures breed from British Columbia to Mexico and have included the islands in that range; they don't build nests but lay one to three brown-splotched eggs in sheltered places on rocks, cliffs, or hollow logs and stumps. Both parents incubate the eggs.

Turkey vultures migrate into our area beginning in mid-March and usually head out again in September to wintering grounds from central California south. They roost communally in tall trees, often gathering in late afternoon and waiting until the air warms enough to create updrafts before moving out again in the morning. The birds' graceful gliding is in sharp contrast to their ponderous efforts on the ground to become airborne; taking off into the wind is vital. Vultures don't call like the bald eagle or red-tail but remain silent, although sometimes they'll hiss or grunt (which doesn't add a whole lot to their appeal).

**Willows** (*Salix* spp.). Water-loving, multitrunked willows offer us one of the first sure signs of spring with their velvety, silvery gray catkins. The short, female catkins (*catkin* means "little cat") appear well in advance of the tree's leaves and have green pistils. Male catkins are usually larger, with yellow stamens soon rising out of the "fur" and filling with pollen. Male and female flowers grow on different trees; pollination is helped along by both wind and insects.

Pollinated female catkins split open in May or June, spreading masses of hairy seeds that will eventually form fast-growing but short-lived trees. The willow's thick root systems prevent soil erosion along stream banks, where beavers feed on its wood and songbirds nest in its branches (hummers may line their nests with catkin fuzz). There are several species of willows in the archipelago, among them the Scouler's, which is our most common pussy willow; the Hooker's, which likes salt water and looks like the Scouler's but has wider leaves that are hairy underneath; and the Pacific, the tallest of our willows (up to 80 feet), with long, narrow, glossy leaves. Willows may interbreed, and it's often difficult to distinguish among them.

**Woodpecker, Pileated** (*Dryocopus pileatus*). This is the largest woodpecker in North America, easily distinguished by its size (16 to 19 inches) and striking red head crest. The sexes look similar, although females have brown coloring instead of

*Pileated woodpecker*

red in the crest and mustache. The pileated's call is similiar to that of the common flicker, an intense series of *kak kak kaks*, but louder and a bit higher-sounding, rising in pitch at the start. Drumming is slow and loud but softer at the end and is used to declare territory and attract mates. Pairs excavate nests in tree holes and lay an average of four white eggs in May.

A resident of the dense coniferous forest, the "rain bird," which favors a diet heavy in carpenter ants, may be detected by rectangular cavities drilled into wood with a strong, chisel-like bill longer than its head. These cavities may be huge, up to 2 feet long and more than half a foot wide, made in the bird's quest to reach ant or termite burrows with its extremely long, barbed tongue. Look for telltale piles of excavated chips littering the ground.

The common flicker has already been described as our most numerous woodpecker; two other species here are the downy, 6 inches long, which favors deciduous woods, and the hairy, a shyer bird about 2 inches bigger, which is more often seen among the conifers. The two have similar color patterns: grayish belly, black back and wings spotted with white, vertical white stripe on the back, and red patch on the back of the male's head. Their rattling, kingfisherlike calls are also similar, although the downy's is softer and descends in pitch at the end.

**Wren, Winter** (*Troglodytes troglodytes*). This tough bit of fluff is often one's only apparent companion on cold-weather walks through island woods. Its rather nondescript brown coloring masks a valiant spirit but blends in well with the forest floor and shrubbery, where the wren makes its home. Listen for a clipped *chip chip* as the stubby-tailed bird skulks through the understory looking for insects and larvae; not until early spring does the wren become bold and musical, trumpeting its song from open perches. Nests are built of mosses and twigs among the roots of trees or in stumps or bushes. Four to seven white eggs dotted with brown are laid sometime between early April and early July; the bird often has two broods per year. Mountain birds swell the resident population in winter.

**Yellow Jacket, Western** (*Vespula vulgaris*). This carnivorous paper-making wasp is an unfortunately common visitor at summer picnics and barbecues. In the spring, fertilized queens come out of hibernation and build small nests, often on the ground or sometimes under the eaves of island homes, and then lay up to five thousand eggs, over half of which are workers. The workers, which are females, soon emerge and forage to feed the remaining larvae; should the spring prove especially rainy, summertime picnics may be relatively free from the pesky bugs because the hive never became large during the waterlogged nesting season. (If the early workers are killed off or prevented from foraging by poor weather, the colony usually does not recover.) Nests are added onto until they contain hundreds of hexagonal cells, sometimes growing as large as a human head. The workers feed the larvae until the fall, when they then discard any worker larvae and concentrate on budding queens and males. New queens emerge in early September, along with males (drones), whose sole function in life appears to be the insemination of these queens. Only fertilized queens winter over, hibernating in wood or under leaves.

**Yew, Pacific** (*Taxus brevifolia*). This small tree is rather slow-growing, sometimes taking up to ninety years to form a trunk at most 6 inches thick and 60 feet high. Common in the understory of moist forests, the yew often looks shrubby and twisted next to its tall neighbors. Short, sharp-tipped, dark green needles grow in two rows similar to those of the grand fir.

In spring, male trees bear clusters of yellow flowers that shed pollen destined for green, budlike female flowers, which ripen to red "berries" in autumn. Bright red coverings surround hard green seeds that birds scatter far and wide in their droppings. The yew's strong wood has been used for archers' bows, and Northwest natives used it for paddles and utensils. The yew achieved notoriety in the 1980s when scientists discovered that a substance called taxol produced in its bark could be used in the treatment of ovarian cancer.

# "BABY SEASON" GUIDELINES

"Baby season" is late spring and summer, a time of year when you may find raccoon kits, chicks, or fawns in the woods and seal pups on the shore. Here are some tips on what to do if you find any young animals that seem to need help.

**Baby Bird out of Its Nest:** Try to find the nest and replace the bird. If this is not possible, keep the nestling warm in a box with air holes in it and a towel on the bottom. Put the box in a quiet place and handle the bird as little as possible. Contact Wolf Hollow Wildlife Rehabilitation Center at (360) 378-5000.

**Nest Full of Baby Birds:** Try to put the nest back in the original location and fix it there. If this is not possible, follow the above procedures and contact Wolf Hollow.

**Deer Fawn:** If it is lying quietly in a safe place, leave it alone and check after 12 hours (or the next morning). Mother deer often leave their fawns for many hours at a time. If the fawn is in an unsafe place, such as at the side of a road, move it to a safer location nearby, handling it as little as possible. Watch for a short time, and check again after 12 hours. If the fawn is wandering around and crying, it is in need of care. Contact Wolf Hollow.

**Baby Raccoons and Otters:** If they are found alone at any time, they have most likely lost their mother and will need care. Contact Wolf Hollow, or bring them to the center as soon as possible.

**Seal Pups:** They should be with their mother, so if you find a pup alone on the shore, call Wolf Hollow. If you can monitor the scene, however, check back after 48 hours to see if the pup is still alone—the mother may simply have been away feeding. If it is alone, call Wolf Hollow. For any pinnipeds—seals, sea lions, or elephant seals—you may also call the Whale Museum at (360) 378-4710.

Please do not attempt to feed or water any baby animals you may find. Improper feeding could harm or kill them.

PLEASE DO WHAT IS BEST FOR THE ANIMALS.
DO NOT ATTEMPT TO RAISE THEM YOURSELF.

*(These guidelines were provided courtesy of Wolf Hollow Wildlife Rehabilitation Center on San Juan Island, [360] 378-5000.)*

# FIELD GUIDES
# AND SUGGESTED READING

The following list is by no means all-inclusive but merely a starting point for your explorations.

**Amphibians**

Leonard, William P., et al. *Amphibians of Washington and Oregon*. Seattle Audubon Society, 1993.

    One of the few books available on local frogs, toads, and salamanders. Great photos, local breeding data, life habits of thirty-three species of Northwest amphibians.

**Birds**

Lewis, Mark, and Fred Sharpe. *Birding in the San Juan Islands*. Seattle: The Mountaineers Books, 1987.

    Indispensable field guide to local birds, with tips on birding spots. Easy to pack along. Drawings are not included for every species, however, so beginning birders should supplement this book with one that includes color plates: good choices are the Golden Press *Birds of North America* or the Nehls field guide below. Most serious birders also like to carry the National Geographic Society's *Field Guide to the Birds of North America*.

Nehls, Harry. *Familiar Birds of the Northwest*. Portland Audubon Society, 1989.

    An easy-to-pack-along guide to local species, with color plates. Use in conjunction with the Lewis and Sharpe book to pinpoint island birds.

Paulson, Dennis. *Shorebirds of the Pacific Northwest*. Seattle: University of Washington Press, 1993.

    Not a field guide but a solid tome full of color photos and identification tips to help you sort out all those scampering shorebirds.

    If, however, hawks are your passion, refer to raptor biologist Bud Anderson's recommendations in "Winter."

**Butterflies**

Neil, W. A., and D. J. Hepburn. *Butterflies Afield in the Pacific Northwest*. Seattle: Pacific Search Books, 1976.

    A slim volume, easily slipped in a pack, that's a photographic guide to over seventy butterflies. Out of print, but look for it in your library or used bookstore.

**Mammals**

Kritzman, Ellen B. *Little Mammals of the Pacific Northwest*. Seattle: Pacific Search Press, 1977.

    Organized by habitat, this book is a good introduction to the often overlooked small mammals, such as shrews, moles, mice, squirrels, chipmunks, beavers, and rabbits. Includes range maps and forty-eight black-and-white and color photos.

Larrison, Earl J. *Mammals of the Northwest*. Seattle Audubon Society, 1976.

Includes all of the species mentioned above, as well as deer, fox, bats, raccoons, marine mammals, and more. Range includes Washington, Idaho, Oregon, and British Columbia. Line drawings of mammals and photos of habitats.

**Marine Life**

Kozloff, Eugene. *Seashore Life of the Northern Pacific Coast*. Seattle: University of Washington Press, 1983.

An encyclopedic text on over six hundred species of coastal plants and animals from northern California to British Columbia, with drawings and color photos. Good reference source, although beginners might get lost in the technical terminology.

Osborne, Richard, et al. *A Guide to Marine Mammals of Greater Puget Sound*. Anacortes: Island Publishers, 1988.

Excellent guide to whales, seals, sea lions, and otters. Gives breeding ranges, behavior, clear descriptions, tips on how and where to observe. Much specific San Juan info. Good photos and info on how to ID animals and distinguish between similar species (sea and river otters, orca and minke whales, California and northern sea lions). Includes list of individual orcas with ID drawings of their dorsal fins and saddle patches, plus a brief history of each whale and its relatives. Individual minkes are also listed.

Smith, Lynwood. *Living Shores of the Pacific Northwest*. Seattle: Pacific Search Books, 1976.

Easy to use if you have a shore plant or animal you want to identify by picture, type of beach it was found on, or tidal zone it was found in, but has no index. Good color photos, lightweight.

Snively, Gloria. *Exploring the Seashore*. Mercer Island: The Writing Works, 1978.

This readable guide includes shorebirds and intertidal plants and animals of Washington, Oregon, and British Columbia. Organized into habitats, the book describes wildlife found in the different zones of rocky shores, sandy and cobble beaches, and mudflats. Detailed line drawings, with color plates of a variety of plants and animals.

Yates. Steve. *Marine Wildlife of Puget Sound, the San Juans, and the Strait of Georgia*. Chester, Conn.: Globe Pequot Press, 1988.

A very usable guide, easy to carry. Includes info on marine mammals, seabirds, fish, invertebrates, and algae, all carefully illustrated.

**Mushrooms**

Graham, Dick. *The Meandering Mushroomer*. Seattle: Hancock House, 1978.

A slim book with color photos of local mushrooms. Easy to flip through to identify what you've got. Describes where and when to find various species and offers comments on edibility. A good starting point.

McKenny, Margaret, and Daniel E. Stuntz. *The New Savory Wild Mushroom*. Seattle: University of Washington Press, 1987.

A more extensive guide to two hundred species of mushrooms found in the Pacific Northwest. Organized into sections describing mushrooms according to types of fruiting bodies. Good color photos.

## Plants

Arno, Stephen F., and Ramona P. Hammerly. *Northwest Trees*. Seattle: The Mountaineers Books, 1977.

In-depth, readable discussions of trees, accompanied by wonderful line drawings depicting the trees' sizes and shapes, as well as details of the leaves and cones. Discussions include Indian lore, commercial uses, and many other interesting tidbits.

Atkinson, Scott, and Fred Sharpe. *Wild Plants of the San Juan Islands*. Seattle: The Mountaineers Books, 1993.

Indispensable guide for those who want to learn the island vegetation. Fine line drawings accompany very readable text. Organized by habitat, the book describes the trees, shrubs, flowers, and grasses most likely to be found in specific areas such as forest or meadow. Not all species are included, however, so you'll want to supplement this book with a more extensive text with color plates.

Domico, Terry. *Wild Harvest: Edible Plants of the Pacific Northwest*. Blaine, Wash.: Hancock House, 1989.

This slender volume provides color plates and line drawings of many local plants. It discusses blooming and fruiting times as well as edibility.

Palmer, George, and Martha Stuckey. *Western Tree Book: A Field Guide for Weekend Naturalists*. Beaverton, Oreg.: Touchstone Press, 1987.

A basic, nontechnical, friendly guide, easy to tote and to use simply by referring to leaf shape. Good line drawings and precise, clear descriptions of fruit, leaves, flowers, bark, twigs, and tree shapes. Also includes Native American uses.

Pojar, Jim, and Andy MacKinnon, eds. *Plants of Coastal British Columbia*. Vancouver, B.C.: Lone Pine Publishing, 1994.

A superb guide to plants found along the coast from Oregon to Alaska. It's all here: trees, shrubs, wildflowers, grasses, mosses, lichens, ferns, and more in 1,100 color photos and 500-plus pages packed with info. Easy to use, although in the extensive wildflower section you'll need to know the plant's name or family for quick reference.

Spellenberg, Richard. *Audubon Society Field Guide to North American Wildflowers, Western Region*. New York: Alfred A. Knopf, 1979.

This is one inclusive guide you might want to use to supplement the Atkinson/Sharpe book. It has over 700 color plates arranged by color so it's quite easy to pinpoint where your search should start. Includes habitat and range info.

Taylor, Ronald J. *Northwest Weeds*. Missoula, Mont.: Mountain Press, 1990.

Beautiful photographs of all the nonnative plants you're likely to see around here, with identifying characteristics, origin, and distribution of each species.

## Wetlands

Crawford, Victoria. *Wetland Plants of King County and the Puget Sound Lowlands*. Seattle: King County Planning Division, 1981.

Good, clear line drawings of wetland trees, shrubs, herbs, grasses, sedges, rushes, and nonflowering plants. Describes vegetation characteristic of various wetland types. Somewhat technical descriptions accompany drawings. Includes Indian and animal use info.

### General

Kozloff, Eugene. *Plants and Animals of the Pacific Northwest*. Seattle: University of Washington Press, 1991.

> Over three hundred color photos and about half that many line illustrations describe just about anything you'll find on a local nature walk, except birds or insects. Trees, shrubs, mammals, fungi, wildflowers, invertebrates—they're all here. Indispensable reference source for this area.

Schwartz, Susan. *Nature in the Northwest*. Englewood Cliffs, N.J.: Prentice-Hall, 1983.

> A good introduction to the natural history of the Northwest that goes beyond the field guide format to discuss the "whys" and "hows" of nature here.

Whitney, Stephen. *Western Forests*. New York: Alfred A. Knopf, 1989.

> A bit heavy to pack around at 670 pages, but this Audubon Society Nature Guide has great color plates of trees, shrubs, birds, mushrooms, mammals, wildflowers, butterflies, insects, reptiles, and amphibians. Info split but easy to access and understand. Includes range maps, mammal prints and signs, bird calls. Well organized.

# BIBLIOGRAPHY

Adams, Richard, and Scott C. Pedersen. "Wings on Their Fingers." *Natural History*, January 1994, 49–54.

Angell, Tony. *Ravens, Crows, Magpies, and Jays*. Seattle: University of Washington Press, 1978.

Angell, Tony, and Kenneth C. Balcomb III. *Marine Birds and Mammals of Puget Sound*. Seattle: University of Washington Press, 1984.

Armstrong, Edward A. *The Folklore of Birds*. Boston: Houghton Mifflin Co., 1959.

Arno, Stephen F., and Ramona Hammerly. *Northwest Trees*. Seattle: The Mountaineers Books, 1977.

Ashwell, Reg. *Coast Salish: Their Art, Culture, and Legends*. Blaine, Wash.: Hancock House, 1989.

Atkinson, Scott, and Fred Sharpe. *Wild Plants of the San Juan Islands*. Seattle: The Mountaineers Books, 1993.

Benoliel, Doug. *Northwest Foraging*. Edmonds, Wash.: Signpost Publications, 1974.

Berrill, N.J., and Jacquelyn Berrill. *1001 Questions Answered about the Seashore*. New York: Dover Publications, 1976.

Berry, James Berthold. *Western Forest Trees*. New York: Dover Publications, 1964.

Blocksma, Mary. *Naming Nature*. New York: Penguin, 1992.

Braun, Ernest, and Vinson Brown. *Exploring Pacific Coast Tide Pools*. Healdsburg, Calif.: Naturegraph Press, 1966.

Burt, W. H., and R. P. Grossenhieder. *A Field Guide to the Mammals*. Boston: Houghton Mifflin Co., 1961.

Cannings, Robert, and Kathleen M. Stuart. *The Dragonflies of British Columbia*. Victoria, B.C.: British Columbia Provincial Museum, 1977.

Caras, Roger. *The Forest*. Lincoln, Nebr.: University of Nebraska Press, 1979.

Carl, G. C. *Guide to Marine Life of British Columbia*. Victoria, B.C.: British Columbia Provincial Museum, 1978.

Clark, Ella. *Indian Legends of the Pacific Northwest*. Berkeley and Los Angeles: University of California Press, 1958.

Comstock, Anna Botsford. *Handbook of Nature Study*. New York: Comstock Publishing Co., 1953.

Crawford, Victoria. *Wetland Plants of King County & the Puget Sound Lowlands*. Seattle: King County Planning Division, 1981.

Cruickshank, Allan, and Helen Cruickshank. *1001 Questions Answered about Birds*. New York: Dover Publications, 1976.

Cvancara, Allan M. *At the Water's Edge: Nature Study in Lakes, Streams, and Ponds*. New York: John Wiley & Sons, 1987.

Dean, Jana, ed. *Wetland Tales*. Olympia, Wash.: Washington State Department of Ecology, 1992.

Dickerson, Mary C. *The Frog Book*. New York: Dover Publications, 1969.

Domico, Terry. *Wild Harvest: Edible Plants of the Pacific Northwest*. Blaine, Wash.: Hancock House, 1989.

Durant, Mary. *Who Named the Daisy? Who Named the Rose?* New York: Congdon & Weed, 1976.

Durrell, Gerald. *The Amateur Naturalist.* New York: Alfred A. Knopf, 1982.

Ehrlich, Paul, et al. *The Birder's Handbook.* New York: Simon & Schuster, 1988.

Einarsen, Arthur. *Black Brant, Sea Goose of the Pacific Coast.* Seattle: University of Washington Press, 1965.

Gallagher, Tim. "Great Horned Owl." *Wild Bird Magazine,* June 1988, 36–40.

Gerber, Peter. *Indians of the Northwest Coast.* New York: Facts on File Publications, 1989.

Gleisner, Donna, et al. "Hummingbirds and How to Attract Them." Olympia, Wash.: Washington State Department of Wildlife, 1989.

Gordon, David George. *Field Guide to the Slug.* Seattle: Sasquatch Books, 1994.

Gruson, Edward S. *Words for Birds: A Lexicon of North American Birds with Biographical Notes.* New York: Quadrangle Books, 1972.

Gunther, Erna. *Ethnobotany of Western Washington.* Seattle: University of Washington Press, 1973.

Haley, Delphine, ed. *Marine Mammals.* Seattle: Pacific Search Press, 1978.

Hansen, Kenneth C. *The Maiden of Deception Pass.* Anacortes, Wash.: Samish Experience Productions, 1983.

Haskin, Leslie L. *Wildflowers of the Pacific Coast.* Portland, Oreg.: Metropolitan Press, 1934.

Headstrom, Richard. *The Living Year.* New York: Ives Washburn, 1950.

Heckman, Hazel. *Island Year.* Seattle: University of Washington Press, 1972.

Heinrich, Bernd. "A Birdbrain Nevermore." *Natural History,* October 1993, 51–56.

Hewlett, Stefani, and K. Gilbey Hewlett. *Sea Life of the Pacific Northwest.* Toronto: McGraw-Hill Ryerson, 1976.

Jewett, Stanley, et al. *Birds of Washington State.* Seattle: University of Washington Press, 1953.

Johnsgard, Paul. *The Hummingbirds of North America.* Washington, D.C.: Smithsonian Institution Press, 1984.

Kirk, Lee Crawley. "Flying Dragons of Summer." *Northwest Parks and Wildlife,* June 1992, 25–27.

Kozloff, Eugene N. *Plants and Animals of the Pacific Northwest.* Seattle: University of Washington Press, 1991.

———. *Seashore Life of the Northern Pacific Coast.* Seattle: University of Washington Press, 1983.

Kritzman, Ellen B. *Little Mammals of the Pacific Northwest.* Seattle: Pacific Search Press, 1977.

Larrison, Earl J. *Mammals of the Northwest.* Seattle: Seattle Audubon Society, 1976.

Larrison, Earl J., and Edward N. Francq. *Field Guide to the Birds of Washington State.* Seattle: Seattle Audubon Society, 1962.

Larrison, Earl J., et al. *Washington Birds: Their Location and Identification.* Seattle: Seattle Audubon Society, 1968.

Lembke, Janet. "A Bird in the Hand." *Audubon Magazine,* November 1991, 10–48.

Leonard, William P., et al. *Amphibians of Washington and Oregon*. Seattle: Seattle Audubon Society, 1993.

Lewis, Mark, and Fred Sharpe. *Birding in the San Juan Islands*. Seattle: The Mountaineers Books, 1987.

Little, Elbert L. *Audubon Society Field Guide to North American Trees, Western Region*. New York: Alfred A. Knopf, 1988.

Lyons, C.P. *Trees, Shrubs, and Flowers to Know in Washington*. Toronto: J.M. Dent & Sons, 1975.

Lyons, Janet, et al. *Walking the Wetlands*. New York: John Wiley & Sons, 1989.

Martin, Laura C. *Wildflower Folklore*. Chester, Conn.: Globe Pequot Press, 1984.

McKenny, Margaret. *Wildlife of the Pacific Northwest*. Portland, Oreg.: Binfords and Mort, 1954.

Merrilees, Bill. *Attracting Backyard Wildlife*. Stillwater, Minn.: Voyageur Press, 1989.

Mueller, Marge, and Ted Mueller. *The San Juan Islands, Afoot and Afloat*. Seattle: The Mountaineers Books, 1995.

Murie, Olaus J. *A Field Guide to Animal Tracks*. Boston: Houghton Mifflin Co., 1975.

Neil, W. A., and D. S. Hepburn. *Butterflies Afield in the Pacific Northwest*. Seattle: Pacific Search Press, 1972.

Nehls, Harry B. *Familiar Birds of the Northwest*. Portland: Portland Audubon Society, 1989.

Nowak, Mariette. "Can Dragons Teach Us to Fly?" *National Wildlife*, April–May 1991, 14–17.

Osborne, Richard, et al. *A Guide to Marine Mammals of Greater Puget Sound*. Anacortes, Wash.: Island Publishers, 1988.

Palmer, E. Lawrence, and H. Seymour Fowler. *Field Book of Natural History*. New York: McGraw-Hill, 1975.

Palmer, George, and Martha Stuckey. *Western Tree Book*. Beaverton, Oreg.: Touchstone Press, 1987.

Peterson, Roger Tory. *A Field Guide to the Western Birds*. Boston: Houghton Mifflin Co., 1961.

Pickwell, Gayle. *Amphibians and Reptiles of the Pacific States*. New York: Dover Publications, 1972.

Platt, Rutherford. *1001 Questions Answered about Trees*. New York: Dover Publications, 1992.

Pohlig, Joni, et al. *The Night People*. Freeland, Wash.: Meeting Ground Journal Publications, 1989.

Pojar, Jim, and Andy MacKinnon, eds. *Plants of Coastal British Columbia*. Vancouver, B.C.: Lone Pine Publishing, 1994.

Ridgway, Sam H., and Richard J. Harrison, eds. *Handbook of Marine Mammals*, vol. 2. New York: Academic Press, 1981

Robbins, Chandler S., et al. *Birds of North America*. New York: Golden Press, 1983.

Rodgers, John. *Shorebirds and Predators*. Vancouver, B.C.: J. J. Douglas, 1974.

Sadler, Doug. *Reading Nature's Clues*. New York: Broadview Press, 1987.

Saling, Ann. *The Great Northwest Nature Factbook.* Seattle: Alaska Northwest Books, 1991.

Schmoe, Floyd. *For Love of Some Islands.* New York: Harper & Row, 1964.

Schwartz, Susan. *Nature in the Northwest.* Englewood Cliffs, N. J.: Prentice-Hall, 1983.

Scott, M. Douglas, and Suni A. Scott. *Heritage from the Wild: Familiar Land and Sea Mammals of the Northwest.* Bozeman, Mont.: Northwest Panorama Publishing, 1985.

Shaw, Winston. "Seals and Sea Kayaks." *Sea Kayaker,* Spring 1991, 14–17.

Skutch, Alexander F. *The Life of the Hummingbird.* New York: Crown Publishers, 1973.

Smith, Howard. *A Naturalist's Guide to the Year.* New York: E.P. Dutton, 1985.

Smith, Lynnwood. *Living Shores of the Pacific Northwest.* Seattle: Pacific Search Press, 1976.

Snively, Gloria. *Exploring the Seashore in British Columbia, Washington, and Oregon.* Mercer Island, Wash.: The Writing Works, 1978.

Spellenberg, Richard. *Audubon Society Field Guide to North American Wildflowers, Western Region.* New York: Alfred A. Knopf, 1979.

Stahlmaster, Mark. *The Bald Eagle.* New York: Universe Books, 1987.

Stauth, Dave. "The Mystery of the Disappearing Amphibians." *Northwest Parks and Wildlife,* August 1993, 46–48.

Stewart, Hillary. *Wild Teas, Coffees, and Cordials.* Vancouver, B.C.: Douglas & McIntyre, 1981.

Suttles, Wayne P. *Economic Life of the Coast Salish of Haro and Rosario Straits.* New York: Garland Publishing, 1974.

Taylor, Ron. *Northwest Weeds.* Missoula, Mont.: Mountain Press, 1990.

Tenneson, Richard. "Shy Seal in a Stormy Sea." *National Wildlife,* December–January 1991, 22–26.

Tufts, Craig. *The Backyard Naturalist.* Washington, D.C: National Wildlife Federation, 1988.

Turner, Nancy J. *Food Plants of British Columbia Indians.* Victoria, B.C.: British Columbia Provincial Museum, 1978.

Udvary, Miklos D. F. *Audubon Society Field Guide to North American Birds, Western Region.* New York: Alfred A. Knopf, 1977.

Underhill, J. E. *Northwestern Wild Berries.* Blaine, Wash.: Hancock House, 1980.

Wahl, Terrence, and Dennis Paulson. *A Guide to Bird Finding in Washington.* Bellingham, Wash.: T. R. Wahl, 1977.

Whitney, Stephen. *Western Forests.* New York: Alfred A. Knopf, 1989.

Yates, Steve. *Marine Wildlife of Puget Sound, the San Juans, and the Strait of Georgia.* Chester, Conn.: Globe Pequot Press, 1988.

Yocum, Charles, and Raymond Dasmann. *Pacific Coastal Wildlife Region.* Happy Camp, Calif.: Naturegraph Publishers, 1965.

# INDEX

# NOTES

# NOTES

# NOTES

# ABOUT THE AUTHOR

Evelyn Adams has lived on Fidalgo Island for 14 years and can be found most mornings slopping through its swamps, fields, and forests with binoculars and notebook. A continuing student of nature, she has explored the San Juans extensively not only on foot but also by sailboat and sea kayak. For 2$^1$/$_2$ years she wrote and published a wildlife newsletter. She now writes a column, "Wild Talk," for the *Anacortes American*.

# ABOUT THE ILLUSTRATOR

Jim Hays lives with his wife and children in rural Western Washington. He has been a freelance illustrator and designer since graduating from the University of Washington in 1962. In recent years, Jim has been spending more time doing projects involving wildlife, and finds tremendous enjoyment in illustrating the animals that he loved to watch as a youth.